1970

This book may be kept

LECTURES ON THE
PHILOSOPHY OF RELIGION

LECTURES

ON THE

PHILOSOPHY OF RELIGION

TOGETHER WITH A WORK ON THE PROOFS
OF THE EXISTENCE OF GOD

By GEORG WILHELM FRIEDRICH HEGEL

TRANSLATED FROM THE SECOND GERMAN EDITION

By THE REV. E. B. SPEIRS, B.D., AND
J. BURDON SANDERSON

THE TRANSLATION EDITED

By THE REV. E. B. SPEIRS, B.D.

IN THREE VOLUMES
VOL. II

NEW YORK
HUMANITIES PRESS INC.

This edition first published in the U.S.A. 1962
Reprinted 1968

Printed in Great Britain

CONTENTS

PART II

PAGE

DEFINITE RELIGION—*continued* 1-323

FIRST DIVISION

THE RELIGION OF NATURE—*continued* 1-65

  II. The division of consciousness within itself—*continued.*

    2. The religion of imagination or phantasy . . 1-47

      a. Its conception 1

      b. The general idea of the objective content of this

        stage 11

      c. Worship or cultus 30

    3. The religion of Being-within-self . . . 48-65

      a. Its conception 48

      b. The historical existence of this religion . . 49

      c. Worship or cultus 59

  III. The religion of nature in transition to the religion

      of freedom 65-122

    1. The religion of the Good, or of light . . 70-82

      a. Its conception 70

      b. This religion as it actually exists . . . 77

      c. Worship or cultus 82

    2. The Syrian religion, or the religion of pain . 82-85

    3. The religion of mystery 85-122

      a. The characterisation of the conception or notion

        of this stage 88

      b. The concrete idea belonging to this stage . . 101

      c. Worship or cultus 109

v

SECOND DIVISION

PAGE

The Religion of Spiritual Individuality . . . 122

    A. The transition to the sphere of spiritual indi-
        viduality 123

    B. The metaphysical conception or notion of this
        sphere 131

        a. The conception of the One 135

        b. Necessity 140

        c. Conformity to an end 148

    C. The division of the subject 166

  I. The religion of sublimity 170-219

    A. The general nature of its conception or notion . 172

    B. The concrete general idea or popular conception . 175

        a. The determination of the divine particularisa-
        tion 175

        b. The form of the world 183

        c. The end God works out in the world . . 189

    C. Worship or cultus 205

        The transition to the stage which follows . 220

  II. The religion of beauty 224-288

    A. The general conception or notion . . . 225

    B. The outward form of the Divine 229

        a. The conflict of the spiritual and the natural . 229

        b. Formless necessity 239

        c. Posited necessity or the particular gods . . 243

    C. Worship or cultus 256

        a. Inner feeling 257

        b. Worship as service 267

        c. Service as reconciliation 278

  III. The religion of utility or of the Understanding 288-323

    A. The general conception of this stage . . 288

    B. This religion as the Roman religion . . 298

    C. Worship or cultus 309

PART III

PAGE

THE ABSOLUTE RELIGION 327

   A. The general aspects of this religion . . . 328

     1. The revealed religion 328

     2. The revealed religion known as revealed . . 335

     3. The religion of truth and freedom . . . 346

   B. The metaphysical notion or conception of the Idea

     of God 348

THE PHILOSOPHY OF RELIGION

PART II

DEFINITE RELIGION

II

THE DIVISION OF CONSCIOUSNESS WITHIN ITSELF
(*continued*)

2. *The Religion of Imagination or Phantasy.*

(a.) *Its Conception.*

The second of the main forms of Pantheism, when this latter actually appears as religion, is still within the sphere of this same principle of the One substantial Power, in which all that we see around us, and even the freedom of man itself, has merely a negative, accidental character. We saw that the substantial Power, in its first form, comes to be known as representing the multitude of esssential determinations, and the entire sphere of these, and not as being in its own self spiritual. And now the question immediately arises as to how this Power is itself determined, and what is its content? Self-consciousness in religion cannot, like the abstract thinking understanding, limit itself to the idea of that Power known only as an aggregate of determinations which merely *are*. In this way the Power is not as yet known as real, as independently existing unity; not as yet as a Principle. Now the opposite form of this

determination is the taking back of the manifold determinateness of existence into the unity of inner self-
determination. This concentration of self-determination
contains the beginning of Spirituality.

1. The Universal, as determining its own self, and not
merely as a multitude of rules, is Thought, exists as
Thought. It is in our thoughts alone that Nature, the
ruling Power which brings forth everything, exists as
the Universal, as this One Essence, as this One Power
which exists for itself. What we have before us in
Nature is this Universal, but not *as* a Universal. It
is in our thought that the truth of Nature is brought
into prominence on its own account as Idea, or more
abstractly as something having a universal character.
Universality is, however, in its very nature Thought,
and as self-determining is the source of all determination. But at the stage at which we now are, and where
the Universal appears for the first time as the determining
agent, as a Principle, it is not as yet Spirit, but abstract
Universality generally. The Universal being known in
this way as Thought, it remains as such shut up within
itself. It is the source of all power, but does not
externalise or make itself manifest as such.

2. Now to Spirit belongs the power of differentiation
and the full development of the difference. Of the system
of this complete development, the concrete unfolding of
Thought on its own account, and that particular unfolding
which as manifestation or appearance is Nature and the
spiritual world, form an inherent part. Since, however,
the Principle which makes its appearance at the present
stage has not as yet got so far as to permit of this
unfolding taking place within that principle itself, it
being rather held fast in simple abstract concentration
only, the unfolding, the fulness of the actual Idea, is
found outside of the Principle, and consequently differentiation and manifoldness are abandoned to the wildest,
most outward forms of imagination. The specialisa-

tion of the Universal manifests itself in a multitude of independent powers.

3. This multiplicity, this wild abandonment, is once more taken back into the original unity. This taking back, this concentration of thought, would complete the moment of spirituality so far as the Idea is concerned, if the original universal thought resolved within its own self upon differentiation, and if it were known as essentially this act of taking back. Upon the basis of abstract thought, however, the taking back itself remains a process devoid of Spirit. There is nothing wanting here, so far as the moments of the Idea of Spirit are concerned, the Idea of rationality is present in this advance. But yet those moments do not constitute Spirit; the unfolding does not give itself the perfect form of Spirit, because the determinations remain merely universal. There is merely a continual return to that Universality which is self-active, but which is held fast in the abstraction of self-determination. We have thus the abstract One and the wildness of extravagant imagination, which, it is true, is recognised in turn as remaining in identity with what is primary, but is not expanded into the concrete unity of the Spiritual. The unity of the intelligible realm reaches the condition of particular independent existence; this last does not, however, become absolutely free, but remains confined within universal Substance.

But just because the unfolding does not as yet return in a true way into the Notion, is not as yet taken back into the Notion by its own inner action, it still retains its immediacy in spite of that return, still belongs to natural religion, and therefore the moments fall apart, and are kept independent and separate relatively to one another. This is the curse of nature. Everywhere we shall find tones that accord with the Notion, with the True, which, however, become the more horrible in the strain as a whole because they continue to retain the character of separateness or mutual exclusion, and because the moments, being independent and objective in their particularity, are looked upon theoretically.

The further question which now presents itself is, What are the forms, the shapes in which this independence appears? We are actually in such a world, consciousness finds itself in an existing world, of such a mutually exclusive character—in a world of sense, and thus has to deal with a world of many-coloured manifoldness. Taking it as a whole, it is thus just "*these,*" these individual things; that is the fundamental determination here. We call "these," Things, and this is the more precise characteristic we assign to the Objective, and by which we distinguish it from Spirit. In a similar way we have in inner life to do with manifold forces, spiritual distinctions and experiences, which the understanding in like manner isolates;—as, for example, this inclination, that passion, this power of memory, that power of judgment, &c. In thinking, too, we have determinations each of which exists for itself, such as positive, negative, being, not-being; this, for our consciousness, which takes things in their sensuous aspect, for our understanding, is independence. In this way we have a view or theory of the universe which is of a prosaic character, because the independence has the form of what is a thing, of forces, faculties of the mind, &c., and consequently its form is abstract. The thought is not Reason here, but Understanding, and is present in that form. But when we so regard the world, what we have is the reflection of understanding, which appears much later, and cannot as yet exist here. Not until prose, not until thinking, has permeated all relations, so that man everywhere assumes the attitude of one who thinks abstractly, does he speak of external things. The thinking in question here is, on the contrary, this Substance only ; it is merely this self-containedness or being at home with self ; it is not as yet brought into exercise, not applied thought, and has not as yet permeated the entire man. The special Powers, which are partly objects, such as the sun, mountains, rivers, or else are more abstract ideas, such as origination, decay, change, assumption of form, and the like, are not as yet taken up into Spirit, are not as yet truly posited as ideal, and yet at the same time, too, are not as yet intelligently distinguished by the understanding from Spirit, and pure Being is still concentrated in that undeveloped state of Substance which is not as yet spiritual Substance.

Now we do not only say things " *are*," but we add in the second place that they stand in manifold relation to one another; they have causal connection, they are dependent on one another: this second moment of the action of understanding cannot be present here. It is the understanding only as pure self-identity, or as a self-consistent process, which conceives of objects under these categories. " Since the one is, therefore the other is," is its way of speaking; and without once turning back, it carries this chain of connection continuously on into the bad or false infinite. Thus the independence we are speaking of has not this form. The form of independence which is present here is no other than the form of that which is the form of concrete self-consciousness itself, and this first mode is therefore the human or animal mode. At this stage there is a filling-up; the concrete makes its appearance as existent, as something which is actually perceived, no longer as Power. In this last the Concrete is posited as merely negative, as in subjection to the Power; it is only the practical element which is objective in the Power, not the theoretical. Here, on the contrary, the theoretical element is set free.

Spirit, as being theoretical, has a double aspect. It relates itself as within itself to itself, and it relates itself to the Things, which " things " are for it universal independence. Thus for Spirit the things themselves break up into their immediate external varied form on

the one hand, and into their free independently existing
Essence on the other. Since this is not as yet a Thing,
nor represents, in fact, the categories of the Understanding, and is not abstract independence produced by thought,
it is the free independence of ordinary conception ; and
this is the idea formed of man, or at least of what has
life, which consequently may be, in a general sense, called
the Objectivity of Imagination. In order to conceive of
the sun, the sky, a tree as existing, as self-sustained, it is
only necessary for us to have a sensuous picture or image
of it, to which nothing which appears heterogeneous has to
be added in order that it may be thus presented to us as
self-sustained or independent. But show or semblance is
a deception. The image, when represented to us as independent, as having Being, and when regarded by us as
such, has for us just the character of Being, of a force, of
a causality, of a form of activity, of a soul; it is in these
categories that it has its independence. But in so far as
the independence has not as yet advanced to the prose of
Understanding, for which the category of force or of cause
is the characteristic quality of objectivity generally, the
apprehension and expression of that independence is this
poetry, which makes the idea of human nature and outward form the supporting basis and Essence of the external
world, or, it may be, even animal form, or the human form
in combination with the animal. This poetry is, in fact,
the rational element in imagination, for this rational element is to be kept firm hold of, although consciousness, as
before stated, has not yet advanced to the category, and
thus the element of independence is to be taken out of the
world which is around us, and, in fact, in direct contrast
to what is not independent, to what is conceived as external. And here it is animal and human existence alone
which is the form, mode, and nature of what is free among
things. The sun, the sea, a tree, and the like, are, as a
matter of fact, without independence as compared with
what lives and is free; and it is these forms of indepen-

dence which in this element of independent existence
constitute the supports of the category for any content
at all. A subjective soul is thus given to Matter, which,
however, is not a category, but is concrete Spirituality
and Life.

The immediate result is that as soon as objects generally and universal thought-determinations have this free
independence, that connection of things in the world
which is the work of understanding is dissolved;—it is
the categories of the relations of necessity, or the dependence of things upon one another in accordance with
their quality, their essential definite character, which
form this connection; all these categories, however, are
absent, and thus nature, with nothing to support or give
it stability, reels at the mercy of imagination. There
may be any sort of unregulated fancy, any kind of chance
occurrence and result; the movement in connection with
any condition of things is not bound and limited by anything whatever; the whole splendour of nature and of
imagination is available as a means of decorating the
content, and the caprice of imagination has absolutely
unbounded scope, and can follow whatever direction it
pleases.

Passion in its natural untrained state possesses but
few interests, and that in which it has an interest it
negates, while on the other hand it pays no attention to
whatever is void of interest. From this standpoint of
imagination, however, all distinctions are taken special
notice of and firmly clung to, and everything which has
an interest for imagination becomes free, independent,
and is exalted to the rank of fundamental thought.

But it is likewise owing to this very imagined independence itself that conversely the peculiar position of
the content and of the definite outward forms disappears;
for since they have a definite finite content, they would
properly have their objective support, their return and
abiding renewal, only in that connection of the under-

standing which has vanished, and by means of which their independence, instead of being a reality, becomes rather a complete contingency. The phenomenal world, the world of appearance, is therefore drawn into the service of imagination. The divine world is a realm of imagination, which becomes all the more infinite and manifold as it has its home in a region where Nature is exuberant; and this principle of passionless imagination, of a fancy built on a theoretical foundation, has enriched the character of the mind and its emotions,—emotions which in this gently hatching warmth are permeated in a pre-eminent degree by a strain of voluptuous and sweet loveliness, but at the same time of feeble softness.

The objective content, too, is not apprehended here in the form of Beauty; those powers, whether general natural objects or the forces of individual feeling, as, for example, love, are not as yet embodied in forms of beauty. To beauty of form belongs free subjectivity, which in the sensuous world and in concrete existence is both free and knows itself to be so.

For the Beautiful is essentially the Spiritual making itself known sensuously, presenting itself in sensuous concrete existence, but in such a manner that that existence is wholly and entirely permeated by the Spiritual, so that the sensuous is not independent, but has its meaning solely and exclusively in the Spiritual and through the Spiritual, and exhibits not itself, but the Spiritual.

Such is true beauty. In living human beings there are many external influences which check pure idealisation, this subsumption of the bodily sensuous element under the Spiritual.

Here this condition does not as yet exist, and for this reason, that the Spiritual is as yet only present in this abstract shape of Substantiality. It is, indeed, unfolded into these particular forms, into special Powers, but the substantiality still exists for itself; it has not permeated and overcome these its particular shapes, this sensuous concrete existence.

Substance is, so to speak, an universal space which has not as yet organised, idealised, and brought under it that with which it is filled up—the particularisation which issued from it.

For this reason, too, the form of beauty cannot be created here, because the content—these particularisations of Substance—is not as yet the true content of Spirit.

Since, then, the limited content is the foundation, and is known as spiritual, the subject—this definite spiritual agent—becomes, owing to this, an empty form. In the Religion of Beauty, the Spiritual, as such, constitutes the foundation, so that the content, too, is the spiritual content. In that religion, statues or pictures, as sensuous matter, are merely the expression of the Spiritual. Here, however, the content is not of a spiritual kind.'

Thus, the art we find here is symbolical art, which does indeed express essential characteristics, but not characteristics of the Spiritual. Hence the unbeautiful, the mad, the fantastic character of the art which makes its appearance here. The symbolism is not the purely Beautiful, just because a content other than spiritual individuality is the basis. Free subjectivity is not the permeating element, and is not essentially expressed by the form. In this phantasy there is nothing fixed, nothing moulds itself into forms of the beauty which is given only by the consciousness of freedom. Speaking generally, what we have here is complete dissolution of form, the restless movement, the manifestation of the self-importance of the individual. Devoid of anything to give it stability, the inner element passes over into external existence, and the unfolding of the Absolute—a process which outdoes itself in this world of imagination —is merely an endless breaking-up of the One into the Many, and an unstable reeling to and fro of all content.

It is the system of universal fundamental determinations, the system determined in and for itself through the Notion, as that of the absolute sovereign powers to which everything returns, and which permeate everything through and through, which alone brings thorough stability into this region of caprice, confusion, and feebleness, into this measureless splendour and enervation. And it is the study of this system which is of the most essential moment. On the one hand, we have to recognise the presence of these determinations through the perverted sensuous form of the capricious, externally determined embodiment, and to do justice to the essential element which lies at their foundation ; and on the other hand, we have to observe the degradation which they undergo. This degradation is partly owing to the mode in which the indifference of those determinations toward one another appears, partly owing to the presence of arbitrary human and externally local sense experience, through which they are transposed into the sphere of the every-day life, where all passions, local features— features of individual recollection—are joined on to them. There is no act of judgment, no feeling of shame, nothing of the higher mutual fitness of form and of content; the every-day existence as such is not made to vanish, and is not developed into beauty. The inequality or disproportion of form and content consists, more strictly speaking, in this that the fundamental determinations are debased, inasmuch as they acquire the semblance of being similar to the disconnected facts of existence, and that conversely the external sensuous representation becomes depraved by means of its form.

From what has now been stated it will be already clear that these determinations of the divine Essence have their existence in the Indian religion. We have here to look away from its vast and characteristically endless mythology and mythological forms, in order to keep to the principal fundamental determinations alone, which are on the one hand *baroque* and wild, and are horrible, repulsive, loathsome distortions, but at the same time prove themselves to have the Notion for their inner source; while in virtue of the development which it gets in this theoretical region, they recall the highest element of the Idea. At the same time, however, they express that definite stuntedness under which the Idea suffers when these fundamental determinations are not brought back again into their spiritual nature.

What constitutes the principal point of interest in this religion of India is the development or explication of form in contrast with an abstract monotheistic religion, and so too with the Greek religion—that is to say, in contrast with a religion which has spiritual individuality as its principle.

(b.) *The general idea of the objective content of this stage.*

What is the first in the Notion, what is true, the universal substantial element, is the eternal repose of Being-within-itself; this Essence existing within itself, which universal Substance is. This simple Substance, which the Hindus call Brāhma, is regarded as the Universal, the self-existing Power; which is not, like passion, turned toward what is other than itself, but is the quiet, lustreless reflection into itself, which is, however, at the same time determined as Power. This abidingly self-enclosed Power in the form of Universality must be distinguished from its operation, from that which is posited by means of it, and from its own moments. Power is the Ideal, the Negative, for which all else exists merely as abrogated, as negated. But the Power, as that which exists within itself, as universal Power, distinguishes itself from its moments themselves, and these therefore appear on the one hand as independent beings, and on the other as moments which even perish in the One. They belong to it, they are merely moments of it, but as differentiated moments they come forward into independent existence, and present themselves as independent Persons—Persons of the Godhead who are God, who are the Whole itself, so that that primary element vanishes in this particular shape or form, but on the other hand they again vanish in the one Power. The alternations—according to which we have now the One, now the distinction as entire totality—are the perplexing inconsistencies which present themselves in this sphere to the logical understanding, but they are at the same time that consistency of reason which is in accordance with the Notion, as contrasted with the consistency of the abstract self-identical understanding.

Subjectivity is Power in itself, as the relation of infinite negativity to itself; it is not, however, only potentially power, but rather it is with the appearance of subjectivity that God is for the first time posited as Power. These determinations are indeed to be distinguished from one another, and stand in relation to the subsequent conceptions of God, and are also of primary importance to the understanding of the preceding ones. They are therefore to be considered more closely.

Power, in fact, at once in religion in the general sense, and in the wholly immediate and crudest religion of nature, is the fundamental determination, as being the infinitude which the finite as abrogated posits within itself. And in so far as this is conceived of as outside of it, as existing at all, it nevertheless comes to be posited merely as something which has proceeded out of that finite as its basis. Now the determination which is all-important here is, that this Power is, to begin with, posited simply as the basis of the particular shapes or existing forms, and the relation to the basis of the inherently existing Essence is the relation of Substantiality. Thus it is merely power potentially—power as the inner element of the existence; and as Essence which has Being within itself or as Substance, it is only posited as the Simple and Abstract, so that the determinations or

differentiations as forms existing in their own right are
conceived of as outside of it. This Essence, which exists
within itself, may indeed be conceived of too as existing
for itself, as Brāhma is self-thinking. Brāhma is the
universal Soul; when he creates, he himself issues as a
breath out of himself; he contemplates himself, and exists
then for himself.

But his abstract simplicity does not at once vanish
owing to this, for the moments, the universality of
Brāhma as such, and the "*I*" for which that universality
exists, these two are not determined as contrasted with
one another, and their relation is therefore itself simple.
Brāhma exists thus as abstractly existing for himself.
The Power and the basis of existences and all things
have, in fact, proceeded out of him and vanished in him.
In saying to himself, "I am Brāhma," all things have
vanished back into him, have vanished in him. Whether
as outside of him, existing independently, or within him,
they have vanished; there is only the relation of these
two extremes. But posited as differentiated determinations, they appear as independent existences outside of
him, since he is primarily abstract, and not concrete in
himself.

The Power posited in this manner potentially only works
inwardly without showing itself as activity. I manifest
myself as power in so far as I am cause and determine,
in so far as I am a subject, when I throw a stone, and
so forth. But this potentially existing Power works in
a universal manner, without this universality being a
subject for itself, a self-conscious subject. These universal modes of working, understood in their true character, are, for instance, the Laws of Nature.

Now Brāhma, as the one, simple, absolute Substance,
is the neuter, or, as we say, the Godhead: Brahmā expresses this universal Essence more as a Person, as a
subject. But this is a distinction which is not constantly
made use of, and in the different grammatical cases this

distinction already spontaneously effaces itself, for the
masculine and neuter genders have many cases which
are similar.   In another respect, too, no great emphasis
is to be laid upon this distinction, because Brahmā as
personified is merely superficially personified in such a
manner that the content still remains this simple substance.

And now distinctions appear in this simple Substance,
and it is worth noting that these distinctions present
themselves in such a way that they are determined in
accordance with the instinct of the Notion.   The First
is totality generally as One, taken quite abstractly; the
Second is determinateness, differentiation generally; and
the Third, in accordance with the true determination, is
that the differences are led back again into unity, into
concrete unity.

Conceived of in accordance with its abstract form, this
Trinity of the Absolute is, when it is formless, merely
Brāhma,—that is, empty Essence.   From the point of
view of its determinations it is a Three, but in a unity
only, so that this threeness is merely a unity.

If we define this more accurately and speak of it under
another form, the Second means that differentiations,
different Powers exist: the differentiation, however, has
no rights as against the one Substance, the absolute unity;
and in so far as it has no rights it may be called eternal
goodness, implying that what has determinate character,—
this manifestation of the Divine,—should indeed exist;
that differentiation too should attain to this, that it *is*.
This is the goodness through which what is posited by
the Power as a semblance or show of Being acquires
momentary Being.   In the Power it is absorbed, yet
goodness permits it to exist independently.

Upon this Second follows the Third—that is, righteousness, implying that the existing determinate element
is not, that the finite attains to its end, its destiny, its
right, which is to be changed, to be transformed, in

fact, into another determinateness; this is righteousness in the general sense. To this, in an abstract way, belong becoming, perishing, originating: for Not-being too has no right; it is an abstract determination in contrast to Being, and is itself the passing over into unity.

This totality, which is the unity, a Whole, is what is called among the Indians *Tri mūrti*—*mūrti* = form or shape—all emanations of the Absolute being called *mūrti*. It is this Highest, differentiated within itself in such a manner that it has these three determinations within itself.

The most striking and the greatest feature in Indian mythology is unquestionably this Trinity in unity. We cannot call this Trinity Persons, for it is wanting in spiritual subjectivity as a fundamental determination. But to Europeans it must have been in the highest degree astonishing to meet with this principle of the Christian religion here : we shall become acquainted with it in its true form later on, and shall see that Spirit as concrete must necessarily be conceived of as triune.

The First, then, the One, the One Substance, is what is called Brahmā. Parabrahma, which is above Brahmā, also makes its appearance; and these are jumbled together. Of Brahmā, in so far as he is a subject, all kinds of stories are related. Thought, reflection, at once goes beyond such a determination as Brāhma, since one having such a definite character is conceived of as One of these Three, makes itself a Higher, which gives itself a definite character in the distinction. In so far as that which is absolute Substance again appears as merely One alongside of others, Parabrahma is expressive of the need of thought to have something yet higher; and it is impossible to say in what definite relation forms of this kind stand to one another.

Brahmā is thus what is conceived of as this Substance out of which everything has proceeded and is begotten, as this Power which has created All. But while the one

Substance—the One—is thus the abstract Power, it at the same time appears as the inert element, as formless, inert matter; here we have specially the forming activity, as we should express it.

The one Substance, because it is only the One, is the Formless: thus this, too, is a mode in which it becomes apparent that substantiality does not satisfy; that is to say, it fails to do so because form is not present.

Thus Brāhma, the one self-identical Essence, appears as the Inert, as that which indeed begets, but which at the same time maintains a passive attitude—like woman, as it were. Krischna therefore says of Brāhma, "Brāhma is my uterus, the mere recipient in which I lay my seed, and out of which I beget All." In the determination, too, "God is Essence," there is not the principle of movement, of production; there is no activity.

Out of Brāhma issues everything,—gods, the world, mankind; but it at once becomes apparent that this One is inactive. In the various cosmogonies or descriptions of the creation of the world, what has just been thus indicated makes its appearance.

Such a description of the creation of the world occurs in the Vedas. In these Brahmā is represented as being thus alone in solitude, and as existing wholly for himself, and a Being which is represented as a higher one then says to him that he ought to expand and to beget himself. But Brahmā, it is added, had not during a thousand years been in a condition to conceive of his expansion, and had returned again into himself.

Here Brahmā is represented as world-creating, but, owing to the fact that he is the One, as inactive, as one who is summoned by another higher than himself, and is formless. Thus the need of another is directly present. To speak generally, Brāhma is this one absolute Substance.

Power as this simple activity is Thought. In the Indian religion this characteristic is the most prominent one of all;

it is the absolute basis and is the One—Brāhma. This form
is in accordance with the logical development. First came
the multiplicity of determinations, and the advance consists in the resumption of determination into unity. That
is the basis. What now remains to be given is partly
something of a merely historical character, but partly,
too, the necessary development which follows from· that
principle.

Simple Power, as the active element, created the world.
The creating is essentially an attitude of thought towards
itself, an activity relating itself to itself, and in no sense
a finite activity. This, too, is expressed in the ideas of
the Indian religion. The Hindus have a great number
of cosmogonies which are all more or less barbarous, and
out of which nothing of a fixed character can be derived.
What we have is not one idea of the creation of the world,
as in the Jewish and Christian religion. In the Code of
Manu, in the Vedas and Puranas, the cosmogonies are constantly understood and presented differently. Notwithstanding this, there is always one feature essentially
present in them, namely, that this Thought, which is
at home with itself or self-contained, is the begetting of
itself.

This infinitely profound and true trait constantly reappears in the various descriptions of the creation of the
world. The Code of Manu begins thus: " The Eternal
with one thought created water," and so on. We also
find that this pure activity is called " the Word," as God
is in the New Testament. With the Jews of later times
—Philo, for example—σοφία is the " First-created," which
proceeds out of the One. The " Word" is held in very
high esteem among the Hindus. It is the figure of pure
activity, definite existence of an externally physical character, which, however, does not permanently remain, but
is only ideal, and immediately vanishes in its external
form. The Eternal created the water, it is stated, and
deposited fruit-bringing seed in it; this seed became a

resplendent egg, and therein the Eternal itself was born again as Brahmā. Brahmā is the progenitor of all spirits, of the existent and non-existent. In this egg, it is said, the great Power remained inactive for a year; at the end of that time it divided the egg by means of thought, and created one part masculine and the other feminine. The masculine energy is itself begotten, and becomes again begetting and active, only when it has practised severe meditation, that is to say, when it has attained to the concentration of abstraction. Thought is therefore what brings forth and what is brought forth; it is the bringer forth itself, namely, the unity of thinking with itself. The return of thinking to itself is found in other descriptions besides. In one of the Vedas, some passages out of which Colebrooke was the first to translate, a similar description of the first act of creation is to be found : " There was neither Being nor nothing, neither above nor below, neither death nor immortality, but only the One enshrouded and dark. Outside of this One existed nothing, and this brooded in solitude with itself; through the energy of contemplation it brought forth a world out of itself; in thinking, desire, impulse first formed itself, and this was the original seed of all things."

Here likewise Thought in its self-enclosed activity is presented to us. But Thought becomes further known as Thought in the self-conscious Essence—in man, who represents its actual existence. 'The Hindus might be charged with having attributed to the One a contingent existence, since it is left to chance whether or not the individual raises itself to the abstract Universal—to abstract self-consciousness. But, on the other hand, the caste of the Brahmans is an immediate representation of the presence of Brāhma ; it is the duty of that caste to read the Vedas, to withdraw itself into itself. The reading of Vedas is the Divine, indeed God Himself, and so too is prayer. The Vedas may even be read unintelligently and in complete stupefaction ; this stupefaction itself is

the abstract unity of thought ; the " I," the pure contemplation of it is perfect emptiness. Thus it is in the
Brahmans that Brāhma exists ; by the reading of the
Vedas Brāhma is, and human self-consciousness in the
state of abstraction is Brāhma itself.

The characteristics of Brāhma which have been indicated seem to have so many points of correspondence
with the God of other religions—with the true God
Himself—that it appears to be of some importance to
point out, on the one hand, the difference which exists,
and on the other, to indicate for what reason the logical
determination of subjective existence in self-consciousness which marks the Indian pure Essence has no place
among these other ideas. The Jewish God is, for example,
the same One, immaterial Substantiality and Power which
exists for thought only ; He is Himself objective thought,
and is also not as yet that inherently concrete One which
He is as Spirit. But the Indian supreme God is merely
the One in a neuter sense, rather than the One Person ;
He has merely potential being, and is not self-conscious ;
He is Brāhma the *Neutrum,* or the Universal determination. Brahmā as subject, on the other hand, is at once
one among the three Persons, if we may so designate
them, which in truth is not possible since spiritual subjectivity as an essential fundamental determination is
wanting to them. It is not enough that the Trimūrti
proceeds out of that primal One, and also returns back
again into that One ; all that is implied in this is that
it is represented merely as Substance, not as Subject.
The Jewish God, on the contrary, is the One exclusively,
who has no other gods beside Him. It is because of
this that He is determined not only as Potentiality, but
also as what alone has Actual Being, as the absolutely
consuming or absorbing element, as a Subject having
infinitude within itself, which is indeed still abstract and
posited in an undeveloped manner, but which is nevertheless true infinitude. His goodness and His righteous-

ness remain so far also merely attributes; or, as the Hebrews frequently express it, they are His names, which do not become special forms or shapes, although too they do not become the content through which the Christian Unity of God is alone the spiritual one. For this reason the Jewish God cannot acquire the determination of a subjective existence in self-consciousness, because He is rather a subject in Himself. To reach subjectivity He does not therefore require an Other in which He should for the first time acquire this determination, but which, because of its being in an Other, would have a merely subjective existence also.

On the other hand, what the Hindu says in and to himself—" I am Brāhma "—must be recognised, in its essential character, as identical with the modern sub-jective and objective " vanity "—with that which the " I " is made into by means of the oft-repeated assertion that we know nothing of God. For the statement that " I " has no affirmative relation to God, that He is a " Beyond " for the " I," a nullity without any content, at once implies that the mere independent " I " is the affirmative for " I." It is of no use to say, " I recognise God as above me, as outside of me; " God is an idea without content, whose sole characteristic, all that is to be recognised or known of it, all which it is to be for me, is wholly and entirely limited to this—that this absolutely indeterminate Being *is*, and that it is the negative of myself. In the Indian, " I am Brāhma," it is not, indeed, posited as the nega-tive of myself, as being in opposition to me. But that apparently affirmative determination of God—that He *is* —is partly in itself merely the perfectly empty abstrac-tion of Being, and therefore a subjective determination only, a determination which has an existence in my self-consciousness only, and which therefore attaches to Brāhma also, and partly in so far as it still is to get an objective meaning, it would already be—and not in concrete determinations only, as, for instance, that God is a subject in and for Himself—something which is known of God, a category of Him, and thus would be already too much. Being, consequently, reduces itself by its own act to the mere "something outside of me," and it is intended expressly, too, to signify the negative of myself, in which negation nothing in fact remains to me but I myself.˙ It is thrashing empty straw to attempt to pass off that negative of myself, that something outside of me or above me, for an alleged, or at least a supposed, recognised objectivity, for to do so is merely to pronounce a negative, and to do this, in fact, expressly through myself. But neither this abstract negation, nor the quality that it is posited through me, and that I know this negation, and know it as negation only, is an objectivity ; nor is it an objectivity, so far, at least, as the form is concerned, even although it is not an objectivity so far as the content is concerned ; for the truth rather is, that is just the empty form of objectivity without content, an empty form and merely subjective supposition. Formerly that which could be described as merely the negative, was called in the Christian world the Devil. Consequently nothing affirmative remains save this subjectively-supposing " I." With a one-sided dialectic it has, by a process of evaporation, sceptically rid itself of all the content of the sensuous and super-sensuous world, and given to it the character of something that is negative for it. All objectivity having become for it vain and empty, what is present is this positive vanity itself—it is that objective "I" which alone is Power and Essence, in which everything has vanished away, into which all content whatever has sunk as finite, so that the " I " is the Universal, the master of all determinations, and the exclusive, affirmative point.

The Indian " I am Brāhma," and that so-called religion, the " I " of the modern faith of reflection, differ from one another in their external relations only ; the former expresses the primitive apprehension of the mind in its naïve form, in which the pure substantiality of its thought comes into existence for self-consciousness, so that it allows all other content whatever to exist beside it, and recognises it as objective truth. In contrast to this, that faith of reflection, which denies all objectivity to truth, holds fast to that solitude of subjectivity alone, and recognises it alone. In this fully developed reflection the divine world, like all other content, is merely something posited by me.

This first relation of the Hindu to Brāhma is set down only in the one single prayer, and since it is itself the existence of Brāhma, the momentary character of this existence at once shows itself to be inadequate to the content, and consequently a demand arises that this existence itself should be rendered universal and lasting like its content. For it is only the momentary time element which appears as the most obvious defect in that existence, it being that alone which stands in relation with that abstract Universality, compares itself with it, and shows itself to be inadequate to it; for in other respects its subjective existence—the abstract "I"—is equal or commensurate with it. But to exalt that merely single look into a permanent seeing means nothing else than to stop the transition from the moment of this quiet solitude into the full present reality of life, of its needs, interests, and occupations, and to preserve oneself continuously in that motionless abstract self-consciousness. This is what, in fact, many Hindus who are not Brahmans (of whom later on) virtually accomplish. They give themselves up with the most persevering callousness to the monotony of an inactivity extending over years, and especially to an inactivity of ten years' duration, in which they renounce all the interests and occupations of ordinary life, and combine with this renunciation the constraint arising from some unnatural attitude or position of the body, as, for example, sitting even on, going with the hands clasped over the head, or else standing, and never even in sleep lying down, and the like.

We now come to the Second in the triad, Krishna or Vishnu ; that is, the incarnation of Brāhma generally. Many and various are the incarnations of this kind which are reckoned up by the Hindus. The general meaning here is that Brāhma appears as man : it cannot, nevertheless, be said that it is Brāhma who appears as man, for this assumption of humanity is not actually held to be the pure form of Brāhma.

Monstrous poetical fictions make their appearance in this region : Krishna is also Brahmā, Vishnu. These popular conceptions of incarnations appear partly to have in them echoes of what is historical, and point to the fact that great conquerors who gave a new shape to the condition of things are the gods, and are thus described as gods. The deeds of Krishna are conquests in connection with which the course of events was sufficiently ungodlike ; indeed, conquest and amours are the two aspects, the most important acts of the incarnations.

The Third is Síva, Mahādeva, the great god, or Rudra : this ought to be the return into self. The First, namely, Brāhma, is the most distant unity, the self-enclosed unity ; the Second, Vishnu, is manifestation (the moments of Spirit are thus far not to be mistaken), is life in human form. The Third should be the return to the First, in order that the unity might appear as returning into itself. But it is just this Third which is what is devoid of Spirit ; it is the determination of Becoming generally, or of coming into being and passing away. It has been stated that change in the general sense is the Third ; thus the fundamental characteristic of Síva is on the one hand the prodigious life-force, on the other what destroys, devastates ; the wild energy of natural life. Its principal symbol is therefore the Ox, on account of its strength, but the most universal representation is the Lingam, which was reverenced among the Greeks as φάλλος, and it is this sign which is to be found in most of the temples. The innermost sanctuary contains it.

Such are the three fundamental determinations : the whole is represented by a figure with three heads, which again is symbolical and wholly without beauty.

The true Third, according to the deeper conception, is Spirit. It is the return of the One- to itself ; it is its coming to itself. It is not merely change, but is the change in which the difference is brought to reconciliation with the First, in which the duality is annulled.

But in this religion, which still belongs to nature, the Becoming is conceived of as mere becoming, as mere change ; not as a change of the difference by means of which the unity produces itself as an annulling of differentiation and the taking of it up into unity. Consciousness, Spirit, is also a change in the First, that is, in the immediate unity. The Other is the act of judgment or differentiation, the having an Other over against one —I exist as knowing—but in such a manner that while the Other is for me, I have returned in that Other to myself, into myself.

The Third, instead of being the reconciler, is here merely this wild play of begetting and destroying. Thus the development issues only in a wild whirl of delirium. This difference, viz., the Third, is essentially based upon the standpoint of natural religion and based upon it in its entirety.

These differentiations are now grasped as Unity—as Trimūrti—and this again is conceived of as the Highest. But just as this is conceived of as Trimūrti, each person too in turn is taken independently and alone, so that each is itself totality, that is, the whole deity.

In the older part of the Vedas it is not Vishnu, and still less Síva, that is spoken of ; there Brāhma, the One, is alone God.

Not only is this principal basis and fundamental determination in the Indian mythology thus personified, but all else too is superficially personified by means of imagination. Imposing natural objects, such as the

Ganges, the Sun, the Himālaya (which is the special dwelling-place of Síva), become identified with Brāhma himself. So too with love, deceit, theft, avarice, as well as the sensuous powers of nature in plants and animals, so that Substance has the form of animals and the like. All these are conceived of by imagination as free and independent, and thus there arises an infinite world of Deities of particular powers and phenomena, which is notwithstanding known as subordinated to something above it. At the head of this world stands Indra, the god of the visible heavens. These gods are mutable and perishable, and are in subjection to the Supreme One; abstraction absorbs them : the power which man acquires by means of these gods strikes them with terror ; indeed, Viśmāvitra even creates another Indra and other gods !

Thus these particular spiritual and natural Powers, which are regarded as deities, are at one time independent, and at another are regarded as vanishing, it being their nature to be submerged in the absolute unity, in Substance, and to spring into existence again out of it.

Thus the Hindus say there have already been many thousand Indras, and there will yet be more; in the same way the incarnations, too, are held to be transient. The substantial unity does not become concrete because the particular Powers return into it, but, on the contrary, it remains abstract unity ; and it also does not become concrete although these determinate existences proceed out of it; rather they are phenomena with the characteristic of independence, and are posited outside of that unity.

To form an estimate of the number and value of these deities is wholly out of the question here ; there is nothing which takes a fixed shape, since all definite form is wanting to this fantastic imagination. These shapes disappear again in the same manner in which they are begotten ; fancy passes over from an ordinary external mode of existence to divinity, and this in like manner returns back again to that which was its starting-point.

It is impossible to speak of miracles here, for all is miracle; everything is dislocated, and nothing determined by means of a rational connection of the categories of thought. Undoubtedly a great deal is symbolical. The Hindus are, moreover, divided into many sects. Among many other differences, the principal one is this, that some worship Vishnu and others Síva. This is often the occasion of bloody wars; at festivals and fairs especially, disputes arise which cost thousands their lives.

Now these distinctions are in a general sense to be understood as meaning that what is called Vishnu even says again regarding itself that it is All, that Brāhma is the womb in which it begets All, and that it is the absolute activity of form, that indeed it is Brāhma. Here this differentiation represented by Vishnu is removed and absorbed.

If it is Síva who is introduced as speaking, then it is he who is absolute totality ; he is the lustre of precious stones, the energy in man, the reason in the soul—in fact, he too in turn is Brāhma. Here all the Powers, even the two other differences, as well as the other Powers, gods of nature and genii, melt into One Person, into one of these differentiations.

The fundamental determination of the theoretical consciousness is therefore the determination of unity, the determination of that which is called Brāhma, Brahmā, and the like. This unity, however, comes to have an ambiguous meaning, inasmuch as Brahmā is at one time the Universal, the All, and at another a particularity as contrasted with particularity in general. Thus Brahmā appears as creator, and then again as subordinate to something else, and he even speaks of something higher than himself—of a universal soul. The confusion which characterises this sphere originates in the dialectic necessarily belonging to it. Spirit, which puts everything in organic connection, is not present here, and therefore if the determinations never make their appearance at all in the form adequate to Spirit, they have to be abrogated as one-sided, and then a fresh form makes its appearance. The necessity of the Notion manifests itself merely as deviation, as confusion, as something which has nothing within itself to give it stability, and it is to the nature of the Notion that this confusion owes its origin.

The One shows itself as fixed or established in its own right, as that which is in everlasting unity with itself. But since this One must advance to particularisation, which, however, remains devoid of Spirit here, all differentiations are called and are in turn Brāhma, are this One within itself, and thus also appropriate the epithet of the One, and so the particular deities are all Brāhma likewise. An Englishman who, by a most careful investigation into the various representations, has sought to discover what is meant by Brāhma, believes that Brāhma is an epithet of praise, and is used as such just because he is not looked on as being himself solely this One, but, on the contrary, everything says of itself that it is Brāhma. I refer to what Mill says in his History of India. He proves from many Indian writings that it is an epithet of praise which is applied to various deities, and does not represent the conception of perfection or unity which we associate with it. This is a mistake, for Brāhma is in one aspect the One, the Immutable, who has, however, the element of change in him, and because of this, the rich variety of forms which is thus essentially his own is also predicated of him. Vishnu is also called the Supreme Brāhma. Water and the sun are Brāhma. Special prominence is given to the sun in the Vedas, and if we were to reckon up the prayers addressed to it, we might suppose that the ancient inhabitants of India found Brāhma in the sun alone, and that they had thus a different religion from that of their descendants. The air, too, the movement of the atmosphere, breath, understanding, happiness are called Brāhma. Mahādeva calls himself Brāhma, and Síva says of himself, " I am what

is and what is not ; I have been everything; I am always
and shall always be ; I am Brahmā and likewise Brāhma ;
I am, the cause which causes, I am the truth, the ox,
and all living things; I am older than all; I am the
past, the present, and the future ; I am Rudra, I am
all worlds," &c.

Thus Brāhma is the One, and is also everything independently which is conceived of as God. Among other
prayers, we find one addressed to speech, in which it says
of itself, "I am Brāhma," the universal supreme soul.
Brāhma is thus this One, which, however, is not exclusively held fast to as this One. He is not such a
Being as we have in our minds when we speak of one
God; this One God is universal unity; here everything
which is independent, which is identical with itself says,
"I am Brāhma."

By way of conclusion, another description may be given
here, in which all the moments which we have hitherto
considered in their divided state and dialectic are expressed unitedly.

Colonel Dow translated a history of India from the
Persian, and in an accompanying dissertation he gives a
translation from the Vedas, and in it there is a description of the creation of the world.

Brima existed from all eternity in the form of immeasurable expansion; when it pleased him to create
the world he said, "Rise up, O Brima!" What was
first had thus been desire, appetite. He says this to
himself. Immediately thereupon a spirit of flames of
fire, having four heads and four hands, issued from h s
navel. Brima looked around and saw nothing but his
own immeasurable image. He journeyed a thousand
years in order to attain a knowledge of his expansion
and to understand it. This fire again is Brima himself,
and he has himself alone for his object as immeasurable.
Now Brima, after the journey of a thousand years, knew
as little about his expansion as he did before. Sunk in

wonderment, he gave up his journeyings and considered what he had seen. The Almighty, who is something different from Brima, had then said to him, " Go, Brima, and create the world ; thou canst not understand thyself ; make something understandable." Brima had asked, " How shall I create a world ? " The Almighty had answered, " Ask me and power shall be given thee." Fire had now issued out of Brima, and he had seen the Idea of all things, which hovered before his eyes, and had said, " Let all which I see become real, but how shall I preserve the things so that they do not go to destruction ? " Upon this a spirit of blue colour proceeded out of his mouth ; this again was Brima himself, Vishnu, Krishna, the maintaining principle, and this he commanded to create all living things, and for their maintenance the vegetable world. Human beings were as yet wanting. Thereupon Brima commanded Vishnu to make mankind. He did this, but the human beings which Vishnu made were idiots with great bellies, without knowledge, like the beasts of the field, without emotions and will, and with sensuous passions only ; at this Brima was wroth and destroyed them. He himself now created four persons out of his own breath, and gave them orders to rule over the creatures. But they refused to do anything else than to praise God, because they had nothing of the quality of mutability or destructibility in them, nothing of the temporal qualities of existence. Brima now became angry. His vexation took the form of a swarthy spirit, which came forth from between the eyes. This spirit sat down before Brima with crossed legs and folded arms, and wept, saying, " Who am I, and what is my dwelling-place to be ? " Brima replied, " Thou shalt be Rudra, and all nature thy dwelling-place ; go and make men." He did so. These men were more savage than tigers, since they had nothing in them but the destructive quality ; they destroyed themselves, for their only emotion was wrath. Thus we see the three gods working separately from one another; what they produce is one-sided only and without truth. Finally, Brima, Vishnu, and Rudra united their forces, and thus created men, ten of them, in fact.

(c.) *Worship.*

Subjective religion—the comprehension of itself by self-consciousness in relation to its divine world—corresponds with the character of that world itself.

As in this world the Idea has developed itself to such an extent that its fundamental determinations have emerged into prominence though they remain mutually external, and as in like manner the empirical world remains external and unintelligible relatively to them and to itself, and therefore abandoned to the caprice of imagination, consciousness too, although developed in all directions, does not attain to the conception of itself as true subjectivity. The leading place in this sphere is occupied by the pure equality or identity of thought, which at the same time is inherently existing creative Power. This foundation is, however, purely theoretical. It is still the substantiality out of which indeed potentially all proceeds, and in which all is retained, but outside of which all content has assumed independence, and is not, so far as regards its determinate existence and standing, made by means of that unity into an objective and universal content. Merely theoretical, formal thought supports the content when it thus appears as accidentally determined; it can indeed abstract from it, but cannot exalt it to the connected unity of a system, and consequently to a connected existence in accordance with law. Thought, therefore, does not really acquire a practical signification here; that is to say, activity and will do not give the character of universality to its determinations; and though form develops itself potentially, indeed, in accordance with the nature of the Notion, still it does not appear in the character of something posited by the Notion, and does not appear as held within its unity. The activity of the will, therefore, does not arrive at freedom of the will—does not arrive at a content which, being determined through the unity of the Notion, would consequently be rational, objective, and in accordance with right. This unity, on the contrary, remains the merely potentially existent substantial Power existing in seclusion, namely, Brahmā, which has let go actuality as mere contingency, and now abandons it entirely to its own wild caprice.

Worship here is first of all a certain attitude of the self-consciousness Brahmā, and then afterwards to the rest of the divine world existing outside of him.

I. As regards the first attitude, that towards Brahmā, we find that it is specially marked off and peculiar exactly in proportion as it keeps itself isolated from the rest of the concrete, religious, and temporal fulness of life.

1. Brāhma is thought, man is a thinking being, thus Brāhma has essentially an existence in human self-consciousness. Man, however, is essentially characterised here as a thinking being, or, in other words, thought as such, and in the first place as pure theory has universal existence here, because thought itself as such, as inherently Power, is given a determinate character, and consequently has in it form generally, namely, abstract form, or the character of determinate Being in general.

Man, indeed, is not only a thinking being, but is here essentially thought; he is conscious of himself as pure thought; for it has just been stated that here thought as such comes into existence ; here man has the general idea of it within himself. In other words, he is actually self-conscious thought, for thought is implicitly Power, but Power itself is just that infinite negativity, that negativity relating itself to itself, which is actual Being, Being-for-self. But Being-for-self, enclosed within the universality of thought generally, exalted in it to free equality with itself, is the soul of a living creature only,

not the powerful self-consciousness imprisoned within
the particularity of desire, but the self of consciousness,
which knows itself in its universality, and which thus
as thinking itself, as forming conceptions within itself,
knows itself as Brāhma.

Or if we proceed from the determination that Brāhma
is Essence as abstract unity, as absorption in self, he has
then his existence in the finite subject too, in the particular Spirit, as this absorption in self. To the Idea of
the true there belongs the universal substantial unity
and identity with self ; but in such a way that it is not
merely the Undetermined, not merely substantial unity,
but is determined within itself.   Brāhma, however, has
the determinateness outside of him.   Thus the supreme
determinateness of Brāhma, namely, consciousness, the
knowing of his real existence, his subjectivity of unity,
can only be the subjective consciousness as such.

This attitude is not to be called worship, for there
is here no relation to the thinking substantiality as to
anything objective, but, on the contrary, the relation is
immediately known along with the determination of my
subjectivity, as " I myself."   In fact, I am this pure
thought, and the " I " itself is indeed the very expression
of it, for " I " as such is this abstract identity of myself
within myself as wholly without determination— " I " as
" I " am merely thought as that which is posited with
the determination of subjective existence reflected into
itself—I am *what thinks*.   Conversely, therefore, it is
conceded, on the other hand, that thought as this
abstract thought has this very subjectivity which " I "
directly expresses as its existence.   For the true thought,
which God is, is not this abstract thought, or this
simple substantiality and universality, but is thought as
the concrete, absolutely full or filled up Idea.   The
thought which is merely the potential existence of the
Idea is just the abstract thought which has merely this
finite existence, namely, in the subjective self-conscious-

ness, and which has not relatively to the latter the objectivity of concrete being in-and-for-self, and therefore is quite justly not held in reverence by it. Every Hindu is himself momentarily Brāhma. Brāhma is this One, the abstraction of thought, and to the extent to which a man puts himself into the condition of self-concentration, he is Brāhma. Brāhma himself is not worshipped; the One God has no temple, has no worship, and no prayer is addressed to him. An Englishman, the author of a treatise on "Idol-worship among the Hindus," makes a number of reflections on the subject, and says, if a Hindu were asked whether he worships idols, he would answer without the least hesitation, "Yes, I worship idols." If, on the other hand, we were to ask a Hindu, whether learned or unlearned, "Do you worship the Supreme Being, Paramesvara? Do you pray to Him? Do you bring Him offerings?" he would then say, "Never." If we were to inquire further, "What is this tranquil devotion, this silent meditation which is enjoined on you and which you practise?" he would then reply, "When I engage in prayer, sit down, cross my legs over one another, fold my hands, and look toward heaven, and concentrate my spirit and my thoughts without speaking, I then say within myself, 'I am Brāhma, the Supreme Being.'"

2. Since in this first attitude we have only one moment of single prayer, of devotion, so that Brāhma is momentary only in his existence, and since this existence is thus inadequate to such content and its universality, the demand arises that this existence should be made into a universal one, such as the content is. The "I," abstractly as such, is the universal, only that this itself is merely a moment in the existence of abstraction; the next demand therefore is that this abstraction, this "I" should be made commensurate with the content. This exaltation means nothing else than the breaking off of the transition from the moment

of still solitude into life, into the concrete present, into concrete self-consciousness. With this, all life and all relations of concrete actual life to the One are to be renounced. The entire living Present, whether that of natural life or of spiritual life, of the family, of the State, of art, of religion, is dissolved in the pure negativity of abstract selflessness.

The highest point which is thus attained to in worship is that union with God which consists in the annihilation and stupefaction of self-consciousness. This is not affirmative liberation and reconciliation, but is, on the contrary, wholly negative, complete abstraction. It is that complete emptying which makes renunciation of all consciousness, will, emotions, needs. Man, so long as he persists in remaining within his own consciousness, is, according to the Hindu idea, ungodly. But the freedom of man justs consists in being with himself—not in emptiness, but in willing, knowing, acting. To the Hindu, on the contrary, the complete submergence and stupefaction of the consciousness is what is highest, and he who maintains himself in this abstraction and has died to the world is called a yogi.

This state is found existing among the people of India, because many Hindus, who are not Brâhmans, undertake and accomplish the task of making themselves into the " I " which is in a completely abstract condition. They renounce all movement, all interests, all inclination, and give themselves up to a still abstraction; they are reverenced and supported by others, they remain speechless in rigid torpor, looking toward the sun or having their eyes closed. Some remain thus during their whole life, others for twenty or thirty years. It is related of one of these Hindus that he had travelled for ten years without ever lying down, having slept standing; during the following ten years he had held his hands above his head, and then he intended to have himself suspended by the feet to swing for three hours and three-quarters over a

fire, and finally to have himself buried for three hours
and three-quarters. He would then have attained to the
highest state, and he who succeeds in reaching such
motionlessness, such lifelessness, is, according to the
opinion of the Hindus, immersed thereby in the inner
life, and exists permanently as Brāhma.

There is an episode in the Ramayana which places us
entirely at this point of view. The story of the life of
Visvamitra, the companion of Rama (an incarnation
of Vishnu), is thus related. There was a mighty king,
who, as being such, had demanded a cow (which is worshipped in India as the generative energy of the earth)
of the Brâhman Vasischtha, as he had got to know of its
wonderful power. Vasischtha refused it; the king thereupon seized it by force, but the cow escaped back again
to Vasischtha, reproached him with having permitted it to
be taken from him, since the power of a Kshatriya (which
the king was) is not greater than that of a Brâhman.
Vasischtha then imposed on the cow the task of assem-
bling a force for him wherewith to resist the king. The
latter confronted him with his entire army, and both
armies were repeatedly overthrown; finally, however, Visvamitra was conquered after his hundred sons too had
been destroyed by means of a wind which Vasischtha had
caused to issue from his navel. Full of despair, he hands
over the government to his only remaining son, and
departs with his consort to the Himalaya mountains,
in order to obtain the favour of Mahādeva (Síva).
Moved by the severity of his exercises, Mahādeva is
prepared to fulfil his wishes. Visvamitra asks to have
the knowledge of the whole science of archery, and this
is granted him. Armed with his bow, Visvamitra in-
tends to coerce Vasischtha; with his arrow he lays
waste his forest. Vasischtha, however, seizes his staff,
the Brâhmanical weapon, and lifts it up; whereupon
the gods are filled with apprehension, for such a force
as this threatened the entire world with destruction.

They entreated the Brâhman to desist. Visvamitra recognises his power, and now resolves to subject himself to the severest exercises in order to attain to that power. He retires into solitude, and lives there a thousand years in abstraction alone with his consort. Brahmā comes to him, and addresses him thus: "I recognise thee now as the first royal sage." Visvamitra, not content with this, begins afresh with his penances. In the meantime an Indian king had come to Vasischtha with the request that he would exalt him in his bodily form to heaven. The request, however, was refused on account of his being a Kshatriya; but on his haughtily persisting in it, he was degraded by Vasischtha to the class of the Tschandala. Upon this he repairs to Visvamitra with the same request. The latter prepares a sacrifice to which he invites all the gods; these, however, decline to come to a sacrifice made for a Tschandala. Visvamitra, however, by an exercise of his strength, lifts up the king to heaven. At the command of Indra, he drops down, but Visvamitra sustains him between heaven and earth, and afterwards creates another heaven, other Pleiades, another Indra, and another circle of gods. The gods were filled with astonishment; they repaired in humility to Visvamitra, and agreed with him about the place they were to assign to their king in heaven. After the lapse of a thousand years, Visvamitra was rewarded, and Brahmā named him the head of the sages, but did not as yet declare him to be a Brâhman. Then Visvamitra recommences his penances; the gods in heaven became envious; Indra attempts to excite his passions (for it is essential for a perfect sage and Brâhman that he should have subjugated his passions). He sends him a very beautiful girl, with whom Visvamitra lives five-and-twenty years, but then withdraws himself from her, having overcome his love. In vain, too, do the gods try to irritate and make him angry. Finally, the Brâhmanic power has to be granted to him.

It is to be observed that this is no expiation for crime; nothing is made good by means of it. This renunciation has not the consciousness of sin as a presupposition. These are, on the contrary, austerities undertaken with a view to attaining the state of Brāhma. It is not penance entered upon for the purpose of atoning to the gods for any kind of crime, transgression, or offence. Penance of the latter kind presupposes the existence of a relation between the work of man, his concrete existence, his actions, and the One God—an idea which is full of content, in which man has the standard and the law of his character and behaviour, and to which he is to conform himself in his will and life. But the relation to Brāhma contains as yet nothing concrete, because he himself is merely the abstraction of the substantial soul; all further determination and content lies outside of him. Thus a worship, as a substantial relation which effectually influences and directs the concrete man, has no place in the relation to Brāhma. If such a relation were present here at all, it would have to be sought in the adoration of the other gods. But just as Brāhma is conceived as the solitary self-enclosed Being, so, too, the exaltation of the individual self-consciousness which strives, by means of the austerities just spoken of, to render its own abstraction something perennial for itself, is rather a flight out of the concrete reality of feeling and living activity. In the consciousness which says, "I am Brāhma," all virtues and vices, all gods, and finally the Trimūrti itself, vanish. The concrete consciousness of one's self and of objective content, which, in the Christian idea of the repentance and conversion of the universal sensuous life, is relinquished, is not characterised here as anything sinful or negative, as it is in the penitential life of Christians and Christian monks, and in the idea of conversion. On the contrary, it comprehends on the one hand, as has just been indicated, the very content, otherwise esteemed as holy; and, on the other hand, we see that the charac-

ter of the religious standpoint under consideration consists just in this, that all the moments drop asunder,
and that the supreme unity casts no reflection into the
fulness of the heart and life.

If the Absolute be conceived of as the spiritually free,
the essentially concrete, then self-consciousness exists as
something essential in the religious consciousness only,
to the extent to which it maintains within itself concrete
movement, ideas full of content, and concrete feeling.
If, however, the Absolute is the abstraction of the " Beyond " or of the Supreme Being, then self-consciousness
too, since it is by nature what thinks, by nature good, is
that which it ought to be.

The man who has thus made himself into the continuously existing Brāhma holds a position equivalent to
that which we have already seen was held by the magician,
namely, that he has won an absolute power over nature,
and is that power.   It is imagined that such a man can
inspire even Indra with fear and apprehension.   In an
episode in Bopp's " Chrestomathie " the story of two
giants is mentioned, who came to the Almighty with a
request for immortality ; but as they had entered upon
their exercises merely with a view to attaining to such
power, he granted their petition only to this extent, that
they are to die only by some act of their own.   They
then exert complete dominion over nature.   Indra becomes
afraid of them, and employs the usual means of inducing
any one to give up such an exercise of power.   He brings
a beautiful woman into existence; each of the giants
wishes to have her for his wife.   In the strife they put
each other to death, and thereby nature is delivered.

3. A characteristic which is quite peculiar remains to
to be considered, and that is, that every Brâhman, every
member of that caste, is esteemed as Brahmā, is regarded
as God by every other Hindu.   This particular way of
viewing the matter, however, is in close connection with
the previous characteristics.   That is to say, each of the

two forms which we have considered is, as it were, a merely abstract, isolated relation of self-consciousness to Brāhma ; the first being only a momentary one, the second only the flight out of life—lasting life in Brāhma being the lasting death of all individuality. The third demand, therefore, is that this relation should not be mere flight, mere renunciation of life, but that it should also be posited in an affirmative manner. The question is, How must the affirmative mode of this relation be constituted ? It can be none other than the form of immediate existence. This is a difficult transition. What is merely inward, merely abstract, is merely outward ; and thus this merely Abstract is the immediate Sensuous, is sensuous externality. Since the relation here is the wholly abstract one to wholly abstract substance, the affirmative relation is in like manner a wholly abstract, and consequently an immediate one. With this we get the concrete phenomenon implying that the relation to Brāhma, the relation of the self-consciousness to him, is an immediate, a natural one, and thus an inborn one, and a relation established by birth.

Man is a thinking being, and is such by nature ; thought is a natural quality of man. But the fact that he is a thinking being generally expresses a quality different from the determination which is here under consideration, from the *consciousness* of thought in general as the absolutely existent. In this form we have in fact the consciousness of thought, and this is then posited as the Absolute. It is the consciousness of absolute Being which is posited here as existing in a natural mode, or, to put it otherwise, which is affirmed and supposed to be inborn ; and its degradation into this form is based upon the entire relation ; for although it is rational knowledge, yet this consciousness is supposed to exist in an immediate form.

Since, then, man is a thinking being, and since the consciousness of thought, as the Universal, the Self-

existent, is distinguished from human thought in general,
while both are something innate, it follows from this that
there are two classes of men, the one including thinking men, men generally, the other including those who
are the consciousness of man, as absolute Being. These
latter are the Brâhmans, those born again, twice born
through birth, first naturally, and then as thinking men.
This is a profound idea. The thought of man is looked
upon here as the source of his second existence, the root
of his true existence, which he gives to himself by means
of freedom.

Brâhmans come into existence as twice born, and are
held in unbounded reverence ; compared with them all
other men are of no value. The entire life of the Brâhmans is expressive of the existence of Brāhma. Their
deeds consist in giving utterance to Brāhma ; indeed, by
right of birth they are the existence of Brāhma. If
any one who is of a lower caste touch a Brâhman, he has
by the very act incurred death. In the Code of Manu
penalties are to be found for offences against Brâhmans.
If, for example, a Sudra utter abusive language to a
Brâhman, an iron staff, ten inches long, is thrust glowing
into his mouth ; and if he attempt to instruct a Brâhman,
hot oil is poured into his mouth and into his ears. A
mysterious power is ascribed to the Brâhmans; it is said
in Manu, " Let no king irritate a Brâhman, for if exas-
perated he can destroy his kingdom, with all his strong-
holds, his armies, his elephants, &c."

The culminating point always is isolated thought as
Brāhma existing solely for itself. This culmination
comes into existence in that immersion in nothingness,
that wholly empty consciousness and contemplation already
spoken of. This Brāhma, however, this highest consciousness of thought, is independent, cut off from all else, and
does not exist as concrete actual spirit; and accordingly
it likewise follows that there is no vital connection with
this unity present in the subject; on the contrary, the

concrete element of self-consciousness is separated from
this region ; the connection is interrupted. This is the
leading characteristic of this sphere of thought, which, it
is true, has in it the development of the moments, but
in such a way that they remain separate from one another,
Self-consciousness being thus cut off, the region in which
it is is devoid of spirit, that is to say, has a merely natural
character as something inborn, and to the extent to which
this inborn self-consciousness is different from the universal one, it is the privilege of certain individuals. The
individual " This " is in an immediate manner the Universal, the Divine. Spirit thus *exists*, but Spirit which
has merely bare Being is devoid of Spirit. By this
means, too, the life of the "this" as "*this*," and its
life in universality are irremediably separated from one
another. In the religions where such is not the case,
that is to say, where the consciousness of the Universal,
of essentiality, appears in the Particular, and is active
in it, freedom of the Spirit takes its rise, and upon
the fact that the Particular is determined by means of
the Universal depends the appearance of uprightness,
morality. In civil law, for example, we find freedom of
the individual in the use he can make of property. I
in this particular relation of actual existence am free ;
the object is held to be mine, as that of a free subject,
and thus the particular existence is determined through
the Universal ; my particular existence is co-related with
this universality. The same holds good of family relations. Morality exists only where unity is what determines the Particular, where all particularity is determined
by the substantial unity. In so far as this is not posited,
the consciousness of the Universal is essentially a consciousness cut off from all else, inactive and devoid of
Spirit. Thus by this isolation the Highest is made into
something unfree and only naturally born.

II. Worship, strictly speaking, is the relation of self-
consciousness to what is essential, to that which exists

in and for itself; it is consciousness of the One *in* this essence, consciousness of one's unity with it. The second relation here is that of consciousness to these very manifold objects. The many deities constitute these objects.

Brāhma has no divine service, no temple, and no altars; the unity of Brāhma is not put in relation to the Real, to active self-consciousness. From what has been stated, namely, that the consciousness of the One is isolated, it follows that nothing is determined by means of reason here in the relation to the Divine; for this would mean that particular actions, symbols, &c., are determined by means of unity. Here, however, the region of the Particular is not determined by this unity, and has thus the character of irrationality, of unfreedom. What we have is merely a relation to particular deities, which represent nature as detached or free. They are, it is true, the most abstract possible moments implicitly determined through the notion, but not taken back into unity in such a manner that the Trimūrti would become Spirit. Their whole significance therefore is merely that of a mode of some particular natural element. The leading characteristic is vital energy or life force, that which produces and which passes away, what returns to life and is self-transformation, and to this natural objects, animals, &c., are linked on as objects of reverence. Thus worship is here a relation to those particular things which are cut off in a one-sided manner from what is essential, and is therefore a relation to unessential things in natural form. Religious action, that is to say, action that is essential, a universal mode of life, is conceived of and carried out in accordance with this, and is known and realised here in this fashion. And here religious action is a content which is unessential and without reason.

Since this element, considered generally, is partly objective, namely, the perception of God, and partly subjective, namely, that which it is essential to do, and

seeing that what is of most importance becomes unessential, the worship is infinite in its range; everything
comes into it, the content is of no importance, it has no
limit within itself; the religious acts are thus essentially
irrational, they are determined in an entirely external
manner. Whatever is truly essential is stable; is, as
regards its form, exempt from the influence of subjective
opinion and caprice. Here, however, the content is this
sensuous contingency, and the action is a merely characterless action, consisting of usages which cannot be
understood, because there is no understanding in it; on
the contrary, a latitude is introduced into it which runs
out in all directions. In so far as all this is trans-
cended, and in so far as there must be satisfaction in
these religious acts, we find this to be attained merely
by means of sensuous stupefaction. The one extreme is
the flight of abstraction, the middle point is the slavery
of unintelligent being and doing, and the other extreme
is capricious extravagance—surely the saddest possible
religion. In so far as flight or escape enters into this
cult, what is actually done represents mere purely external accomplished action, mere activity, and to this are
added the wildest intoxication and orgies of the most
fearful kind. Such is the necessary character of this
worship, a character which it acquires owing to the fact
that the consciousness of the One is broken up in this
way, for the connection with the rest of concrete existence is interrupted, and everything becomes disconnected.
In the region of imagination are found wildness and freedom, and here fancy has free scope. Thus we find most
beautiful poetry among the Indian peoples, but it always
rests upon the craziest foundation; we are attracted by
its loveliness, and repelled by the confusion and nonsense
in it.

The delicate sensibility and charm of the tenderest
feelings and this infinite resignation of personality, must
necessarily possess supreme beauty under such conditions

as are peculiar to this standpoint, because it is only this feeling which, resting thus upon a foundation so devoid of rationality, is moulded exclusively into forms of beauty. But since this feeling of abandonment is without the element of right, it, for this very reason, is seen to alternate with the most extreme harshness, and thus the moment of the independent existence of personality passes over into ferocity, into forgetfulness of all established bonds, and issues in the trampling under foot of love itself.

The whole content of Spirit and of nature generally is allowed to break up in the wildest way. That unity which occupies the leading position is indeed the Power out of which all proceeds and into which all returns; but it does not become concrete, does not become the uniting bond of the manifold powers of nature, and in like manner does not become concrete in Spirit, nor the bond of the manifold activities of Spirit and of emotional experiences.

In the first case, when the unity becomes the bond of natural things, we call it necessity; this is the bond of natural forces and phenomena. We look upon natural properties, things, as being, though independent, essentially linked together; laws, understanding, are in Nature, so that in this way the phenomena are co-related.

But that unity remains in solitary and empty independence, and accordingly that fulness which it acquires is wild, extravagant disorder. In the spiritual world, in like manner, the Universal, thought, does not become concrete, determining itself within itself. Thought determining itself within itself, and abrogating and preserving the determinate element in this universality—pure thought as concrete, is Reason.

Duty, right, exist in thought only. These determinations when they appear in the form of universality are rational in respect to the truth, the unity just spoken of, and likewise in respect to the will. That One, that solitary unity, however, does not become such concrete unity, reason, rationality.

For this reason there is no right, no duty present here, for the freedom of the will, of the Spirit, just consists in being present with itself in determinateness. But here this being present or at home with itself, this unity, is abstract, is devoid of determinate character. And here is one source of the fantastic polytheism of the Hindus.

It has been remarked that the category of Being is not found here; the Hindus have no category for what we call independent existence in things, or what we express when we say " they are," " these are." Man, to begin with, knows himself only as existing independently, he therefore conceives of an independent object of nature as existing with his independence, in the mode of independence which he has in himself, in his Being, in his human form, as consciousness.

Here fancy makes everything into God. This is what we see in its own fashion among the Greeks, too, where all trees and springs are made into dryads or nymphs. We are accustomed to say that the beautiful imagination of man gives soul and life to everything, conceives everything as endowed with life, that man wanders among his like, anthropomorphises everything, by his beautiful sympathy shares with everything that mode of beauty which is his own, and thus, as it were, presses everything to his heart as having animated life.

But the liberality of the Hindus in the wild extravagance of their desire to share their mode of existence, has its foundation in a poor idea of themselves, in the fact that the individual has not as yet within himself the content of the freedom of the Eternal, the truly and essentially existent, and does not as yet know his content, his true nature, to be higher than the content of a spring or of a tree. Everything is squandered on imagination, and nothing reserved for life.

With the Greeks this is more a play of fancy, while

among the Hindus there is no higher feeling of themselves present. The idea which they have of Being is only that which they have of themselves ; they place themselves upon the same level with all the productions of nature. This is because thought lapses so completely into this abstraction.

These natural powers, then, whose being is thus conceived of as anthropomorphic and as conscious, are above the concrete man, who, as having a physical nature, is dependent upon them, and his freedom is not as yet distinguished from this his natural aspect.

It is implied by this that the life of man has no higher value than the being of natural objects, the life of any natural thing ; the life of man has value only if it is in itself or essentially, higher ; but among the Hindus human life is despised, and is esteemed to be of little worth—there a man cannot give himself value in an affirmative, but only in a negative manner.

Life acquires value only by the negation of itself. All that is concrete is merely negative in relation to abstraction, which is here the ruling principle. From this results that aspect of Hindu worship according to which men sacrifice themselves, and parents their children. To this is due, too, the burning of wives after the death of their husbands. Such sacrifices have a higher value when they take place with express reference to Brāhma, or to any god whatever, for the latter is Brāhma likewise.

It is esteemed among the Hindus a sacrifice of high value when they mount to the snow clefts of the Himalaya, where the sources of the Ganges are, and cast themselves into the springs. Such actions are not penances on account of crime, nor are they sacrifices with a view to making amends for any evil deed, but merely sacrifices to give oneself value, and this value can be attained only in a negative way.

With the position which is here given to man animal-worship is closely connected. An animal is not a conscious spirit, but in this concentration of absence of consciousness man is really not far removed from the brutes. By the Hindus action is not conceived as definite activity, but as simple energy which works through every-thing. Special activity is despised; it is only stupefaction which is held in esteem, and in this state it is clearly the animal life alone which is left remaining. And if no freedom, no morality, no good customs be present, then the power is only known as inward, torpid power, which belongs likewise to the brutes, and to them in the most complete degree.

Since man when he exists in this way is without free-dom, and has no intrinsic worth, we find bound up with this in the sphere of concrete extension that unspeakable and infinitely varied superstition, those enormous fetters and limitations above referred to. The relation of man to external natural things, which is of little consequence to Europeans, that dependence on them, becomes some-thing fixed, something permanent. For superstition has its foundation just in this, that man is not indifferent toward external things; and he is not so if he has no freedom within himself, if he has not the true indepen-dence of spirit. All that is indifferent is fixed, while all that is not indifferent, all that belongs to right and morality, is thrown away and abandoned to caprice.

Of this character are the directions which the Brâh-mans have to observe, and of a similar character, too, is the narrative of Nala in the Mahabharata. Just as super-stition is of limitless extent owing to this want of free-dom, so too it follows that no morality, no determination of freedom, no rights, no duties have any place here, so that the people of India are sunk in the most complete immorality. Since no rational determination has been able to attain to solidity, the entire condition of this people could never become a legitimate one, a condition inherently justified, and was always merely a condition on sufferance, a contingent and a perverted one.

3. The Religion of Being-within-self.

(a.) *Its conception.*

The general basis here is still the same as that which is peculiar to the Indian religion ; what advance there is merely consists in the necessity felt that the characteristics of the Indian religion should be brought together again out of their wild, lawless independence, out of their merely natural state of dispersion, placed in their inner relation, and have their unstable chaos reduced to a state of rest.   This religion of Being-within-self is the concentration and tranquillisation of spirit as it returns out of the arid disorder of the Indian religion into itself and into essential unity.

The essential unity and the differences have hitherto continued to keep apart to such an extent that the latter were essentially independent, and only vanished in the unity in order at once to reappear in all their independence.   The relation of the unity and the differences was an infinite progression, a perennial alternation of the vanishing of differences in unity, and their reappearance in their own essential independence.   This alternation is now arrested, because that which is potentially contained in it, namely, the coming together of the differentiations in the catagory of unity, is actually posited.

In its character as this Being-within-itself, for which all relation to another is now precluded, the essence is essentiality existing within itself, reflection of negativity into itself, and is thus that which is at rest within itself and persists.

However defective this determination may be, for the Being-within-itself is not as yet concrete, is only the disappearance of the independent differences, yet we are on firm ground here ; it is a true determination of God which constitutes the foundation.

If we compare this general conception with the assumption that we know nothing of God, then this religion, however poor and mean it may seem, yet stands higher than that which asserts that God cannot be known. For in such a case there can be no possibility of worship, since a man can only worship what he knows, what he has a rational knowledge of. *Is colit Deum qui eum novit,* is an example in frequent use in the Latin grammar. Self-consciousness has at least here an affirmative relation to this object, for the very essence of being-within-itself is thought itself, and this is the real essential element in self-consciousness, and therefore there is nothing unknown in it, nothing which is " beyond." It is in presence of its own essence in an affirmative form, since it at once knows this essence as its own essential nature; but it also conceives it as an object, so that it distinguishes this being-within-itself, this pure freedom, from itself, from this particular self-consciousness. For this last is contingent, empirical, independent Being, being for self, determined in a manifold way. This is the fundamental determination.

Substance is universal presence, but as essentiality existing within itself, it must be known concretely too in an individual concentration. This embodiment and definite form is still in accordance with the standpoint of natural religion, the immediate form of the Spiritual, and has the form of a single definite self-consciousness. Thus, as compared with the previous stage, there is an advance made here from fantastic personification split up into a countless multitude of forms, to a personification which is enclosed within definite bounds, and is actually present. A human being is worshipped, and he is as such the god who assumes individual form, and in that form gives himself up to be reverenced. Substance in this individual existence is power, sovereignty, the creating and maintaining of the world, of nature, and of all things—absolute Power.

(b.) *The historical existence of this religion.*

It is as the religion of Foe that this religion has an historical existence; it is the religion of the Mongols, the Thibetans in the north and west of China, also of the Burmese and Cingalese, where, however, that which is elsewhere called Foe is designated Buddha. It is, in fact, the religion which we know under the name of Lamaism. It is the most widely spread of religions, and has the greatest number of adherents. Its worshippers are more numerous than those of Mahomedanism, which again counts more adherents than the Christian religion. As in the Mahomedan religion, a simple Eternal constitutes the fundamental idea and the characteristic quality of the inner element, and this simplicity of its principle is of itself sufficient to bring diverse nationalities under its sway.

Historically, this religion appears rather later than that form in which the absolute Power is what rules. The French missionaries have translated an edict of the Emperor Hia-King by which he suppressed many monasteries, because those who lived in them did not till the ground and paid no tribute. Here the Emperor says, in the beginning of the edict, " Under our three famous dynasties the sect of Foe was not heard of. Only since the dynasty of Hang has it come into existence."

The general conception of this religion in its more definite features is as follows.

1. The absolute foundation is the stillness of being-within-itself, in which all differences cease, in which all determinations of the natural existence of Spirit, all particular powers, have vanished. Thus the Absolute, as being-within-itself, is the Undetermined, the annihilation of all particularity, so that all particular existences, all actual things, are merely something accidental, are merely Form having no significance.

2. Since reflection into itself as the Undetermined (and this too is in harmony with the standpoint of natural religion) is merely immediate reflection, it is expressed in this form as a principle ; nothing and not-being is what is ultimate and supreme. It is nothing alone which

has true independence; all other actuality, all particularity, has none at all. Out of nothingness everything has proceeded; into nothingness everything returns. Nothing, nothingness is the One, the beginning and the ending of everything. However diverse men and things may be, there is but the One principle—nothingness—out of which they proceed, and it is form alone which constitutes the quality, the diversity.

That man should think of God as nothingness must at first sight seem astonishing, must appear to us a most peculiar idea. But, considered more closely, this determination means that God is absolutely nothing determined. He is the Undetermined; no determinateness of any kind pertains to God; He is the Infinite. This is equivalent to saying that God is the negation of all particularity.

When we consider the forms of expression which we hear used, and which are current at the present day, namely, " God is the Infinite, is Essence—pure, simple Essence, the Essence of Essences and Essence only "—we find that such expressions are either entirely or nearly identical in signification with the statement that God is nothingness. In like manner, when it is said that man cannot know God, God is thus for us emptiness, indefiniteness.

That modern mode of definition is therefore merely a milder expression for " God is nothingness." That, however, is a definite, a necessary stage : God is the Indeterminate, the indeterminateness in which immediate Being and its apparent independence are abrogated and absorbed, and in which they have vanished away.

3. God, although actually conceived of as nothingness, as Essence generally, is yet known as a particular immediate human being, as Foe, Buddha, Dalailama. Such a conjunction may appear to us the most offensive, revolting, and incredible of all, that a man with all his sensuous needs should be looked upon as God, as He who eternally creates, maintains, and produces the world.

When in the Christian religion God is worshipped in human form, that is something altogether different; for the divine Essence is there beheld in the man who has suffered, died, risen again, and ascended to heaven. That is not man in his sensuous, immediate existence, but man who has taken on the form of Spirit. The most startling contrast, however, is when the Absolute has to be worshipped in the immediate finite nature of a human being; this is an even more isolated individualisation than the animal itself is. And what is more, humanity has within itself the requirement that it should rise higher, and hence it seems repugnant that this demand should be suppressed, and man's aspiration tied down to continuance in ordinary finite existence.

We must, however, learn to understand this general conception, and in understanding it we justify it: we show how it gets its foundation, its element of rationality, a place within reason; but it is also implied in this that we perceive its defectiveness. In dealing with religions, we must learn to perceive that what is in them is not mere nonsense, mere irrationality. What is of more importance than this, however, is to recognise the element of truth, and to know how it is in harmony with reason; and that is more difficult than to pronounce a thing to have no sense in it.

Being-within-itself is the essential stage, so that we may advance from immediate, empirical singularity to the determination of essence, of essentiality, to the consciousness of Substance, of a substantial Power which governs the world, causes everything to originate and come into being in accordance with rational laws of connection. So far as it is substantial, inherently existent, it is a power which works unconsciously; and just because of this it is undivided activity, has universality in it, is universal power. And in order to make this intelligible to ourselves, we must recall the expressions activity of nature, spirit of nature, soul of nature. We do not mean by these that the spirit of nature is conscious spirit, nor in using them are we thinking of anything conscious. The natural laws of plants, animals, of their organisation and action, are devoid of consciousness: these laws are the substantial element, are their nature, their notion; they are this implicitly, are the reason that is immanent in them, but without consciousness.

Man is Spirit, and his spirit determines itself as soul, as this unity of what has life. This its life force, which in the unfolding of his organised existence is one only, permeating and sustaining everything, this activity is present in man so long as he lives, without his knowing it or willing it; and yet his living soul is the cause, the originating agency, the Substance, which produces it. Man, this living soul, knows nothing of this; he does not will this circulation of the blood, does not prescribe it to himself; yet he does it: it is *his deed.* Man is the acting, working power in that which goes on in his organism. This unconscious active rationality or unconscious rational activity is the ruling of the world by νους; among the ancients the νους of Anaxagoras. This is not conscious reason. By modern philosophers, especially by Schelling, this rational activity has been also called perception or intuition—God as intuitive intelligence. God, intelligence, reason as intellectual intuition, is the eternal creation of nature, what is called the maintenance of nature; for creation and preservation are inseparable. In perception we are immersed in the objects; they fill us. This is the lower stage of consciousness, this immersion in the objects; to reflect upon them, to arrive at general ideas, to originate points of view, to attach certain determinations to certain objects—to judge—is no longer perception as such.

Such then is this standpoint of substantiality, of intellectual perception or intuition. This is really the standpoint of Pantheism in the true sense of the word, this Oriental knowledge, consciousness, thought of this abso-

lute unity, of the absolute Substance and the activity of
this Substance within itself, an activity in which all that
is particular, that is individual, is merely something
transient, vanishing, and does not represent true independence.

This Oriental conception stands in contrast to that of
the West, in which man, like the sun, sets into himself,
into his subjectivity.   Here individuality is the leading
category, the fact, namely, that it is the individual which
is independent.   As with the Orientals it is the Universal which is the truly independent, so in this form of
consciousness we find the singularity or individuality of
things, of mankind, occupying the foremost place; indeed,
the Occidental mode of conception is capable of going so
far as to assert that finite things are independent, that
is to say, absolute.

The expression Pantheism has the same ambiguity
which attaches to Universality. Ἐν καὶ Πᾶν means
the One All, the All, which remains absolutely One;
but Πᾶν means also Everything, and thus it is that it
passes over into that idea which is devoid of thought,
and is a poor and unphilosophical one.

Thus Pantheism is understood as meaning the divine
nature of *all things*, not the divine nature of *all*: for in
the case of *all* being deified, if God were All, there is
only one God ; in the All, particular things are absorbed,
and are merely shadows, phantoms; they come and go,
the very nature of their being is to vanish.

Philosophy is, moreover, asked to confess that it is
Pantheism in the first of these two senses, and it is
theologians especially who use this kind of language.

The ambiguity of Universality is precisely the same.
If it be taken in the sense of the universality of reflection, it is in that case allness; and in the next place, this
is taken to mean that individuality remains independent.
But the Universality of Thought, the substantial universality, is unity with itself, in which all that is indivi-

dual, that is particular, is merely ideal, and has no true Being.

This substantiality is the fundamental determination of our knowledge of God too, but it is only the fundamental determination, the foundation not being yet the True. God is the absolute Power, we must say that; He alone is Power. Everything which pretends to say of itself that it is, that it has reality, is annulled, absorbed, is only a moment of the absolute God, the absolute Power. God alone is; God alone is the One true reality.

In our religion too this lies at the foundation of the idea of God. The omnipresence of God, if it is no empty word, directly expresses substantiality; the latter underlies it. But stupidity continues to prate of these profound religious expressions as a mere matter of memory, and is not at all in earnest about them. As soon as true Being is ascribed to the finite, as soon as things are independent, God is shut out from them; then God is not omnipresent at all, for if God is omnipresent, it will at once be said that *He* is real, and not the things.

He is therefore not beside the things, in the pores, like the God of Epicurus, but actually in the things: and in this case the things are not real, and this presence in them is the ideality of the things. For that feeble way of thinking, on the other hand, things are invincible; they are an impregnable reality. Omnipresence must have a true meaning for the spirit, heart, thought; Spirit must have a true interest in it. God is the subsistence of all things.

Pantheism is a bad expression, because it is possible to misunderstand it so that $\Pi\tilde{a}\nu$ is taken in the sense of allness or totality, not as universality. The philosophy of Spinoza was a philosophy of substantiality, not of Pantheism.

God is in all higher religions, but especially in the Christian religion, the absolutely One Substance. He is,

at the same time, however, subject too, and that represents a further stage. As man has personality, the
characteristic of subjectivity, personality, spirit, absolute
spirit, enters into God. This is a higher characteristic,
but Spirit nevertheless remains Substance, is the One
Substance notwithstanding.

This abstract Substance, which is the ultimate principle of the philosophy of Spinoza, this Substance which
is *thought of*, which is only for thought, cannot be the
content of the religion of a people, cannot be the faith
of a concrete spirit. Spirit is concrete; it is only abstract thought which remains in one-sided determinateness of this kind, in that of Substance.

The concrete spirit supplies the deficiency, and this
deficiency is that subjectivity is wanting, that is to say,
spirituality or the spiritual element. Here at the stage
of natural religion, however, this spirituality does not
yet exist as such, is not yet thought-out spirituality,
universal spirituality, but sensuous, immediate spirituality; here it is a man, as sensuous, external, immediate
spirituality, and therefore in the form of the spiritual life
of a definite human being, of an empirical, individual consciousness. Now if this man remains in contrast with
this Substance, with the inherently universal Substance,
then it must be remembered that man as living substantiality is really this inherent substantial reality in himself, which is determined by his bodily existence; it
must be possible to think that this life force is in a substantial way active life within him. This point of view
contains universal Substantiality in an actual form.

Here the idea presents itself that a man is universal
Substance in his act of meditation, when he is occupied
with himself, when he is absorbed in himself; not merely
in his active life, but in his absorption in self, in the
centre of the νους, of the νους posited as the centre, but
in such a way that the νους is not conscious of itself in
its determination and development.

This substantiality of the *νοῦς*, this absorption represented in one individual, is not the meditation of a king,
who has in his consciousness the thought of the admini-
stration of his empire ; but rather implies that this absorption in self is as abstract thought potentially active
substantiality, the creation and preservation of the world.

The subjective form is not as yet exclusive here : only
in the interpenetration of spirituality, subjectivity, and
substance does God become essentially One. Thus Substance is certainly One ; but Subjectivity, these outward
embodiments, are several, and it is their very nature to
be several : for this assumption of outward form is conceived of as itself in relation to substantiality, as something essential in fact, while yet at the same time it is
also conceived of as something that is accidental.

For opposition, contradiction, first appears only in
consciousness, in will, in a particular act of intelligence,
and for this reason there cannot be several worldly rulers
in one land. But this spiritual activity, although it has
spiritual form for its definite existence or actual embodiment, is yet merely activity of substance, and does not
appear as conscious activity, as conscious will.

Thus there are several, that is to say, three principal
Lamas : the first, Dalailama, is to be found in Lassa, to
the north of the Himalayas. There is another Lama in
Little Thibet, in Tischu-Lombu, in the neighbourhood of
Nepaul. Finally, in Mongolia there is yet a third Lama.

Spirit can, indeed, have one outward form only, and
this is man, the sensuous manifestation of Spirit. But
if the inner element is not determined as Spirit, the form
at once becomes accidental or indifferent. The eternal
life of the Christian is the Spirit of God itself, and the
Spirit of God just consists in self-consciousness of oneself
as the Divine Spirit. At this stage, on the other hand,
Being-within-itself is still devoid of determination, is not
as yet Spirit. It is immediate Being-within-itself; the
eternal as this Being-within-itself has as yet no content,

so that we cannot speak of the form as corresponding to the inner nature. The indifference of the form extends here even to the objectively eternal. Death even is no interruption as regards the substantial Essence; as soon as ever a Lama dies, another is at hand at once, so that the Essence is the same in both, and he can be sought for directly, being recognisable by certain marks. Thus we have a description by the English ambassador Turner of the Lama in Little Thibet; he was a child of two or three years old, whose predecessor had died on a journey to Pekin, to which place he had been summoned by the Chinese Emperor. A regent, the minister of the previous Dalailama, who is designated his cup-bearer, took the place of this child in the affairs of government.

There is a difference between Buddhism and Lamaism. What they have in common has been already indicated, and those who worship Foe and Buddha worship the Dalailama also. It is, however, more under the form of some dead person, who yet has also a present existence among his successors, that the latter is worshipped. Of Foe, too, in like manner, it is related that he had incarnated himself eight thousand times, and had been present in the actual existence of a human being.

Such are the fundamental determinations which result from what is here the divine nature, and which alone result from it, since this itself is still confined entirely to the undeveloped abstraction of calm, characterless Being-within-itself. On this account all further embodiment and mental representation of it is made entirely dependent, partly on the accidental element of empirical historical events, and partly on that of ungoverned imagination. The details of it belong to a description of the countless confused imaginings about certain incidents connected with, or things that have befallen these deities, their friends and disciples, and yield material which, so far as its substance is concerned, has but little interest or value, and indeed, for the reasons already stated, has not the interest of the Notion.

In regard to worship, we have not to do here with external ceremonies and customs. It is the essential element alone which is to be described here, namely, how Being-within-itself, the principle of this stage, appears in the actual consciousness.

(c.) *Worship or cultus.*

This religion of substantiality has influenced the character of the peoples who profess it in the degree in which they have made exaltation above the immediate individual consciousness a thorough-going requirement.

1. Since the One is conceived of as the Substantial, this immediately involves elevation above desire, above the individual will, above savagery—involves immersion in this inwardness, this unity. The image of Buddha is in this thinking position: the feet and arms are folded over one another so that one toe goes into the mouth, representing this returning into self, this self-absorption. The character of the peoples who profess this religion is that of calmness, gentleness, obedience, which is superior to savagery, to passion.

But it is the Dalailama above all who is the manifestation of perfect and satisfied Being-within-itself. His leading characteristics are repose and gentleness, with which he combines insight and a thoroughly noble manner of existence. Nations worship him, regarding him in the fair light of one living in pure contemplation, the absolute Eternal being present in him. If the Lama has to direct his attention to eternal things, he is then exclusively occupied with the beneficent office of bestowing consolation and help; his primary attribute is to forget and to have mercy. That child which was in Little Thibet when the English ambassador already mentioned arrived there, was, it is true, still being suckled, but was a lively intelligent child, behaved with all possible dignity and propriety, and seemed already to have a consciousness of his higher dignity. And the ambassador could not sufficiently praise the regent for his noble bearing and passionless repose. The preceding Lama, too, had been a discerning, worthy, high-minded man. That, however, an individual should have substance concentrated in himself, and should outwardly display this worthy and noble character, are two things which are in close relation to each other.

In so far as the stillness of Being-within-itself is the extinction of all that is particular, is nothingness, this state of annihilation is the highest state for man, and his destiny is to immerse himself in this non-existence, eternal repose, in nothingness—in fact, in the substantial, where all determinations cease, and there is no will, no intelligence. By persistent immersion and meditation within himself man is supposed to become like to this principle, to come to be without passion, without inclination, without action, and to arrive at a condition in which he desires nothing and does nothing.

There is no question here of virtue, vice, reconciliation, immortality ; the holiness of a man consists in his uniting himself in this extinction, in this silence, with God, with nothingness, with the Absolute. The highest state consists in the cessation of all bodily motion, of all movement of the soul. When this level has been reached, there is no descent to a lower grade, no further change, and man has no migration to fear after death, for he is then identical with God. Here, therefore, we have expressed the theoretical moment that man is something substantial, exists for himself. The practical element is that he wills ; if he wills, then that which is is an object for him which he alters, upon which he impresses his form. The practical value of religious feeling is determined in accordance with the content of that which is regarded as the True. In this religion, however, this theoretical element is still present, namely, that this unity, purity, nothingness is absolutely independent in relation to con-

sciousness, that it is its nature not to act in opposition
to the objective, not to give it form, but to leave it to
itself, so that this stillness is produced in it. This is
the Absolute ; man has to make himself nothingness. The
value of man consists in this, that his self-consciousness
has an affirmative relation to that theoretical substantiality. This is the opposite of that relation which, since
the object has no determination for it, is of a merely
negative nature, and for that very reason is *only* affirmative, as being a relation of the subject to its own
inwardness, which is the power to transmute all objectivity into a negative, that is to say, is affirmative in its
" vanity " alone.

That still, gentle state of mind has, in the first place,
momentarily in worship the consciousness of such eternal
repose as essential divine Being, and this gives the tone
and character to the rest of life. But self-consciousness
is at liberty too to make its entire life a permanent state
of that stillness and contemplation without existence ; and
this actual withdrawal from the eternal conditions of the
needs and activities of life into the tranquil inner region,
and the consequent attainment of union with this theoretical substantiality, must be considered as the supreme consummation. Thus great religious associations take their
rise among these peoples, the members of which live in
community in repose of the spirit, and in tranquil contemplation of the Eternal, without taking part in worldly
interests and occupations.

If a man assumes this negative mental attitude, defends
himself not against what is external, but only against
himself, and unites himself with nothingness, rids himself of all consciousness, of all passion, he is then exalted
to the state which among Buddhists is called Nirvana.
In this condition man is without gravity, he has no
longer any weight, is not subject to disease, to old age,
to death; he is looked upon as God Himself; he has
become Buddha.

2. If by transplanting himself into this state of abstraction, this perfect solitude, this renunciation, nothingness, a man attains to this, that he is undistinguishable from God, eternal, identical with God, then the ideas of immortality and transmigration of souls enter as an essential element into the doctrines of Foe, of Buddha. This standpoint is, strictly speaking, higher than that at which the adherents of Tâo are supposed to make themselves Shan, immortal.

While this is given out as the highest destiny of man, namely, to make himself immortal by means of meditation, by returning into himself, it is not at the same time asserted that the soul in itself as such is persistent and essential, that the spirit is immortal, but only that man makes himself for the first time immortal by this abstraction, this exaltation, that he ought, in fact, to make himself such. The thought of immortality is involved in the fact that man is a thinking being, that he is in his freedom at home with himself; thus he is absolutely independent; an "Other" cannot break in upon his freedom : he relates himself to himself alone ; an Other cannot give itself valid worth within him.

This likeness or equality with myself, " I," this self-contained existence, this true Infinite, is accordingly what, in the language peculiar to this point of view, is immortal, is subject to no change; it is itself the Unchangeable, what is within itself alone, what moves itself only within itself. " I," is not dead repose, but movement—movement, however, which is not called change, but is eternal rest, eternal transparency within itself.

Since God is known as the essential, is thought of in His essentiality, and since Being-within-itself, and self-contained Being or Being-with-itself is a true determination, so in relation to the subject this Being-within-itself, this essentiality is known as its nature, the subject being inherently spiritual. This essentiality attaches to the soul, to the subject too ; it becomes known that the soul is immortal, that its nature is to have a pure existence, but not as yet to exist in the strict sense as this purity— that is, not as yet to exist as spirituality. On the contrary, this essentiality still strictly implies that the mode of existence continues to be sensuous immediacy, which, however, is merely accidental.

Immortality, therefore, means that the soul which is at home with itself or self-contained, as being something essential, is at the same time existing. Essence without existence is a mere abstraction ; essentiality, the Notion, must be thought of as existing. Thus realisation, too, belongs to essentiality, but the form of the realisation is still sensuous existence, sensuous immediacy. Now transmigration of souls means that the soul still persists after death, but in another mode of existence, a sensuous mode. The soul being still abstractly conceived of as Being-within-itself, the form assumed is a matter of indifference. The spirit is not known as concrete, is only abstract essentiality, and thus determinate Being ; the phenomenal appearance is merely the immediate sensuous shape, which is contingent, and is human or animal form. Human beings, animals, the whole world of life, become the many-hued garment of colourless individuality. Being-within-itself, the Eternal, has as yet no content, and therefore, too, no standard for form.

The idea that man passes into such forms, is accordingly united with the thought of morality, of desert. That is to say, the relation of man to the principle, to nothingness, implies that in order to be happy he must labour by means of continuous speculation, meditation, musing upon himself, to become like to this principle, and the holiness of man consists in uniting himself in this silence with God. The loud voices of worldly life must become mute ; the silence of the grave is the element of eternity and holiness. In the cessation of all movement or motion of the body, all movement of the soul, in this extinction of oneself happiness consists. And when a man has reached this stage of perfection, then there is no more change, his soul has no longer to fear transmigration, for he is identical with the god Foe.   The soul is exalted into the region of nothingness, and thus delivered from bondage to external sensuous form.

In so far, however, as a man has not, by renunciation, by sinking into himself, attained to this felicity—though this latter is indeed in him, for his spirit is this potentiality—he is still in need of duration, and so of bodily existence too, and in this way the idea of metempsychosis takes its origin.

3. It is here, accordingly, that the aspects of power and of magic combine with this idea, and the religion of Being-within-itself runs out into the wildest superstition. The theoretical relation, owing to the fact that it is, properly speaking, inherently empty, is reversed and changes into the practical one of magic.   The mediation of priests here comes in, and they represent at once the Higher, and the power above the forms or shapes which man assumes.   The adherents of Foe are in this respect superstitious to the utmost degree.   They believe that man passes into all possible forms, and that the priests are those who, living in the supersensuous world, determine the form which the soul is to take on, and are therefore able to keep it from assuming ill-omened shapes.   A missionary tells a story of a dying Chinese who had sent for him, and complained that a Bonze (these are the priests, those who know, to whom is known what is happening in the other world) had told him that just as he was now in the service of the Emperor, so would he remain in it after death likewise; his soul would pass into an imperial post-horse; he must then perform his duties faithfully, not kick, not bite, not stumble, and content himself with a small amount of food.

The dogma of metempsychosis is also the point at which the simple worship of Being-within-itself transforms itself into an idolatry of the most varied description. In this dogma we have the foundation and origin of that infinite multitude of idols and images which are everywhere worshipped where Foe holds sway. Four-footed beasts, birds, creeping things, in a word, the lowest forms of animal life, have temples and are worshipped, because the god inhabits each one of them in his new births, and any and every animal body may be inhabited by the soul of man.

III.

NATURAL RELIGION IN TRANSITION TO THE RELIGION OF FREEDOM.

As regards its necessity, this transition is based upon the fact that the truth which in the preceding stages is potentially present as the foundation is here actually brought forward and posited. In the Religion of Phantasy and that of Being-within-itself, this subject, this subjective self-consciousness, is identical, though in an immediate manner, with that substantial unity which is called Brāhma or characterless nothingness. This One is now conceived of as unity determined within itself, as implicitly subjective unity, and at the same time as this unity in its character as implicitly totality. If the unity be inherently determined as subjective, it then contains the principle of Spirituality in itself, and it is this principle which unfolds itself in the religions which are based upon this transition.

Further, in the Indian religion the One, the unity of Brāhma, and determinateness, the many Powers of the Particular, this appearance of differences, stood in a relation to each other which implied that at one time the differences were held to be independent, and at another that they had disappeared and were submerged in unity. The dominant and universal characteristic was the alter-

nation of origination and passing away ; the alternation
of the annulling and absorption of the particular Powers
in the unity, and of procession out of unity.   In the
Religion of Being-within-itself this alternation was indeed
brought to rest in so far as the particular differences fell
back into the unity of nothingness, but this unity was
empty and abstract, and the truth is, on the contrary,
the unity which is concrete within itself and is totality,
so that even that abstract unity, together with the element of difference, enters into the true unity in which the
differences are posited as annulled, as ideal, negative, and
non-self-subsisting, but at the same time as preserved.

   The unfolding of the moments of the Idea, the self-
differentiation of the thought of absolute Substance, was
therefore hitherto defective, in so far as the forms or
shapes lost themselves on the one hand in hard fixity,
while on the other it was merely by flight that unity
was reached, or to put it otherwise, the unity was merely
the disappearance of the differences.   Now, however, the
reflection of manifoldness into itself appears, implying
that Thought itself contains determination within itself,
so that it is self-determination, and determination has
only worth and substantive content in so far as it is
reflected into this unity.   Together with this, the notion
of freedom, objectivity, is posited, and the divine Notion
thus becomes the unity of the finite and infinite.   The
Thought which only exists within itself, pure Substance,
is the Infinite, and the finite, in accordance with the
thought-determination, is the many gods ; while the unity
is negative unity, abstraction, which submerges the Many
in this One.   But this last has gained nothing by this ;
it is undetermined as before, and the finite is only affirmative outside of the Infinite, not within it, and hence so
soon as it is affirmative it is finitude which is devoid
of rationality.   But now the finite, the determinate in
general is taken up into infinitude, the form is commensurate with the substance, the infinite form is identical

with the substance, which determines itself within itself, and is not merely abstract Power.

The other equally essential determination is that with this the separation of the empirical self-consciousness from the Absolute, from the content of the Highest, for the first time takes place, that here for the first time God attains true objectivity. At the former stages it is the empirical self-consciousness immersed in itself which is Brāhma, this abstraction within self, or, in other words, the Highest is present as a human being. Thus substantial unity is still inseparable from the subject, and in so far as it is still something imperfect, is not as yet in its very nature subjective unity; it still has the subject outside of it. The objectivity of the Absolute, the consciousness of its independence in its own right, is not present.

Here this breach between subjectivity and objectivity takes place for the first time, and it is here that objectivity for the first time properly deserves the name of God; and we have this objectivity of God here because this content has determined itself by its own act to be potentially concrete totality. The meaning of this is that God is a Spirit, that God is the Spirit in all religions.

When, as happens with special frequency at the present day, we hear it said that subjective consciousness forms a part of religion, the idea expressed is a correct one. We have here the instinct that subjectivity belongs to religion. But people have an idea that the spiritual can exist as an empirical subject, which then as empirical consciousness can have a natural thing for its God, and this means that spirituality can come into consciousness *only*, and God, too, as a natural existence, can be an object for this consciousness.

Thus, on the one side, we have God as a natural existence; but God is essentially Spirit, and this is the absolute characteristic quality of religion in general, and therefore the fundamental characteristic, the substantial basis, in every form of religion. The natural thing is presented in a human fashion, and also as personality, as spirit, as consciousness; but the deities of the Hindus are still superficial personifications—the personification by no means implies that the object, God, is known as Spirit. It is these particular objects, the sun, a tree, which are personified. The incarnations of the deities, too, have their place here; the particular objects have, however, an independence, and because they are particular and natural objects the independence is only a fictitious one.

But the Highest is Spirit, and it is from the empirical subjective spirit in the first instance that this spiritual determination and independence is derived, either where it gets a definite shape, or where Brāhma has his existence in and through immersion of the subject in itself. Now, however, it is no longer the case that man is God or God is man—that God exists merely in an empirico-human mode; on the contrary, God is truly objective in His own nature, is in His very Being totality, concretely determined in Himself, that is to say, known as being in His real nature subjective, and thus is He for the first time essentially an Object, and stands over against man in general.

The return to the thought that God appears as man, as God-man, we shall find later on; but it is here that this objectivity of God has its beginning.

Now if the Universal be conceived as determination of self within self, then it comes into opposition with what is Other than itself, and represents strife with the Other of itself. In the religion of Power there is no opposition, no strife, for the accidental has no value for Substance.

Power now determining itself by its own act, has not, indeed, these determinations as something finite. On the contrary, what is determined exists in its complete and independent truth. By means of this, God is determined as the Good; goodness is not laid down as a predicate here, but He is simply the Good. In what has no determinate character there is neither good nor evil. The Good, on the other hand, is here the Universal, but with one purpose or end—a determinate character, which is commensurate with the universality in which it is.

To begin with, however, the self-determination of self is at this stage exclusive. Thus the Good comes into relation with what is Other, the Evil, and this relation is strife—dualism. Reconciliation, here a becoming or something that ought-to-be only, is not as yet thought of as in and pertaining to this Goodness itself.

Here it is at once posited as a necessary consequence that the strife comes to be known as a characteristic of Substance itself. The Negative is posited in Spirit itself, and this is compared with its affirmation, so that this comparison is present in felt experience, and constitutes pain, death. And here, finally, the strife, which dies away, is the wrestling of Spirit to come to itself, to attain to freedom.

From these fundamental determinations the following divisions of this transition stage result:—

1. The first determination is that of the Persian religion. Here the actual Being of the Good is still of a superficial kind, consequently it has a natural form, but a natural existence which is formless—Light.

2. The form of religion in which strife, pain, death itself actually appear in the Essence—the Syrian religion.

3. The struggling out of the strife, the going onward to the true destiny of free spirituality, the overcoming of evil, complete transition to the religion of free spirituality —the Egyptian religion.

Speaking generally, however, the characteristic common to these three forms of religion is the resumption of wild, unrestrained totality into concrete unity. This giddy whirl, in which the determinations of unity are precipitated into externality and contingency, where out of unity, as out of Brāhma, this wild notionless world of deities proceeds, and where the development, because it is not proportionate to the unity, breaks up into confusion—this state, devoid of anything to give it steadfastness, has now passed away.

This resumption into substantial unity, which is inherently subjective, has, however, two forms. The first form of resumption is that seen in the religion of the Parsees, and it takes place in a pure, simple manner. The other is the fermenting process, seen in the Syrian and Egyptian religions, where the fermentation of totality mediates itself into unity, and unity comes into existence in the strife of its elements.

I. *The Religion of the Good or of Light.*

(a.) *Its notion or conception.*

I. The resumption is as yet the pure simple one, but for that reason it is also abstract. God is known as the absolutely existent, which is determined within itself.

Here the determinate character is not an empirical, manifold one, but is just what is pure, universal, what is equal to itself; a determination of Substance, by which it ceases to be Substance, and begins to be subject. This unity, as self-determining, has a content, and that this content is what is determined by unity, and is in conformity with it, is the universal content, is what is called Good or the True; for those are only forms which belong to the further distinctions of knowing and willing, which in the highest form of subjectivity are but one truth, particularisations of this One truth.

The fact that this Universal is determined by the self-determination of Spirit, and by Spirit and for Spirit, is the side upon which it is Truth. In proportion as it is posited by Spirit, is a self-determination commensurate with its unity, is its own self-determination by which it

remains true to itself in its universality, and in consequence of which no other determinations present themselves unless that unity itself, is it the Good. It is therefore the true content which has objectivity, the Good,
which is the same as the True. This Good is at the same
time self-determination of the One, of absolute Substance,
and in being such it directly remains absolute Power—
the Good as absolute Power. Such is the determination
of the content.

2. It is just in this determination of the Absolute, and
in the fact that it is self-determination and the Good, in
which even concrete life is able to behold its affirmative
root, and to become conscious of itself in a true manner,
that there lies the connection with the concrete, with the
world, with concrete empirical life generally. Out of
this Power all things proceed. We had this determination of the Absolute in the foregoing forms, where it
implied that this mode of self-determination, as a mode of
determination, contains abstract determination, is not self-
determination, what has returned into itself, what remains
in identity, the True and Good in the universal sense,
but is the act of determination generally. Power, as
such, is neither good nor wise ; it has no end in view,
but is merely determined as Being and Not-being ; it is
characterised by wildness, by modes of acting savouring
of madness in fact. For this reason Power is intrinsically what is without determination.

This moment of Power is also present, but as something subordinated. Thus it is concrete life, the world
in manifold existence ; but that which is all-important
is that in the Good, as self-determination, is contained
this absolute characteristic, namely, the connection of the
Good with the concrete world.

Subjectivity, particularity generally, is in this Substance,
in the One itself, which is the absolute subject. This
element, which belongs to the particular life, this determinateness is at the same time posited in the Absolute

itself, and in being so is an affirmative co-relation or
connection of the Absolute, of the good and true, of the
Infinite with that which is called the finite.

The affirmative connection in the earlier forms of
religion exists in part only in this pure absorption, in
which the subject says, " I am Brāhma," but it is an
absolutely abstract connection, which only exists by
means of this stupefaction, this relinquishment of all
concrete actuality of Spirit, by means of negation. This
affirmative connection is merely, as it were, a simple
thread; for the rest, it is the abstract negative, this
sacrifice, this self-immolation ; that is to say, instead of
connection there is merely flight from the concrete.

But with this affirmative connection, where determinate existence is taken up into universality, it is stated
that things themselves are good ; the Good is present
Substance in them, and that which is good is their life,
their affirmative Being. So far as they remain good,
they belong to this realm of the Good ; they are from the
very first received into favour ; it is not that a part only
are these twice-born, as in India. On the contrary, the
finite is composed of what is good, and is good. And,
indeed, good is taken in the proper sense, and is understood with reference to an external end, an external
comparison. That is in accordance with an end which
is good for something, so that the end lies outside of the
object. Here, on the other hand, good is to be understood as meaning that it is the Universal determined
within itself. Good is so determined within itself ; the
particular things are good, they serve their own purpose,
are adequate to themselves, not merely to an Other. The
Good is not for them a " Beyond,"—Brāhma again.

3. This Good, although it is indeed subjective itself,
is inherently determined as Good, and is commensurate
with substantial unity, with Universality itself, yet this
determination is itself still abstract. The Good is concrete within itself, and yet this determinate existence of

concrete Being is itself still abstract. In order that the Good be not abstract, there must be the development of form, the positing of the moments of the Notion. In order to exist as rational Idea, to be known as Spirit, its determinations, the negative element, the distinctions as representing its powers must be posited, known, by means of the thought in it.

The Good may be made use of in various ways, or, to put it otherwise, human beings have good intentions. Here the question presents itself, "What is good?" There is a demand for further definition and explanation of the Good. Here we still have Good as abstract, as something one-sided, and consequently as an absolute antithesis to an Other, and this Other is Evil. In this simple relation the negative is not as yet comprehended within what rightly belongs to it.

We thus have two principles, the well-known Oriental dualism—the realms of good and evil. This is the grand opposition which has here reached this universal abstraction. In the varied character of the deities previously referred to, there is undoubtedly manifoldness, difference ; but the fact that this duality has become the universal principle is quite another thing, for the difference confronts itself as this dualism.

The Good is indeed the True, the Powerful, but is at war with Evil in such a way that Evil stands over against it as an absolute principle, and remains standing over against it. The evil ought, it is true, to be overcome, to be equated, but what ought to be *is* not. The ought-to-be, the ideal, is a force which cannot realise itself ; it is a certain weakness and impotence.

This dualism, understood as distinction or difference in its entire universality, is the interest alike of religion and philosophy, and it is, in fact, when put in terms of Thought that this opposition acquires its universality. At the present time dualism is a form of thought too ; but when we speak of dualism, the forms referred to are of a weak and slight kind. The modern antithesis of finite and infinite is just that of Ahriman and Ormazd— it is just the same Manicheism as we have here.

From the moment that we take the finite as independent, so that the infinite and finite stand opposite to one another in such a way that the infinite has no part with the finite, and the finite cannot pass over to the infinite, then that is the same thing as this dualism, only that when we so conceive of the relation, we have not the intention of forming, nor the heart to form a conception of these opposites in accordance with their entire content.

The finite when, in its further determination, it asserts itself as finite over against the infinite, the Universal, and in so doing declares itself opposed to the infinite, is the Evil. We find accordingly that some stop short at this standpoint, which is marked by an utter absence of thought, and in accordance with which a valid existence is allowed both to the finite *and* the infinite. But God is only one principle, one power, and the finite, and for that very reason Evil, has no true independent existence.

But further, Good, by virtue of its universality, has moreover a natural mode of determinate existence, a mode of existence for an Other, namely, Light, which is pure manifestation. As the Good, that which is self-identical or commensurate with itself, is subjectivity in its pure identity with itself in the spiritual sphere, so is Light this abstract subjectivity in the sensuous sphere. Space and time are the primary abstractions in the sphere of externality or mutual exclusion, but the concrete physical element in its universality is Light. If, therefore, the essentially Good, because of its abstract character, comes to have the form of immediateness, and consequently of naturalness (for immediateness is the natural), then this immediate Goodness, which has not as yet purified itself and raised itself to the form of absolute spirituality, is Light. For Light is in the natural world pure manifestation, determination of self by self, but in an entirely simple, universal manner.

If Brāhma had to be represented in a sensuous fashion, he could only be represented as abstract space. Brāhma has not as yet, however, the force within himself to be independently represented, but has as his realisation the empirical consciousness of man.

The fact that the Good at which we have arrived is still supposed to have essentially a natural form, although certainly it is nature in the pure form of Light, presents a certain difficulty. But Nature cannot possibly be left out by Spirit; it essentially belongs to Spirit.

God, too, as inherently concrete, as pure Spirit, is at the same time essentially Creator and Lord of nature. Thus the Idea in its Notion, God in His essential Being itself, must posit this reality, this external existence which we call Nature. The moment of naturalness, therefore, cannot be dispensed with, only it exists here as yet in an abstract form—in this immediate unity with thè Spiritual, the Good, just because the Good is as yet this abstraction.

The Good contains determinateness within itself, and in determinateness is the root of natural existence. We say, "God creates the world." Creation is this subjectivity to which determinateness in general pertains. It is in this activity or subjectivity that the essential character of nature lies, and indeed in the more definite relation which implies that that nature is something created. This does not, however, as yet exist here. What is present here is abstract determinateness.

This determinateness has essentially the form of nature generally, of Light, and of immediate unity with the Good ; for the Immediate is itself just the Abstract, because determinateness is merely this universal, undeveloped determinateness.

Light, accordingly, has darkness standing over against it. In Nature these two characteristics are separate from one another in this fashion. This is the impotence of nature, namely, that light and its negation lie side by side, although, indeed, light is the power to drive away darkness. This determination in God is itself as yet that element of impotence which, because of its abstraction, is not as yet able to contain and endure the opposition, the contradiction within itself, but has the Evil alongside of it. Light is the Good and the Good is light; this is the indivisible unity which we have here.

But light is in conflict with darkness, with evil, which it is to overcome, though ideally only, for it does not actually succeed in doing this.

Light is an infinite expansion, it is as rapid as Thought; but in order that its manifestation be real, it must strike upon something that is dark. Nothing is made manifest by pure light; only in this Other does definite manifestation make its appearance, and with this, Good appears in opposition to Evil. This manifestation is a determining but not as yet concrete development of determination; the concreteness of determination is therefore outside of it, because of its abstraction it has its determination in the Other. Without the opposition Spirit does not exist, and in the development of Spirit the point of importance is merely as to the position this opposition assumes relatively to mediation and to the original unity.

Thus the Good in its universality has a natural form, namely, this pure manifestation of nature, Light. The Good is the universal determinateness of things. Since it is thus abstract subjectivity, the moment of particularity or singularity, the moment, the mode, by which it is for Other, is itself as yet in sensuous perception something externally present, which, however, may come to be adequate to the content, for all particularity is taken up into the Universal; particularity of this more precise kind, in accordance with which it is the mode of perception, the mode of immediateness, is then capable of seeming adequate to the content. Brāhma, for example, is merely abstract thought; looked upon in a sensuous way, he would, as has been already stated, correspond merely with the perception of space, a sensuous universality of perception which is itself merely abstract. Here, on the contrary, the substantial element is commensurate with the form, and the latter is then physical universality—light, which has darkness over against it. Air, breath, &c., are also determinations which are physical, but they are not in this way the Ideal itself, are not universal individuality, subjectivity. It is in light which manifests itself that we have the moment of self-determination, of individuality, of subjectivity. Light appears as light generally, as universal light, and then as nature in a particular specific form ; nature in the form of special objects reflected into itself as the essential element of particular things.

Light must not here be understood as meaning the sun. It may indeed be said that the sun is the most prominent light, but it stands beyond and above us as a particular body, as a special individual object. The Good, the light, on the contrary, has within itself the root of subjectivity, but only the root ; accordingly, it is not posited as thus individual, existing apart by itself ; and thus light is to be taken as subjectivity, as the soul of things.

(b.) *This religion as it actually exists.*

This Religion of Light or of the immediate Good is the religion of the ancient Parsis, founded by Zoroaster. There still exist some communities who belong to this religion in Bombay and on the shores of the Black Sea, in the neighbourhood of Baku, where those naphtha springs are specially frequent, in the accidental proximity of which some have imagined they find an explanation of the fact that the Parsis have chosen fire as an object of worship. From Herodotus and other Greek authors we derive some information regarding this religion, but it is only in later times that a more accurate knowledge of it has been arrived at by the discovery of the principal and funda-

mental books (Zend-Avesta) of that people by the French-
man Anquetil du Perron:[1] these books are written in
the ancient Zend language, a sister language to Sanscrit.

Light, which is worshipped in this religion, is not a
symbol of the Good, an image or figure by which the
Good is represented; it might, on the contrary, just as
well be said that the Good is the symbol of light.
Neither of the two is outward sign or symbol, but they
are directly identical.

Here among the Parsis worship makes its appearance.
Substantiality here exists for the subject in its particularity: man as a particular form of the Good stands over
against the universal Good, over against light in its pure,
as yet undisturbed, manifestation, which the Good as
natural concrete existence is.

The Parsis have also been called fire-worshippers.
This designation is to a certain degree incorrect, for the
Parsis do not direct their worship to fire as devouring
material fire, but only to fire as light, which as the truth
of the material appears in an outward form.

The Good as an object, as something having a sensuous shape, which corresponds with the content which
is as yet abstract, is Light. It has essentially the
signification of the Good, the Righteous; in human form
it is known as Ormazd, but this form is as yet a superficial personification here. Personification exists, that is
to say, so long as the form as representing the content
is not as yet inherently developed subjectivity. Ormazd
is the Universal, which in an external form acquires subjectivity; he is light, and his kingdom is the realm of light.

The stars are lights appearing singly. What appears
being something particular, natural, there at once springs
up a difference between that which appears and that

---

[1] It was in 1754 that Anquetil du Perron saw a facsimile of four leaves
of the Oxford MS. of the Vendêdâd Sâdah, and after years of heroic effort
and persevering toil, in 1771 he published the first European translation of
the Zend-Avesta—Tr. S.

which is implicit, and what is implicit then becomes a something Particular, a genius also. Just as universal light is personified, so particular lights come to be personified too. Thus the stars are personified as genii; in one aspect they are what appears, and then are personified as well; they are not differentiated, however, into light and into the Good; on the contrary, it is the collective unity which is personified: the stars are spirits of Ormazd, of the universal light, and of the inherently existing Good.

These stars are called the *Amshaspands*, and Ormazd, who is universal light, is also one of the Amshaspands. The realm of Ormazd is the realm of light, and there are seven Amshaspands in it. These might perhaps suggest the planets, but they are not further characterised in the Zend-Avesta, and in none of the prayers, not even in those directed to them individually, are they more particularly specified. The lights are the companions of Ormazd, and reign with him. The Persian State itself, too, similarly with this realm of light, is described as the kingdom of righteousness and of the Good. The king, too, was surrounded by seven magnates, who formed his council, and were thought of as representatives of the Amshaspands, in the same way as the king was conceived to be the representative of Ormazd. The Amshaspands govern, changing place day by day, in the realm of light with Ormazd; consequently what is posited here is merely a superficial distinction of time.

To the Good or the kingdom of light belongs all that has life; that which in all beings is good is Ormazd; he is the life-giving element through thought, word, and deed. Here we still have Pantheism in so far as the Good, light, substance, is in everything; all happiness, blessing, felicity meet together in it; whatever exists as loving, happy, strong, and the like, that is Ormazd. He bestows the light on all beings, upon trees as upon noble men, upon animals as upon the Amshaspands.

The sun and the planets are the first chief spirits or
deities, a heavenly people, pure and great, shielding all,
beneficent to all, shedding benediction upon all—being
rulers by turns over the world of light. The whole
world is Ormazd in all its stages and varied existence,
and in this kingdom of light all is good. To light
belongs everything, all that lives, all essential being,
all spiritual existence, the action, the growth of finite
things, all is light, is Ormazd. In this is not merely
sensuous life, life in general, but strength, spirit, soul,
blessedness. In the fact that a man, a tree, an animal
lives and rejoices in existence, possesses an affirmative
nature, is something noble, in this consists their glory,
their light, and this it is which is the sum and essence of
the substantial nature of every individual existence.

The manifestation of light is worshipped, and in connection with this the element of locality has a value
for the Parsi. Advantage is taken, for example, of the
plains upon which naphtha wells abound. Light is
burnt upon the altars; it is not a symbol, but is rather
the presence of the ineffable, of the Good. All that is
good in the world is thus reverenced, loved, worshipped,
for it is esteemed as the son, the begotten of Ormazd, in
which he loves himself, pleases himself. In like manner
hymns of praise are addressed to all pure spirits of mankind. These are called *Fravashis*,[1] and are either beings
still in the body and still existing, or dead beings, and
thus Zoroaster's Fravashi is entreated to watch over them.
In the same way animals are worshipped, because they
have life, light in them. In worshipping these, the genii,
spirits, the affirmative element of living nature, is brought
into prominence and reverenced as the ideals of the particular kinds of things, as universal subjective forms,
which represent the Divine in a finite way. Animals
are, as already stated, objects of worship, but the ideal

---

[1] The word which Hegel uses is *Ferver*, but he evidently means
Fravashis.

is the heavenly bull, which, among the Hindus, is the symbol of procreation, and stands beside Síva. Among fires, it is the sun that is specially worshipped ; among mountains, too, there is a similar ideal—Alborg, the mountain of mountains. Thus in the Parsi's view of things there exists an active present world of the Good, ideals which are not beyond this world, but are in existence, are present in actual things.

Everything that is alive is held in reverence as Good, but only the good, the light in it, not its particular form, its finite transitory mode of existence. There is a separation between the substantial element and what belongs to the perishable. A distinction is posited in man too ; a something higher is distinguished from the immediate corporeal, natural, temporal, insignificant character of his external Being, of his existence. This is represented by the Genii, *Fravashis*. Among trees, there is one which is specially marked off—*Hôm*, the tree from which flow the waters of immortality. Thus the State is the manifestation of the substantial, of the realm of light, the prince being the manifestation of the supreme light, while the officials are the representatives of the Spirits of Ormazd. The above distinction is, however, a surface one ; the absolute one is that between Good and Evil.

It may be also mentioned that one among the helpers of Ormazd is *Mitra*, the μεσίτης, mediator. It is curious that Herodotus, even in his time, makes special mention of this Mitra ; yet in the religion of the Parsis, the characteristic of mediation, reconciliation does not seem as yet to have become prominent. It was not until a later period that the worship of Mithras was more generally developed in its complete form, as the human spirit had become more strongly conscious of the need of reconciliation, and as that need had become keener and more definite.

Among the Romans in Christian times Mithras-worship

was very widely spread, and so late as the Middle Ages we meet with a secret Mithras-worship ostensibly connected with the order of the Knights-Templars. Mithras thrusting the knife into the neck of the ox is a figurative representation belonging essentially to the cult of Mithras, of which examples have been frequently found in Europe.

(c.) *Worship.*

The worship belonging to this religion results directly from the essential character of the religion. The purpose of it is to glorify Ormazd in his creation, and the adoration of the Good in everything is its beginning and end. The prayers are of a simple and uniform character, without any special shades of meaning. The principal feature of the cultus is that man is to keep himself pure as regards his inner and outer life, and is to maintain and diffuse the same purity everywhere. The entire life of the Parsi is to be this worship; it is not something isolated, as among the Hindus. It is the duty of the Parsi everywhere to promote life, to render it fruitful and keep it gladsome; to practise good in word and deed in all places; to further all that is good among mankind, as well as to benefit men themselves; to excavate canals, plant trees, give shelter to wanderers, build waste places, feed the hungry, irrigate the ground, which, from another point of view, is itself subject and *genius.*

Such is this one-sidedness of abstraction.

2. *The Syrian Religion, or the Religion of Pain.*

We have just been considering the ideas of strife and of victory over evil. We have now to consider, as representing the next moment or stage, that strife as Pain. " Strife as pain" seems a superficial expression; it implies, however, that the strife is no longer an external opposition only, but is in a single subject, and within that subject's own feeling of itself. The strife is, accord-

ingly, the objectifying of pain. Pain is, however, in
general terms the course or process of finitude, and, from
a subjective point of view, brokenness of heart. This
process or course of finitude, of pain, strife, victory, is a
moment or stage in the nature of Spirit, and it cannot
be absent in the sphere under consideration, in which
power continuously determines itself toward spiritual
freedom. The loss of one's own self, the contradiction
between self-contained Being and its "Other," a contradiction which annuls itself by absorption into infinite
unity—for here we can think of true infinitude only—the
annulling of the opposition, these are the essential determinations in the Idea of Spirit which now make their
appearance. It is true that *we* are now conscious of the
development of the Idea, of its course as well as of
its moments or stages, whose totality constitutes Spirit.
This totality, however, is not as yet posited, but obtains
expression in moments which in this sphere present themselves successively.

The content not being as yet posited in free Spirit,
since the moments are not as yet gathered together into
subjective unity, it exists in an immediate mode, and is
thrown out into the form of Nature; it is represented by
means of a natural progressive process, which, however,
is essentially conceived of as symbolical, and consequently
is not merely a progressive process in external nature,
but is an universal progressive process as contrasted with
the point of view which we have hitherto occupied, and
from which not Spirit but abstract Power is seen to be
what rules. The next element in the Idea is the moment
or stage of conflict. It is the essential nature of Spirit
to come to itself out of its otherness and out of the
overcoming of this otherness, by the negation of the
negation. Spirit brings itself forth; it passes through
the estrangement of itself. But since it is not as yet
posited as Spirit, this course of estrangement and return
is not as yet posited ideally, and as a moment or stage

of Spirit, but immediately, and therefore in the form of what is natural.

This determination, as we have seen it, has acquired a definite form in the religion of the Phœnicians and in the religions of anterior Asia generally. In these religions the Process which has been spoken of is contained, and in the religion of the Phœnicians the succumbing to death, the estrangement of the god from himself, and his resurrection are brought into special prominence. The popular conception regarding the Phœnix is well known : it is a bird which burns itself, and from out of its ashes there comes a young Phœnix in new vigour and strength.

This estrangement, this otherness, defined as a natural negation, is death, but death that is at the same time annulled, since out of it there issues a revival and renewal of life. It is the eternal nature of Spirit to die to self, to render itself finite in Nature, and yet it is by the annulling of its natural existence that it comes to itself. The Phœnix is the well-known symbol of this. What we have here is not the warfare of Good with Evil, but a divine process which pertains to the nature of God Himself, and is the process in one individual. The more precise form in which this progressive process definitely appears is represented by Adonis. This representation has passed over to Egypt and Greece, and is mentioned in the Bible, too, under the name of Thammus (תַּמּוּז), Ezek. viii. 14, "And behold there sat women weeping for Thammus." One of the principal festivals of Adonis was celebrated in spring; it was a service in honour of the dead, a feast of mourning which lasted several days. For two whole days Adonis was sought for with lamentation ; the third day was a joyous festival, when the god had risen again from the dead. The entire festival has the character of a solemn feast of Nature, which expires in winter and awakens again in spring. Thus in one aspect this is a natural process, but looked

at in the other aspect it is to be taken symbolically
as a moment of God, as descriptive of the Absolute in
fact

The myth of Adonis is associated even with Greek
mythology. According to the latter, Aphrodite was the
mother of Adonis. She kept him as a child of tender
years concealed in a little chest, and took this to Ais.
Persephone, however, would not give back the child out of
the chest when the mother demanded it. Zeus decided
the dispute by ordering that each of the goddesses was
to keep Adonis for a third part of the year. The last
third was to be left to his own choice; he preferred to
spend that time also with the universal mother and his
own, namely, Aphrodite. As regards its direct interpretation, this myth, it is true, has reference to the seed
lying under the ground, and then springing up out of it.
The myth of Castor and Pollux, whose abode is alter-
nately in the nether world and upon the earth, has
also reference to this. Its true meaning, however, is
not merely the alternation of Nature, but the transition
generally from life, from affirmative Being, to death, to
negation, and then again the rising up out of this negation—the absolute mediation which essentially belongs
to the notion or conception of Spirit.

Here therefore this moment of Spirit has become
religion.

3. *The Religion of Mystery.*

The form which is peculiar to the religions of anterior
Asia is that of the mediation of Spirit with itself, in
which the natural element is still predominant; the form
of transition where we start from the Other as representing what Nature in general is, and where the transition
does not yet appear as the coming of Spirit to itself.
The further stage at which we have now arrived is where
this transition shows itself as a coming of Spirit to itself,
yet not in such a way that this return is a reconciliation,

but rather that the strife, the struggle, is the object, as a moment, however, of the Divinity itself.

This transition to spiritual religion contains, it is true, concrete subjectivity within itself ; it is, however, the free, unregulated play of this simple subjectivity; it is the development of it, yet a development which is still, as it were, in a wild and effervescent state, and has not as yet arrived at a state of tranquillity, at the true spirituality which is essentially free.

As in India the parts of this development were seen in an isolated state, so here the determinateness is in its detached state, but in such wise that these elementary powers of the Spiritual and the Natural are essentially related to subjectivity, and so related that it is one single subject which passes through these moments.

In the Indian religions, also, we had origination and passing away, but not subjectivity, return into the One, not One which itself passes through these forms and differences, and in them and from out of them returns into itself. It is this higher Power of subjectivity which, when developed, lets the element of difference go out of itself, but when enclosed within itself holds fast, or rather overpowers the difference.

The one-sidedness of this form consists in the absence of this pure unity of the Good, of the state of return, of self-contained Being. This freedom which we have here merely goes forth, merely impels itself forwards, but is not as yet, so to speak, complete, perfect, is not as yet such a beginning as would bring forth the end, the result. It is, therefore, subjectivity in its reality, not as yet, however, in true, actual freedom, but in a state of fermentation going in and out of this reality.

The dualism of light and darkness begins to come to unity here, and in such a way that this dark, this negative element, which, when intensified, even becomes evil, is included within subjectivity itself. It is the essential nature of subjectivity to unite opposite principles within itself, to be the force or energy which is able to endure this contradiction, and to dissolve it within itself.

Ormazd has always Ahriman confronting him ; we also find the idea, it is true, that Ahriman is at last overcome, and Ormazd alone reigns; but that is merely expressed as something in the future, not as anything that belongs to the present. God, Essence, Spirit, the True, must be present, not transported in idea into the past or the future. The Good—and this is the most immediate demand—must also be posited in actual fact as real power in itself, and being conceived of as universal, must thus be conceived of as real subjectivity.

What we have at the present standpoint is this unity of subjectivity, and the fact that by means of these distinguished moments, affirmation passes through negation itself, and ends with return into itself and reconciliation ; in such a way, however, that the action of this subjectivity is more the mere effervescence of it than the subjectivity which has actually attained to itself completely, and already reached its consummation.

One single subject constitutes this difference, a something concrete in itself, one development. Thus this subjectivity imports itself into developed powers, and so unites them that they are set free. This subject has a history, is the history of life, of Spirit, of movement within itself, in which it breaks up into the differentiation of these powers, and in differentiation this subject converts itself into what is heterogeneous relatively to itself.

Light does not become extinct, does not set, but here it is one single subject, which alienates itself from itself, is arrested in the negativity of itself, but reinstates itself by its own act in and from out of this estrangement. The result is the conception of free Spirit, not yet, however, as true ideality, but, to begin with, as merely the impulse to bring the ideality into actual existence.

Here we have reached the ultimate determination of

natural religion in this sphere, and in fact the stage which constitutes the transition to the religion of free subjectivity. When we examine the stage of Parsiism, we perceive it to be the resumption of the finite into the essentially existent unity in which the Good determines itself. This Good is, however, only implicitly concrete, the determinateness is essentially simple, not as yet determination made manifest; or, in other words, it is still abstract subjectivity, and not as yet real subjectivity. Accordingly, the next moment is, that outside of the realm of the Good, Evil has been given a determinate character. This determinateness is posited as simple, not developed; it is not regarded as determinateness, but merely as universality, and therefore the development, the difference is not as yet present in it as differentiated; what we find rather is that one of the differentiated elements falls outside of the Good. Things are good merely as lighted up on their positive side only, not, however, on the side of their particularity also. We now, in accordance with the Notion, approach more nearly to the realm of real actual subjectivity.

(a.) *The characterisation or determination of the Notion of this stage.*

Material is not wanting for the determinations; on the contrary, even in this concrete region that material presents itself with a determinate character. The difference lies merely in this, namely, whether the moments of totality exist in a purely superficial, external form, or whether they have their being in the inner and essential element; that is to say, whether they exist merely as superficial form and shape, or are posited, and thus thought of as the determination of the content. It is this that constitutes the enormous difference. In all religions we meet with the mode of self-consciousness, to a greater or less degree, and further with the predicates of God, such as omnipotence, omniscience, &c. Among the Hindus and Chinese we meet with sublime descriptions of God, so that higher religions have no superiority over them in this respect: these are so-called pure conceptions of God (such, for example, as those in Friedrich von Schlegel's " *Weisheit der Indier* "), and are regarded as survivals of the perfect original religion. In the Religion of Light, too, we have already found that evil in an individual form is everywhere done away with. Subjectivity we have observed everywhere at the same time in the concrete determination of self-consciousness. Even at the stage of magic, the power of self-consciousness was above Nature. What really constitutes the special difficulty in the study of religion is that we have not to do here, as in logic, with pure thought-determinations, nor with existing ones, as in Nature, but with such as are not wanting in the moment of self-consciousness, of finite spirit in fact, since they have already run their course through subjective and objective Spirit. For religion is itself the self-consciousness of Spirit regarding its self, and Spirit makes the different stages of self-consciousness themselves, by which Spirit is developed into the object of consciousness for itself. The content of the object is God, the absolute Totality, and therefore the entire manifoldness of matter is never wanting. It is necessary, however, to seek more precisely for definite categories, which form the differences of the religions. This difference is especially sought for in the mode of working of the Essence; this last is everywhere, and yet is not; it is further made to turn on the question as to whether there is or is not *one* God. This distinction is just as little to be relied upon, for even in the Indian religion there is to be found One God, and the difference then merely consists in the mode in which the many divine forms bind themselves together into unity. There are several Englishmen who hold that the ancient Indian religion contains the idea of the unity of God as a sun or universal soul. But predicates of the understanding such as these don't help us here.

When such predicates are given to God, we do not by the help of these determinations get a knowledge of Him in His true nature. They are even predicates of finite Nature, for it, too, is powerful, is wise. Taken as representing a knowledge of God, they would be extended over finite matter through the All. In this way, however, the predicates lose their definite meaning and are transient, like the *Trimūrti* in Brāhma. What is essential is contained in the One, in what is substantial, immanent; it is essential determination, which is conceived and known as such. These are not the predicates of reflection, not external form, but Idea (*Idee*).

Thus we have already had the determination of subjectivity, of self-determination, but merely in a superficial form, and not yet as constructing the nature of God. In the Religion of Light, this determination was abstract universal personification, because in the Person the absolute moments are not contained as developed or unfolded. Subjectivity is just abstract identity with self, is Being-within-itself, which differentiates itself, but which is likewise the negativity of this difference, which latter maintains itself in the difference, does not let it escape out of itself, retains its sway over it, is in it, but in it independently, has the difference within. it momentarily.

1. If we consider this in relation to the next form, subjectivity is this negativity which relates itself to itself, and the negative is no longer outside of the Good, but rather it must be contained, posited in the affirmative relation to self, and thus is, in fact, no longer the Evil. Therefore the negative, Evil, must now no longer exist outside of the Good. It is just the essential nature of Good to be Evil, whereby of course Evil no longer remains Evil, but as Evil relating itself to itself, annuls its evil character and constitutes itself into Good. Good is that negative relation to itself as its other by which it posits Evil, just as the latter is the movement which

posits its negation as negative, that is to say, which annuls it. This double movement is subjectivity. This is no longer that which Brāhma is; in Brāhma these differences merely vanish, or, in so far as the difference is posited, it is found as an independent god outside of Brāhma.

The first and essentially universal form of subjectivity is not the perfectly free, purely spiritual subjectivity, but is still affected by Nature. It is thus, it is true, universal Power, but power which merely exists implicitly, such as we have hitherto met with. As subjectivity it is, on the contrary, posited actual power, and is so conceived of when it is taken as exclusive subjectivity.

The distinction lies between power which is implicit and power so far as it is subjectivity. This last is posited power, is posited as power existent in its own right. We have already had power under every form. As a first fundamental determination it is a crude power over what has a bare existence; then it is the inner element only, and the distinctions or differences appear as self-sustained existences outside of it; existences which have, it is true, proceeded out of it, but which outside of it are independent, and which would have vanished, in so far as they were comprehended in it. Just as distinctions vanish in Brāhma, in this abstraction, when self-consciousness says, "I am *Brāhma*," and from that moment everything that is divine, all that is good, has vanished in him, so the abstraction has no content, and the latter, in so far as it is outside of it, moves unsteadily about in a state of independence. In relation to particular existences, power is the active agent, the basis; but it remains the inner element merely, and acts in a universal way only. That which universal power brings forth, in so far as it is implicit, is also the Universal, the Laws of Nature; these belong to the power which is potentially existent. This power acts; it is implicit power, its working likewise is implicit, it acts unconsciously, and existing things, such as sun, stars, sea, rivers, men, animals, &c., appear as independent exis- tences; their inner element only is determined by the power. Power can only show itself in this sphere as in opposition to the laws of nature, and here, accordingly, would be the place of miracles. But among the Hindus there are no miracles, for they have no rational intelli- gent Nature. Nature has no intelligent co-relation; everything is miraculous, and therefore there are no miracles. These latter cannot exist until the God is determined as Subject, and as Power which has indepen- dent Being, and works in the manner characteristic of subjectivity. Where potentially existent Power is repre- sented as subject, it is of no consequence in what form it appears; accordingly it is represented in human beings, in animals, &c. That vital force acts as immediate power cannot in any case be denied, since as power which is implicitly existent it works invisibly without showing itself.

From this power actual power must be distinguished; the latter is subjectivity, and in it two principal charac- teristics are to be observed.

The first is that the subject is identical with itself, and at the same time posits definite distinct determina- tions within itself. There is one subject of these dis- tinctions; they are the moments of one subject. The Good is thus the universal self-determination which is so entirely universal that it has the very same undiffe- rentiated extent as Essence; determination is, in fact, not posited as determination. To subjectivity belongs self- determination, and this means that the determinations present themselves as a plurality of determinations; that they have this reality in relation to the Notion, in con- trast to the simple self-involved Being of subjectivity. But at first these determinations are still enclosed within subjectivity, are inner determinations.

The second moment is that the subject is exclusive,

is negative relation of itself to itself, as power is, but in relation to an Other. This Other is capable, too, of appearing as independent, but it is involved in this that the independence is only a semblance of independence, or else it is of such a kind that its existence, its embodiment, is merely a negative relatively to the power of subjectivity, so that this last is what is dominant. Absolute power does not hold sway; where there is the exercise of ruling authority, the Other is swallowed up. Here the latter abides, but obeys, serves as a means.

The unfolding of these moments has now to be further considered. This process is of such a kind that it must arrest itself within certain limits, and for this reason especially, that we are as yet only in the transition to subjectivity; the latter does not appear in a free and truthful form; there is still an intermixture here of substantial unity and subjectivity. On the one hand, subjectivity does indeed unite everything; on the other hand, however, since it is as yet immature, it leaves the Other outside, and this intermixture has therefore the defect of that with which it is still entangled, namely, the religion of nature. In reference to the nature of the form in which Spirit has its self-consciousness concerning itself as the object of its consciousness, the stage now before us presents itself as the transition from the earlier forms to the higher stage of religion. Subjectivity does not as yet exist on its own account or for itself, and is consequently not yet free, but it is the middle point between substance and free subjectivity. This stage is therefore full of inconsistencies, and it is the problem of subjectivity to purify itself. This is the stage of Mystery or enigma.

In this fermenting process all the moments present themselves. For this reason the consideration of this standpoint of thought possesses especial interest, because both stages, the preceding one of the religion of nature and the following one of free subjectivity, appear here in their principal moments, the two being not yet severed. Accordingly there is here merely what is mysterious and confused, and by means of the Notion alone can the clue be obtained which indicates to which side such heterogeneous elements tend to come together, and to which of the two sides the principal moments belong.

The God is still the inner nature here, implicit power, and for that reason the form this power may wear is accidental, is an arbitrary one. This merely implicitly existent power may be invested with this or the other human or animal form. The power is unconscious, active intelligence, which is not spiritual. It is mere Idea, not subjective Idea, however, but vitality void of consciousness—in fact, life. This is not subjectivity, is not self, in fact; but if life is to be presented as outward form at all, the form that lies nearest at hand for the purpose is that of some living creature. Within life in general the living, in fact, lies hidden; *what* particular living creature, what animal, what human being this may be is a matter of indifference. We thus find zoolatry present at this stage, and, indeed, in the greatest variety : in different localities different animals are held in reverence or worshipped.

From the point of view of the Notion it is of more importance that the subject is determined immanently within itself, is in its reflection into itself, and this determination is no longer the universal Good, though it certainly is the Good, and thus has Evil over against it. The next stage, however, is that actual subjectivity posits differences in its determination, that differentiated Good is posited here, an inner content ; and this content is of a definite and not of a merely general or universal character. Not until differences can exist for me, not until possibility of choice is present, and only to the extent in which this is the case, is the subject an actual subject, or, in other words, does freedom begin. In this way the subject stands for the first time above particular ends, is

free from particularity, when the latter has not the range
of subjectivity itself, is no longer universal Good. It is
another thing when the Good is at the same time made
determinate, and is exalted into infinite wisdom. Here
a plurality of Good is determined, and thus subjectivity
occupies a position of superiority, and it appears as its
choice to desire one thing or the other; the subject is
posited as deciding, and it appears as the determining of
ends and of actions.

The God as substantial unity does not appear as acting;
he annihilates, begets, is the basis of things, but does not
act. Brāhma, for example, does not act; independent
action is either merely imagined, or else pertains to the
changing incarnations. Yet it is only a limited end or
purpose which can come in here; the subjectivity is
merely the primal subjectivity, of which the content
cannot as yet be infinite truth.

It is at this point, too, that the outward form is determined as human, and thus there is a transition of the
god from the animal to human form. In free subjectivity
the form which directly corresponds with such a conception is the human one alone; it is no longer life only,
but free determination in accordance with ends, therefore
the human character appears as the form, it may be a
particular subjectivity, a hero or an ancient king, &c.
Here where the particular ends make their appearance
as in the first form of subjectivity, the human form is
not of the indefinite kind represented by Ormazd. On
the contrary, specialised forms make their appearance,
which have special ends, and are characterised by an
element of locality. The principal moments coincide
with this. That is to say, to speak more precisely,
developed definite character must show itself in the
subject; the definite ends of action are limited, defined,
are not determinateness in its totality. Determinate
character must, however, show itself in the subject in
its totality too; developed subjectivity must be beheld

in it.   The moments are not, however, the totality of
the form, but present themselves in the first place as a
sequence, as a course of life, as different states of the
subject.   Not until later does the subject as absolute
Spirit arrive at the stage at which its moments are
potential or implicit totality.   Here the subject is still
formal, still limited as regards determinate character,
although Form in its entirety belongs to it, and thus
there is still this limitation, that the moments are developed into form as states only, and not each one for
itself as a totality ; and it is not eternal history which
is beheld in the subject as constituting the subject's
nature, but merely the history of states or conditions.
The first is the moment of affirmation, the second is
negation, the third is the return of negation into itself.

2. The second moment is the one which is of most
importance here.   Negation shows itself as a certain
state of the subject ; it is its alienation, death, in fact.
The third is restoration, return to sovereignty.   Death is
the most immediate way in which negation shows itself
in the subject, in so far as the latter has merely natural
form generally, and also definitely existing human form.
Further, this negation has besides the further characteristic that since what is here is not eternal history, is not
the subject in its totality, this death comes to individual
existence as it were by means of an Other, and from
without, by means of the evil principle.

Here we have God as subjectivity generally, and the
most important moment in it is that negation is not
found outside, but is already within the subject itself,
and the subject is essentially a return into itself, is self-
contained existence, Being which is at home with itself.
This self-contained condition includes the difference which
consists in positing and having an Other of itself—negation—but likewise, in returning into itself, being with
self, identical with itself in this return.

There is One subject ; the moment of the negative, in

so far as it is posited as natural in the character of what belongs to nature, is death. It is therefore the death of the god, and this characteristic presents itself for the first time here.

The negative element, this abstract expression, has very many determinations—it is change, in fact; change also contains partial death. In the natural sphere this negation shows itself as death; thus negation is still in the natural sphere, and not as yet purely in Spirit, in the spiritual subject as such.

If it is in Spirit, this negation shows itself in the human being itself, in Spirit itself as this determination, namely, that its natural will is for it another will; it distinguishes itself in its essence, in its spiritual character from its natural will. This natural will is here negation, and man comes to himself, is free Spirit, in overcoming this natural character, in having the natural particularity, this Other of rationality reconciled with rationality, and so being at home with himself, not outside of himself.

It is only by means of this movement, of this course of thought, that such inner harmony, such reconciliation, comes to exist. If the natural will shows itself as Evil, then negation shows itself as something *found*. Man, in the act of raising himself to his true nature, finds this natural determination to be something opposed to what is rational.

A higher conception, however, is that negation is that which is posited by Spirit. Thus God is Spirit, in that He begets His Son, the Other, posits the Other of Himself, yet in Him is still with Himself, and beholds Himself, and is eternal love. Here the negation is likewise the transient or vanishing element. This negation in God is therefore that definite essential moment. Here, however, we have only the general idea of subjectivity, subjectivity in the general sense. Thus it comes to pass that the subject itself passes through these different states as its own states, in such a way that this negation is immanent in it. Then this determination, in so far as this negation appears as a natural state, enters as the determination of death, and the god appears here in the character of subjectivity in his eternal history, and shows himself to be the absolute Affirmative, which itself dies —the moment of negation. He becomes alienated from himself, loses himself, but through this loss of himself finds himself again, returns to himself.

In this religion, then, it is one and the same subject which passes through these different determinations. The negative, which we had in the form of the Evil One, Ahriman, implying that negation does not belong to the self of Ormazd, belongs here to the self of the god.

We have already had negation in the form of death too. In Hindu mythology there are many incarnations; Vishnu especially is the history of the world, and is now in the eleventh or twelfth incarnation. The Dalailama in like manner · dies; Indra, too, the god of the natural sphere dies, and there are others who die and come back again.

But this dying is different from the negativity which is in question here, namely, death in so far as it pertains to the subject. As regards this difference, all depends on the logical determinations. In all religions analogies may be found, such ideas as those of God becoming man and of incarnations. The name Krishna has even been put side by side with that of Christ. Such comparisons, however, although the objects compared have something in common, some similar characteristic, are utterly superficial. The essential thing on which all depends is the fuller characterisation of the distinction, which last is overlooked.

Thus the thousandfold dying of Indra is of a different kind from that above referred to. The Substance remains one and the same; it forsakes merely the particular individual body of the one Lama, but has directly chosen for itself another. This dying, therefore, this negation, has nothing to do with Substance, it is not posited in the Self, in the subject as such. The negation is not an actual inner moment, an immanent determination of Substance, and the latter has not the pain of death within itself.

Here, for the first time, we have the death of the god as something within himself, implying that the negation is immanent in his essential nature, in his very self, and it is precisely owing to this that this god is essentially characterised as Subject. The nature of a subject is to give itself this otherness within itself, and through negation of itself to return to itself, to produce itself.

This death appears at first as something undignified; we have the idea that it is the lot of the finite to pass away, and in accordance with this idea death, in so far as it is spoken of in connection with God, is only transferred to Him as a determination out of the sphere of that finite which is inadequate to Him. God does not in this way get to be truly known, but rather is debased by the determination of negation. Over against that assertion of the presence of death in the divine stands the demand that God should be conceived of as a supreme Being, only identical with himself, and this conception is reckoned as the highest and most honourable, so that it is only at the end that Spirit reaches it. If God be thus conceived as the Supreme Being, He is without content, and this is the poorest possible idea of Him, and quite an antiquated one. The first step of the objective attitude is the step to this abstraction, to Brāhma, in whom no negativity is contained. Good, light, is likewise this abstraction, which has the negative only outside of itself as darkness. From this abstraction an advance is already made here to the concrete idea of God, and in this way the moment of negation enters, at first in this peculiar or special mode as death, inasmuch as God is now beheld in human form. And thus the moment of death is to be ranked high, as an essential moment of God Himself—as immanent in Essence. To self-determination belongs the moment of inner, not outward negativity, as is already implied in the expression "self-determination." The death which here comes into prominence is not like the death of the Lama, of Buddha, of Indra, and other Indian deities, whose negativity is an external one, and approaches them as a power that is external to them. It is a sign that there has been an advance toward conscious spirituality, to knowledge of freedom, to the knowledge of God. This moment of negation is an absolutely true moment of God. Death, then, is a peculiar special form, in which negation makes its appearance in an outward shape. By reason of the divine totality the moment of immediate form must become recognised in the divine Idea, for to it there must be nothing wanting.

Thus the moment of negation is immanent in the divine Notion, because it essentially belongs to it in its outward manifestation. In the other religions we have seen that the essential nature of God is merely determined as abstract Being-within-itself, absolute substantiality of Himself. There death is not thought of as belonging to substance, but is regarded merely as external form, in which the god shows himself. It is quite otherwise when it is an event which happens to the god himself, and not merely to the individual in whom he presents himself. It is thus the essential nature of God which comes into prominence here in this determination.

3. But now, further, we have in close connection with this the idea that God restores himself, rises from the dead. The immediate god is not God. Spirit is alone what, as being free in itself, exists by its own act, what posits itself. This contains the moment of negation. The negation of the negation is the return into self, and Spirit is the eternal return into self. Here then at this stage we come upon Reconciliation. Evil, death, is represented as vanquished, God is consequently

once more reinstated, restored again, and as thus eternally returning into himself is he Spirit.

(b.) *The concrete idea belonging to this stage.*

In this religion, as it actually exists in the religion of the Egyptians, there occur an infinite variety of forms or figures. But the soul or animating principle of the Whole is what constitutes the chief characteristic, and it is brought into prominence in the principal figure. This is Osiris, who in the first place, it is true, has negation opposed to him as external, as other than himself, as Typhon. This external relation is not, however, permanent in the sense of being only a strife such as that carried on by Ormazd; on the contrary, negation makes its entrance into the subject itself.

The subject is slain, Osiris dies, but he is eternally restored again, and he is thus posited in popular conception as born a second time, this birth not having a natural character, but being posited as something apart from what is natural or sensuous. He is consequently posited, defined as belonging to the realm of general ideas, to the region of the Spiritual, which endures above and beyond the finite, not to the natural sphere as such.

Osiris is the God of popular conception, the God conceived of or mentally represented in accordance with his inner character. Accordingly in the idea that he dies, but is likewise restored, it is expressly declared that he is present in the realm of general ideas as opposed to mere natural being.

But he is not only conceived of in this way; he becomes *known* too as such. That does not mean the same thing. As represented in the form of idea, Osiris is defined as the ruler in the realm of Amenthes; as he is lord of the living, so also is he lord of what no longer continues in sensuous existence, but of the continuously existing soul, which has severed itself from the body, from what is sensuous, perishable. The kingdom of the dead is the realm where natural being is overcome, the

realm of ideas or ordinary thought where what is preserved is precisely that which has not natural existence.

Typhon, Evil, is overcome, and likewise pain, and
Osiris is the judge in accordance with law and justice.
Evil is overcome, is condemned; and with this the act
of judgment makes its first appearance, and does so as
what decides; that is to say, Good has the power to
assert itself, and to annihilate the non-existent, the evil.

If we say Osiris is a ruler of the dead, the dead are in
this case just such as are not held to be in the sensuous
natural sphere, but have independent continuous existence in a region beyond what is sensuous and natural.
Connected with this is the fact that the individual subject is known as continuous, as something withdrawn
from the region of the transitory, as something having
a fixed, independent existence, something distinguished
from what is sensuous.

That is a thoroughly weighty saying of Herodotus regarding immortality, namely, that the Egyptians were
the first to declare that the soul of man is immortal. We
find this continued life, this metamorphosis in India and
China, but this, like the continued life of the individual,
the immortality of the Hindus, is itself merely something subordinate and unessential. What is with them
highest is not an affirmative permanent duration, but is
Nirvana, continuous existence in the state of annihilation
of the Affirmative, or only a semblance of affirmation,
the being identical with Brāhma.

This identity, this union with Brāhma, is at the same
time a melting away into this unity, which is, it is true,
seemingly affirmative, and yet is in itself utterly devoid
of determination and without differentiation. But what
we have here as a logical deduction is this: the highest
form of consciousness is subjectivity as such; this is
totality, and is able to exist independently in itself; it
is the idea of true independence or self-existence.

We call that independent or self-sustained which is

not in a condition of opposition, which rather overcomes that opposition, does not contain a finite over against itself, but has this opposition within itself, yet at the same time has conquered there. This determination of that subjectivity which is objective, which pertains to the objective, namely, to God, is also the determination of the subjective consciousness. This consciousness knows itself as subject, as totality, true independent existence, and consequently as immortal. With this knowledge the higher destiny of man dawned upon consciousness.

This negation of the negation, namely, that death is slain, that the evil principle is vanquished, is thus a determination of supreme moment. Among the Parsis that principle is not overcome, but the Good, Ormazd, stands opposed to the Evil, Ahriman, and has not yet arrived at this reflection. It is here in the Egyptian religion that the vanquishing of the evil principle is for the first time posited.

Herewith, accordingly, that determination comes in which was mentioned above, and which we have already recognised, namely, that this one who is born again, is represented directly afterwards as having departed; he is ruler in the kingdom of Amenthes; as he is Lord of the living, so also is he Judge of the dead in accordance with right and justice. Here for the first time right and morality come in, in the determination of subjective freedom; both, on the contrary, are wanting in the God of substantiality. So then there is a penalty or punishment here, and the individual worth of man, which determines itself in accordance with morality and right, comes into prominence.

Around this Universal play an infinite number of popular conceptions of deities. Osiris is only one of these conceptions, and according to Herodotus is even one of the latest; but it is principally in the realm of Amenthes as ruler of the dead, as Serapis, that he has risen above all other gods as an object of supreme interest.

Herodotus, following the statements of the priests, gives a series of Egyptian gods, and Osiris is to be found here among the later ones. But the further development of the religious consciousness takes place also within a religion itself, and we have already seen in the Indian religion that the worship of Vishnu and Síva is of later date. In the sacred books of the Parsis Mithras is put among the other Amshadspans, and stands on the same level with them; but Herodotus already gives prominence to Mithras, and at the time of the Romans, when all religions were brought to Rome, the worship of Mithras was one of the principal religions, while the service of Ormazd had not anything like the same importance.

Among the Egyptians, too, in the same manner Osiris is said to be a deity of later date. It is well known that in the time of the Romans, Serapis, a special form of Osiris, was the principal deity of the Egyptians, and yet, although it was in later times that the idea of him dawned upon the human mind, he is none the less the deity in whom the totality of consciousness disclosed itself.

The antithesis contained in the Egyptian view accordingly next loses its profound meaning and becomes a superficial one. Typhon is physical evil and Osiris the vitalising principle; to the former belongs the barren desert, and he is conceived as the burning wind, the scorching heat of the sun. Another antithesis is the natural one of Osiris and Isis, the sun and the earth, which is regarded as the principle of procreation generally. Thus Osiris too dies, is vanquished by Typhon, and Isis seeks everywhere for his bones: the god dies, here again is this negation. The bones of Osiris are then buried; he himself, however, has now become ruler of the kingdom of the dead. Here we have the course of living nature, a necessary cycle returning into itself. The same cycle belongs also to the nature of Spirit, and the fate of Osiris exhibits the expression of it. Here again the one signifies the other.

To Osiris the other deities attach themselves; he is the uniting point, and they are only single moments of the totality which he represents. Thus Ammon is the moment of the Sun, which characteristic also pertains to Osiris. There are besides a great number of deities which have been called the deities of the calendar, because they have a relation to the natural revolutions of the year. Particular periods of the year, like the vernal equinox, the early summer, and the like, are brought into prominence and personified in the deities of the calendar.

Osiris, however, signifies what is spiritual, not only what is natural; he is a lawgiver, he instituted marriage, taught agriculture and the arts. In these popular conceptions are found historical allusions to ancient kings: Osiris consequently contains historical features too. In the same way the incarnations of Vishnu seem to point to the conquest of Ceylon in the history of India.

Just as the special characteristics represented by Mithras as being the most interesting were brought into prominence, and the religion of the Parsis became the worship of Mithras, so Osiris has become the central point here; not, however, in the immediate, but in the spiritual and intellectual world.

What has been said implies that subjectivity exists at first in the form of idea or ordinary thought here. We have to do with a subject, with a spiritual being conceived after a human fashion. This subject is not, however, a man in his immediate character, his existence not being posited in the immediacy of human thought, but in that of popular conception or ordinary thought.

It is a content which has moments, movement in itself, by means of which it is subjectivity, but is also in the form, on the plane of spirituality, exalted above the Natural. Thus the Idea (*Idee*) is posited in this region of general conception, but is marked by the deficiency consequent on its being merely a conception formed by subjectivity, by subjectivity as resting on an abstract basis.

The depths of the universal antithesis are not in it as yet; subjectivity is not yet grasped in its absolute universality and spiritual nature. Thus it is superficial, external universality.

The content which is in idea or ordinary thought is not bound to time; it is posited in the region of Universality. The sensuous particularity which implies that a thing exists at a definite time or in definite space is stripped off. Everything, since it rests on a spiritual basis, owing to the presence of general ideas, has universality, although very little of the sensuous is stripped off—as, for example, in the idea of a house. The Universality is thus external Universality only, the possession of certain common features.

That external Universality is still the predominating principle here, is intimately connected with the fact that the foundation, this idea of Universality, is not as yet absolutely immersed in itself, is not as yet a filled up or concrete basis in itself, which absorbs everything, and by means of which natural things are posited ideally.

In so far as this subjectivity is the Essence, it is the universal basis, and the history which the subject is becomes known at once as movement, life, as the history of all things, of the immediate world. And so we have the distinction which is implied in the fact that this universal subjectivity is also the basis for the Natural. It is the inner Universal, that which is the Substance of the Natural.

We have, therefore, two elements here, the Natural element and the inner Substance, and in this we have what characterises symbolism. To natural Being a foundation other than itself is attributed; what is immediate and sensuous acquires another substance. It is no longer itself as immediate, but represents or means something Other than itself, which is its substance, its meaning.

Now in this abstract relation of things the history of Osiris is the inner essential history of the Natural too—of the nature of Egypt. To this belong the sun, its course in the heavens, the Nile, which fertilises and which fluctuates. The history of Osiris is therefore the history of the sun; the sun goes onward till it reaches its culminating point, then it returns; its rays, its strength, become feeble, but afterwards it begins to lift itself up again—it is born anew.

Thus Osiris signifies the sun and the sun Osiris, the sun being conceived of as this cycle. The year is considered as the single subject, which in its own history runs its course through these diverse states. In Osiris what belongs to nature is conceived of as being a symbol of the subject's history.

Thus Osiris is the Nile, which increases, renders everything fruitful, overflows, and through the heat—here the evil principle comes into play—becomes small and impotent, then again recovers its strength. The year, the sun, the Nile are conceived as this cycle which returns into itself.

The special aspects of such a course are represented as existing momentarily apart and in independence, as a multitude of gods who indicate particular aspects or moments of this cycle. Now, if it be said that the Nile is the inner element, that the meaning of Osiris is the sun, the Nile, and the other gods are calendar deities, such a statement would not be without truth. The one is the kernel, the other what outwardly represents it, the sign, the signifier, by means of which this inner element manifests itself externally. At the same time, however, the course of the Nile is universal history, and they may be taken as standing to each other in a reciprocal relation, the one as the inner element and the other as the form of representation or of apprehension.

What really is that inner element is Osiris, the subject, this cycle which returns into itself.

In this mode of representing the truth it is the symbol which is the dominant factor. We have an independent inner element which has an external mode of existence, and these two are distinct from one another. It is the inner element, the subject, which is free here, which has become independent, in order that that inner element may be the substance of what is external, and may not be in contradiction with it, may not be a dualism, but be the signification, the independently self-existing idea, in contrast to the sensuous mode of existence in which last it constitutes the central point.

The representation of subjectivity in this definite shape as the central point is closely connected with the impulse to give the idea visible form. The idea as such must express itself, and it is man who must bring this meaning out of himself and give it a visible form. The immediate has already vanished if it is supposed to appear under the conditions of sense-perception or in some particular mode of immediacy, and the general idea is under the necessity of giving itself completeness in this way. If the general idea thus integrates itself, this immediacy must be of a mediated character, a production of man.

Formerly we had visibility, immediacy in a natural unmediated mode, where Brāhma has his existence, the mode of his immediacy in thought, in the immersion or sinking down of man into himself. Such was the case too where the Good is light, and therefore in the form of an immediacy which exists in an immediate mode.

Since here, however, the starting-point is ordinary thought or idea, this must give itself to a definite sensuous form, and must bring itself to immediacy. It is, however, a mediated immediacy, because it is an immediacy posited by man. It is the inner element which

is to be brought to immediacy : the Nile, the course of
the year, are immediate existences, but they are symbols
only of the inner element.

Their history, as natural, is gathered up and comprised
within idea, this unification, this course appearing as one
subject, and the subject itself is intrinsically the returning movement already spoken of. This cycle is the
subject, which idea is, and which as the subject is to
make itself perceptible by sense.

(c.) *Worship or cultus.*

The impulse just described may be regarded as representing in general the cultus of the Egyptians, this
endless impulse to work, to describe or represent outwardly what is as yet only inward, contained in idea, and
for this reason has not become clear to the mind. The
Egyptians worked on for thousands of years. First of
all they put their soil into order; but the work which
has relation to religion is the most amazing that has
ever been accomplished, whether upon the earth or
under it. Think of the works of art still in existence,
but in the form of parched and arid ruins, which, however, on account of their beauty and the toil which their
construction represents, have been a source of astonishment to all the world.

It has been the task, the deed of this people to produce these works ; there was no pause in this production ;
we see the spirit labouring ceaselessly to render its idea
visible to itself, to bring into clearness, into consciousness, what it inwardly is. This restless industry of an
entire people is directly based upon the definite character
which the god has in this religion.

First of all we may recall how, in Osiris, spiritual
moments too are revered, such as justice, morality, the
institution of marriage, art, and so forth. Osiris is,
however, in a special sense the lord of the realm of the
dead, judge of the dead. A countless number of pictures
or representations are to be found in which Osiris is

delineated as judge, while before him is a scribe, who is reckoning up for him the deeds of the soul brought into his presence. This realm of the dead, that of Amenthes, constitutes a principal feature in the religious conceptions of the Egyptians. As Osiris, the life-giving, was opposed to Typhon, the annihilating principle, and was the sun of the earth, so the antithesis of the living and the dead makes its first appearance here. The realm of the dead is just as fixed a conception as the realm of the living. The realm of the dead discloses itself when natural Being is overcome; it is just there that what has no longer natural existence persists.

The enormous works of the Egyptians which still remain to us are almost entirely those only which were destined for the dead. The celebrated labyrinth had as many chambers above as beneath the ground. The palaces of the kings and priests have been transformed into heaps of rubbish, while their tombs have bid defiance to time. Deep grottos extending several miles in length are to be found hewn in the rock for the mummies, and all the walls are covered with hieroglyphics. But the objects which excite the greatest admiration are the pyramid-temples for the dead, not so much in memory of them, as in order to serve them as burial-places and as dwellings. Herodotus says that the Egyptians were the first who taught that souls are immortal. It may occasion surprise that, although the Egyptians believed in the immortality of the soul, they yet devoted so much care to their dead: one might think that man, if he holds the soul to be immortal, would no longer have special respect for his body. But, on the contrary, it is precisely those peoples who do not believe in an immortality who hold the body in slight esteem after its death, and do not provide for its preservation. The honour which is shown to the dead is wholly dependent upon the idea of immortality. If the body falls into the power of the forces of nature, which are no longer restrained by the soul, yet still man does not wish, at least that nature, as such, should be that which exerts its power and physical necessity over the exanimated body, that noble casket of the soul. Man's desire is, on the contrary, that he himself should exert this power over it. Men accordingly endeavour to protect it against nature as such, or give it themselves, by their own free will, as it were, back to the earth, or else annihilate it by means of fire. In the Egyptian mode of honouring the dead and preserving the body, there is no mistaking the fact that man knew himself to be exalted above the power of nature, and therefore sought to maintain his body against this power, in order to exalt it above it too. The methods followed by peoples in their treatment of the dead stands in the closest connection with the religious principle, and the different customs which are usual at burial are not without bearings of very great importance.

In order then to understand the peculiar position of Art at this stage, we have to recollect that subjectivity does, as a matter of fact, begin to appear here, but as yet only so far as its basis is concerned, and that its conception or idea still passes over into that of substantiality. Consequently the essential differences have not yet mediated and spiritually permeated each other; on the contrary, they are as yet mixed together. Several noteworthy features may be specified which elucidate this intermixture and combination of what is present and of living things with the Idea of the Divine, so that either the Divine is made into something present, or on the other hand into something human; and in fact here even animal forms become divine and spiritual moments Herodotus quotes the Egyptian myth that the Egyptians had been ruled by a succession of kings who were gods. In this there is already the mixing together of the ideas that the god is known as king, and again the king as god. Further, we see in the countless number of the representations of art which portray the consecration of kings, that the god appears as the consecrator and the king as the son of this god ; then the king himself too is found represented as Ammon.   It is related of Alexander the Great that the oracle of Jupiter Ammon declared him to be the son of that god.   This is quite in accordance with the Egyptian character, for the Egyptians said the very same of their kings.   The priests were esteemed at one time as the priests of the gods, and then as God himself also.   Many monuments and inscriptions remain even from later times, where the Ptolemaic king is always and only called the son of god, or God himself.   The same thing happened in the case of the Roman Emperors.

Astonishing certainly, yet considering the mixture of the conception of substantiality with that of subjectivity, no longer inexplicable, is that Zoolatry the practice of which was carried out by the Egyptians in the most rigid manner.   In various districts of Egypt special animals were worshipped, such as cats, dogs, monkeys, and so forth ; and this worship was even the occasion of wars between the various districts.   The life of such animals was held absolutely sacred, and to kill them was to incur severe punishment.   Further, dwelling-places and estates were granted to these animals, and provisions laid up for them : indeed, it even happened in a time of famine that human beings were permitted to die rather than that those stores should be invaded.   The apis was most of all held in reverence ; for it was believed that this bull represented the soul of Osiris.   In the coffins in some of the pyramids, apis bones were found carefully preserved.   Every form of this religion and every shape taken by it is mingled with zoolatry.   This worship of animals is undoubtedly connected with what is most offensive and hateful.   But it has been already shown in connection with the religion of the Hindus how man could arrive at the stage in which he worships an animal.   If God be not known as Spirit, but rather as power in general, then this power is unconscious activity—universal life, it may be. This unconscious power then appears under an out-ward form, and first of all in that of an animal. An animal is itself something devoid of consciousness, it leads a dull, still life within itself, as compared with human caprice or free-will, so that it may appear as if it had within itself this unconscious power which works in the whole.

Especially peculiar and characteristic, however, are the forms under which the priests or scribes so frequently appear in plastic representations and paintings with animal masks; and the same is the case with the em-balmers of mummies. This duplicate form,—an external mask concealing another form underneath it,—intimates that the consciousness is not merely sunken in dull, animal life, but also knows itself to be separated from it, and recognises in it a further signification.

In the political state of Egypt, too, we find the struggle of Spirit seeking to extricate itself from immediateness. Thus history frequently mentions the conflicts of the kings with the priestly caste, and Herodotus speaks of these even from the earliest times. King Cheops caused the temple of the priests to be shut up, while other kings reduced the priestly caste to complete subjection and excluded them from all power.

This opposition is no longer Oriental; we see here the human free-will revolting against religion. This emerg-ence from a state of dependence is a trait which it is essential to take into account.

It is especially, however, in naïve and highly pic-torial representations in artistic forms that this strug-gling on the part of Spirit and its emergence from Nature, are expressed. It is only necessary to think of the image of the Sphinx, for example. In Egyptian works of art everything, indeed, is symbolical; the significance in them reaches even to the minutest details; even the number of pillars and of steps is not reckoned in accord-

ance with external suitability to ends, but means either
the months, or the feet that the Nile has to rise in order
to overflow the land, or something of a similar kind.
The Spirit of the Egyptian nation is, in fact, an enigma.
In Greek works of art everything is clear, everything
is evident; in Egyptian art a problem is everywhere
presented; it is an external sign, by means of which
something which has not been yet openly expressed is
indicated.

Even if, however, at this standpoint Spirit is still in
a state of fermentation, and still has the drawback of a
want of clearness, and if even the essential moments of
religious consciousness are in part mingled with one
another, and partly in this intermingling, or rather on
account of this intermingling, are in a state of mutual
strife, yet it is still free subjectivity which here takes
its rise, and thus it is precisely here that art too, more
correctly speaking fine art, must of necessity make its
appearance and is needful in religion.   Art, it is true, is
imitation, but not that alone; it may, notwithstanding,
arrest itself at that, but it is then neither fine art nor
does it represent a need belonging to religion.   Only as
fine art does it pertain to the Notion of God.   True art
is religious art, but art is not a necessity where God
has still a natural form; for example, that of the sun
or of a river.   It is also not a necessity in so far as
the reality and visibility of God are expressed in the
outward shape of a man or of an animal, nor when the
mode of manifestation is light.   It begins, it is true,
when, as in the case of Buddha, the actual human form
has dropped away, but still exists in imagination; and
thus it has a commencement where there is imaginative
conception of the divine form, as, for example, in images
of Buddha; in this case, however, the Divine is regarded
as at the same time still present in the teachers, his
followers.   The human form in the aspect in which it
is the appearance of subjectivity, is only then necessary

when God is determined as subject. The need begins
to exist when the moment of Nature, of immediacy, is
overcome, in the conception of subjective self-determination or in the conception of freedom—that is to say,
at the standpoint which we have now reached. Inasmuch as the mode of definite Being is determined by
means of the inner element itself, the natural form is
no longer sufficient, nor is the imitation of it sufficient
either. All peoples, with the exception of the Jews
and Mahommedans, have images of their gods; these,
however, do not belong to fine art, but are mere personifications of conceptions or ideas, signs of merely
conceived or imagined subjectivity, where this last
does not as yet exist as immanent determination of
the Essence itself. Figurate conception or idea has an
external form in religion, and from this what is known
as pertaining to the Divine Essence is to be essentially
distinguished. In the Hindu religion God has become
man; it is in totality that Spirit is always present:
whether, however, the moments are looked upon as
belonging to the Essence or as not belonging to it, is
what makes all the difference.

It thus becomes a necessity to represent God by
means of fine art when the moment of naturalness is
overcome, when Spirit exists as free subjectivity, and its
manifestation, its appearance in its definite existence, is
determined by means of Spirit from within, and exhibits
the character of something which is a spiritual production. Not until God Himself has the determination of
positing the differences under which He appears, out of
His own inner Being, not until then does art enter as
necessary for the form given to the god.

In connection with the introduction here of art, two
moments specially deserve attention: first, that God is
presented in art as something capable of being beheld
by sense; secondly, that as a work of art the god is
something produced by human hands. To our notions,

both of these represent modes which are inadequate to
the Idea of God — so far, that is to say, as they are
supposed to be the sole mode ; for of course we are all
aware that God has been outwardly visible to sense,
though only as a transient moment. Art, too, is not
the ultimate mode of our worship. But for the stage
of that subjectivity which is not as yet spiritualised,
which is thus itself as yet immediate, existence which
is visible in an immediate way is both adequate and
necessary. Here this is the entirety of the mode of
manifestation of what God is for self-consciousness.

Thus art makes its appearance here, and this implies
that God is apprehended as spiritual subjectivity. It is
the nature of Spirit to produce itself, so that the mode
of definite existènce is one created by the subject, an
estrangement or externalisation which is posited by the
act of the subject itself. That the subject posits itself,
manifests itself, determines itself, that the mode of
determinate Being or existence in a definite form is one
posited by Spirit, is implied when art is present.

Sensuous existence, in which God is visibly beheld,
is commensurate with His Notion ; it is not a sign, but
expresses in every point that it is produced from within,
that it corresponds with thought, with the inner Notion.
But it has the defect of being still a sensuously visible
mode,—that the mode in which the subject posits itself
is sensuous. This defect is the consequence of its being
as yet subjectivity in its first form, the primal free
Spirit ; its determination is its first determination, and
thus its freedom is that of what is as yet natural,
immediate, primal determination ; that is to say, the
moment of Nature, of sense.

The other point is that the work of art is produced
by human beings. This, too, is inadequate to our Idea
of God. That is to say, infinite, truly spiritual subjectivity, that which exists for itself as such, produces itself
by its own act, posits itself as Other, namely, as its out-

ward form or shape, and this last is posited by means of subjectivity itself, and produced freely. But this its assumption of form, which to begin with as the I = I, is as yet reflected into itself, must also have the determination of differentiation expressly in such a way that this differentiation is merely determined by means of subjectivity, or, in other words, that it merely appears in this which is at first still something external. This first freedom further comes to have an additional element, namely, that the outward embodiment produced by the subject is taken back into subjectivity. What is First is thus the creation of the world; what is Second is the reconciliation, namely, that it reconciles itself in itself with the true First. In the subjectivity which is before us at this stage, this return is not as yet present, its mode of existence being as yet of an implicit character; its existence as subject is found outside of it in the form of Being-for-other. The Idea is not as yet there; for to it belongs that the Other should of its own act reflect itself into the primal unity. This second part of the process which pertains to the divine Idea is not as yet posited here. If we consider the determination as end or aim, then the primal action of subjectivity regarded as an end is still a limited end; it has reference to this particular people, this definite particular end, and if it is to become universal, a truly absolute end, the return is essential, and the doing away with what is merely natural in respect of the outward form is essential likewise. Thus, the Idea is first present when this second part of the process is added to the first, the part which annuls the natural character, the limitation of the end, and it is owing to this that it becomes for the first time an universal end. Here Spirit as regards its manifestation is only the half way of Spirit; it is still one-sided finite Spirit, in other words, subjective Spirit, subjective self-consciousness; it is the outward form of the god, the mode of his existence for an " Other." The work of art is merely something accomplished, posited by the finite spirit, by the subjective spirit, and for this reason the work of art must be executed by man. This explains why it is necessary that the manifestation of the gods by means of art is a manifestation fashioned by human hands. In the religion of absolute Spirit the outward form of God is not made by the human spirit. God Himself is, in accordance with the true Idea, self-consciousness which exists in and for itself, Spirit. He produces Himself of His own act, appears as Being for " Other ;" He is, by His own act, the Son ; in the assumption of a definite form as the Son, the other part of the process is present, namely, that God loves the Son, posits Himself as identical with Him, yet also as distinct from Him. The assumption of form makes its appearance in the aspect of determinate Being as independent totality, but as a totality which is retained within love ; here, for the first time, we have Spirit in and for itself. The self-consciousness of the Son regarding Himself is at the same time His knowledge of the Father ; in the Father the Son has knowledge of His own self, of Himself. At our present stage, on the contrary, the determinate existence of God as God is not existence posited by Himself, but by what is Other. Here Spirit has stopped short half way. This defect of art, namely, that the god is made or fashioned by man, is also felt in those religions in which this is the highest manifestation, and attempts are made to remedy the defect, not, however, in an objective, but in a subjective way. Images of the gods must be consecrated ; alike by the Negro and the Greek they are consecrated, that is to say, the divine Spirit is put into them by a process of conjuration. This results from the consciousness, the feeling of defect ; but the mode of remedying it is one which is not contained in the objects themselves, but comes to them from without. Even among the Catholics such consecration takes place ; of pictures, for example, relics, and the like.

This explains the necessity there is that art should make its appearance here, and the moments indicated are those from which it results that the god exists as a work of art. Here, however, art is not yet free and pure; it is not as yet even in the process of transition to fine art. In this perverted state it still presents itself in such a way that outward forms which belong to immediate nature, and which are not produced by Spirit, such as the sun, animals, &c., do just as well as any other for self-consciousness. The artistic form which breaks forth out of an animal, the form of the Sphinx, is more a mixture of artistic form and animal form. Here a human countenance looks forth upon us from the body of an animal; subjectivity is as yet not clear or manifest to itself. The artistic form is therefore not as yet purely beautiful, but is more or less imitation and distortion. The general character of this sphere is the intermingling of subjectivity and substantiality.

The artistic activity of this whole people was not as yet absolutely pure fine art, but rather the impulse towards the fine art. Fine art contains this determination, namely, that Spirit must have become in itself free—free from passion, from the natural life in general, from a condition of subjugation or thraldom produced by means of inner and outer Nature; it must feel the need to know itself as free, and thus to exist as the object of its consciousness.

In so far as Spirit has not yet arrived at the stage of thinking itself free, it must picture itself as free, must have itself before itself as free Spirit in sensuous perception. If it is thus to become an object for sensuous perception in the mode of immediacy, which is a product, this involves that its definite existence, its immediacy, is wholly determined by means of Spirit, has entirely such a character as implies that here it is a free spirit which is described.

This, however, is precisely what we call the Beautiful, in which all externality is absolutely significant and characteristic, and determined by the inner element as representing that which is free. We have here a natural material which implies that the features in it are simply tokens of the Spirit which is essentially free. The natural moment must, in fact, be overcome, that it may serve for the expression, the revelation of Spirit.

While the content in the Egyptian characteristic quality is this subjectivity, the impulse present here toward fine art is one which is worked out architecturally for the most part, and has at the same time endeavoured to pass over to beauty of form. Inasmuch, however, as it was only impulse, beauty itself as such has not as yet actually appeared here.

Such then is the source of this conflict between the signification and the material of the external form in general; it is only the attempt, the effort, to stamp the inward Spirit upon the outward embodiment. The pyramid is an independent crystal, in which a dead man dwells; in the work of art, which is pressing forward toward beauty, the inner soul is impressed upon the externality of the form employed.

What we have here is simply the impulse, because the signification and actual representation, the mental idea and the actual definite form of existence, are in fact opposed to one another in this difference, and this difference exists because subjectivity is, to begin with, merely universal, abstract, and is not yet concrete, filled up subjectivity.

The Egyptian religion thus actually exists for us in Egyptian works of art, since what these tell us is bound up with what is historical, and which has been preserved to us by ancient historians. In recent times especially, the ruins of the land of Egypt have been explored in a variety of ways, and the dumb language of the statues, as also of the mysterious hieroglyphics, has been studied.

If we must recognise the superiority of a people which has laid up its Spirit in works of language over one which has only left dumb works of art behind it for posterity, we must at the same time recollect that here among the Egyptians no written documents are in existence, for the reason that Spirit had not as yet clarified itself, as it were, but was struggling to clear itself of alien elements, and this in an external way, as appears in the works of art. At last, it is true, after prolonged study, advance has been made in the deciphering of hieroglyphics, but, on the one hand, there is still a part of this work which is unaccomplished, and on the other hand, they always remain hieroglyphics. Numerous rolls of papyrii have been found beside the mummies, and it was at first believed that a great treasure had been discovered in these, and that we had come upon important disclosures. These papyrii are, however, nothing else than a species of archives, and contain for the most part deeds of purchase regarding pieces of land, or have reference to objects which the person deceased had acquired.

It is, therefore, principally the extant works of art whose language we have to decipher, and from which a knowledge of this religion may be obtained.

Now, if we contemplate these works of art, we find that everything in them is wonderful and fantastic, but always with a definite meaning, which was not the case among the peoples of India. We thus have the immediateness of externality here, and the meaning, the thought. We have all these elements together in the tremendous conflict of the inner with the outer; there is a tremendous impulse on the part of what is inner to work itself free, and what is outer exhibits to us this struggle of Spirit.

The form is not as yet exalted into form that is free and beautiful, not as yet spiritualised into clearness, transparency; the sensuous, the natural, is not as yet so perfectly transfigured into the spiritual as to be merely an expression of the spiritual, so that this organisation and its features might be mere signs, merely the signification of the spiritual. To the Egyptian principle this transparency of the natural, of the external element of outward embodiment, is wanting; what remains is only the task of becoming clear to self, and the spiritual consciousness as being the inner element merely seeks to struggle out of naturalness and be free.

The most important representation by which the essential nature of this struggle is made perfectly plain is the statue of the goddess at Sais, who was represented veiled. It is symbolised in that statue, and in the inscription in her temple, " I am what was, is, and shall be ; my veil has been lifted by no mortal," it is expressly declared that Nature is something differentiated within itself, namely, an Other in contrast to its outward appearance as that immediately presents itself, an enigma. It has an inner element, something that is hidden. " But," it is stated further in this inscription, " the fruit of my body is Helios." This as yet hidden essence therefore expresses clearness, the sun, the becoming clear to oneself, the spiritual sun in the form of the son who is born of her. It is this clearness which is attained to in the Greek and Jewish religion, in the former in art and in the beautiful human form, in the latter in objective thought. The enigma is solved ; the Egyptian Sphinx, according to a deeply significant and admirable myth, was slain by a Greek, and thus the enigma has been solved. This means that the content is man, free, self-knowing Spirit.

SECOND DIVISION

THE RELIGION OF SPIRITUAL INDIVIDUALITY.

The Religion of Nature is the most difficult to get a grasp of, because it lies farthest from our ordinary thought, and is the crudest and most imperfect form of religion. The natural element has such a variety of shapes within itself, that in the form of naturalness and immediateness the universal absolute content is broken up.

A.

TRANSITION TO THE SPHERE OF SPIRITUAL INDIVIDUALITY.

What is higher is also deeper; in it the separate moments are grasped together in the ideality of subjective unity; the want of connection which characterises immediacy is annulled, and the separate elements are brought back into subjective unity. For this reason it is necessary that what has the quality of naturalness should manifest such a multiplicity of outward shapes, which exhibit themselves as indifferent and mutually exclusive, as independent and individual forms of existence.

The general characteristic is free subjectivity which has satisfied its impulse, its inner desire. It is free subjectivity which has attained to dominion over the finite generally, over the natural and finite elements of consciousness, whether physical or spiritual, so that now the subject, that is, Spirit as spiritual subject, becomes known in its relation to the natural and the finite, while the latter are in part merely subservient to Spirit, and in part the garment of Spirit, and are present concretely in Spirit. Further, as outwardly representing Spirit, the natural and finite merely serve as a manifestation and glorification of Spirit. Spirit in this freedom, power, reconciliation with itself, exists on its own account, free and untrammelled in the natural; the external, the finite, is distinguished from these finite-natural and spiritual elements, from what belongs to the region of empirical, changeable consciousness, as well as to that of external existence.

Such is the general fundamental characteristic of this stage. Spirit being free, and the finite only an ideal moment in it, it is posited as inherently concrete, and inasmuch as we look upon Spirit and the freedom of Spirit as concrete, what we have is rational Spirit; the content constitutes the rationality of Spirit.

This determinateness first referred to, looked at from the point of view of its content, is in its formal aspect this, namely, that the natural, the finite, are simply witnesses to Spirit, are simply subservient to its manifestation. Here we have the religion within which rational Spirit is the content.

The next step in advance, therefore, is that the free form of subjectivity, the consciousness of the Divine, comes into view in an unalloyed and independent form, in the character of free subjectivity, so far as this can be in the first form of spirituality which has become free. That this last, however, is known exclusively for itself, or, in other words, that the Divine is determined on its own account as subjectivity, represents a purifying from the natural, which has been already referred to in the previous discussion. The subject is exclusive; it is the principle of infinite negativity, and since as regards its content it is universal, it leaves nothing existing independently beside it which is devoid of Spirit, or is merely natural; and in like manner nothing which is merely substantial, essentially devoid of form. Subjectivity is infinite Form; and as such, it no more leaves to Form which is not free, that is to say external naturalness, any independent existence along side of it, than it does to empty, pure, undetermined substantiality. The fundamental determination is that God becomes known as freely determining Himself within Himself; still formally, it is true, but yet already freely within Himself. We are able to recognise this emergence of free subjectivity in religions and in the peoples to which such religions belong, principally by observing whether among such peoples universal laws, laws of freedom, justice, and morality, constitute fundamental determinations and have the predominance. God conceived of as subject is conceived of as spontaneously determining himself, i.e., His self-determinations are the laws of freedom; they are the determinations of self-determination, and are of such a kind that their content belongs only to the form of free self-determination, and with this is necessarily connected the fact that freedom constitutes the content of the laws. When we perceive this, the element of naturalness or immediacy retires into the background, and inherently universal ends show themselves—ends which are inherently universal, although externally they may be quite unimportant, or, so far as their range is concerned, are not yet universal, just as a man who acts from ethical motives may perform his actions within a sphere extremely restricted, so far as its general content is concerned, and yet be essentially moral. The brighter sun of Spirit makes the natural light pale before it. Thus we pass outside of the circle of the Religion of Nature. We come to gods who are essentially founders of states and marriage, founders of peaceful life, producers of art which originates solely with them, gods who preside over oracles and states, and who originate and protect law and morality. The peoples who have reached that stage in the development of self-consciousness in which subjectivity is recognised to be the ideality of the natural, have thereby crossed over into the sphere of ideality, into the kingdom of the soul, and have come to the region belonging to the realm of Spirit. They have torn from their eyes the bandage of sensuous perception, escaped from the trackless maze which is devoid of thought, they have laid hold of thought, of the Intellectual Sphere, and have made and secured for themselves the solid ground in what is inward. They have laid the foundations of the sanctuary which in its very nature is firm and stable.

The progress made up to this point has been as follows :—We started from the natural desires as seen in the religion of magic, from the authority and power of these desires over Nature, gained simply by individual will which is not determined by thought. The second stage was occupied by the theoretical determination of the independence of objectivity, in which accordingly all the moments were set free and released, and reached the state of independence. In the third stage was found the theoretical or self-determining element, which took back into itself these moments thus released, so that the practical element is thus made theoretical, the Good self-determination, and, finally, the blending of substantiality and subjectivity.

If we now ask,—How has the idea of God been defined so far? What is God? What have we learned about Him? The answer is as follows :—

In accordance with the abstract form of the metaphysical Notion we began thus: God is the unity of the Infinite and the Finite, and our sole concern is to find out how particularity and determinateness, *i.e.*, the finite, is incorporated with the infinite. What result have we as regards this point so far reached? God is the infinite in general, what is identical with itself, substantial power. When we start by saying this, it is not implied that finitude is as yet posited as contained in it, and it is, to begin with, the purely immediate existence of the infinite self-consciousness. From the fact that God is just infinitude, substantial power, it follows, and it is consciously implied in it, that the substantial Power alone is the truth of finite things, and that their truth consists only in this, that they return into the substantial unity. God is thus, to begin with, the Power referred to, a definition which, being purely abstract, is extremely imperfect. The second position is that God is the substantial Power in Himself, pure Being-for-self, separate from the manifoldness of the finite. This is substantiality which is reflected into itself, and this is the essential conception of God. With this idea of substantiality which exists within itself and distinguishes itself from the finite, we have reached higher ground, but here the determination of the true relation of the finite to the substantial Power, whereby the latter would itself come to be the infinite, does not yet exist. This inherently existing substantiality is accordingly Brāhma, and the independently existing finite is represented by the many gods. The third position is that in which the finite is posited as identical with substantiality, so that its sphere is of similar extent to that of the latter, and is pure universal form, as substantiality itself is. This is God conceived of as The Good.

Spiritual subjectivity, the conception at which we have now arrived, is the absolutely free power of self-determination, so that this is nothing else than the Notion, and has no content but the Notion; and in this self-determination there is nothing beyond the fact that it contains itself. This self-determination, this content, is accordingly as universal, as infinite, as the Power itself. This universal Power, which now shows itself active in the form of self-determination, we may call Wisdom. In so far as we have to do with spiritual subjectivity we have to do with self-determination, with an end, and these are as universal as the Power, and are thus wise ends. Determination in accordance with an end is directly involved in the conception of free subjectivity. Action which is in accordance with an end is inner self-determination, *i.e.*, it is determination by means of freedom, by means of the subject, for there is nothing within but just the subject itself.

This self-determination maintains itself in external existence, natural being has no longer any worth in its immediacy, it belongs to the Power, is a transparent medium for it, and has no value for itself. In so far as it takes on an external form—and it must externalise itself, subjectivity must give itself reality—it is simply free self-determination which maintains itself in realising itself, in external existence, in the natural sphere. In the case of action which is in conformity with an end, nothing comes out of it unless what is already there. Immediate existence, on the other hand, is bereft of power, as it were, is form only, is the mode only in which the end is present in it, and it is the end which is the inner element.

We find ourselves here accordingly in the sphere of the End, and action which is in conformity with an end is wise action, since wisdom consists in acting according to ends which hold good universally; and no other content is actually present in it, for it is free subjectivity which determines itself.

The general conception here is that of subjectivity, of power which works in accordance with ends, which is active in fact. Subjectivity, speaking generally, consists in being active, and the end must be a wise one, it must be identical with what determines it, with the unlimited Power.

1. What we have first to consider here is the relation of the subject to Nature, to natural things, and more particularly to what we previously called Substantiality, the Power which has only potential being. This remains something inward, but subjectivity is Power which has independent actual being, and is different from Power which has potential being and from its reality, namely, Nature. This Power which has potential being, Nature, is now degraded to the condition of something powerless, something dependent relatively to the underived Power, or, to put it more definitely, it is made a means. Natural things are deprived of their own independent existence. Hitherto they had a direct share in Substance, while now they are in the subjective Power separated from substantiality, distinguished from it, and are regarded as only negative. The unity of the subjective Power is outside of them, is distinguished from them. They are only means or modes which have no more value beyond serving for manifestation; they are the material of manifestation and are subject to what manifests itself in them; they may no longer show themselves directly, but must reveal a something higher in them, namely, free subjectivity.

2. But what is the more definite determination connected with the idea of wisdom? It is, to begin with,
undetermined so far as the end is concerned. We do
not as yet know of what it consists, what the ends of
this Power are, and do not go beyond the undefined
phrase, the wisdom of God. God is wise, but what are
His ways, His ends? In order that we may be able to
say what they are, the ends must be already before us
in all their determinateness and definiteness, *i.e.*, in their
development as a distinction of moments. So far we
have here only determination in accordance with ends
in general.

3. Since God is above all things real, we cannot, in
considering Him, stop short at this indeterminateness in
wisdom. The ends must be determined. God as subject
manifests Himself, acts, which means that He comes
forward into actual existence, into reality. At an earlier
stage the unity of infinitude and finitude was regarded
as simply immediate, and was thus the first and best of
finite things, sun, hill, river, &c., and the reality was of
an immediate kind. Here it is also necessary that God
be in a definite place, *i.e.*, that His end be definite and
determined.

In reference to the reality of the end there are two
points which call for notice. The first is contained in
the question, What is the sphere in which this end can
be present? The end, as being something inward, is
merely subjective, is only thought or idea. God, however, as subjective Power, is not simply will, intention,
&c., but rather immediate Cause. This sphere of the
realisation of the actual existence of the end is self-consciousness or the finite spirit. End is determination in
general, and here we have determinations which are
merely abstract and not as yet developed. The finite
spirit is accordingly the sphere in which the divine end
shows itself. Since it is only now that we first reach
the thought of the determination of wisdom in general,

we have not any content, anything definite, whereby to express what is wise. The end is potential, is yet undetermined in the notion of God, and so we have to take a second and further step, and show that the end must become actual, must be realised. There must, therefore, be determination in it, but the determination is not as yet developed. The determination as such, the development, has not as yet taken an actual form within the Divine Essence, and for this reason the determination is finite, external, an accidental or particular end. In so far as it exists, it exists in an undefined form in the divine notion, but so far as it is determined it is an accidental and entirely limited end ; or, to put it otherwise, what constitutes it is something outside of the divine notion, an end which can be distinguished from it, not the divine end in all its completeness in and for itself, *i.e.*, not an end which would be developed from its own inner nature, and would in its particular forms express the determinateness of the divine notion.

In studying the Religion of Nature, we saw that in it goodness was as universal as power; but speaking generally, it does not go beyond expressing the idea of substantial immediate identity with the Divine Essence, and all things accordingly are good and full of light. Here, in the determination of subjectivity, of Power which has independent existence, the end is distinguished from the notion, and the definite form given to the end is just for this reason merely accidental, because the difference has not yet been taken back into the divine notion, is not yet considered as equivalent to it. Here, therefore, we have only ends which, so far as their contents are concerned, are finite, and are not as yet adequate to express the divine notion. Finite self-consciousness is thus, to begin with, the region in which they are realised. This is the fundamental characteristic of the standpoint we have got to.

B.

THE METAPHYSICAL CONCEPTION OR NOTION OF
THIS SPHERE.

It is the pure abstract thought-determination which forms the basis here. We abstract as yet from idea or mental representation, as also from the necessity of the realisation of the Notion, a necessity which does not exactly belong to idea, but is rather one which the Notion itself renders necessary. Here we have the metaphysical notion in its relation to the form taken by the Proofs of the Existence of God. The special characteristic of the metaphysical notion, as contrasted with the foregoing, lies in this, that in the case of the latter we started from the unity of the Infinite and the finite. The Infinite was absolute negativity, undeveloped Power, and the thought involved in the first sphere and its essence were limited to this definition of infinitude. In that sphere the notion, so far as we are concerned, was undoubtedly that of the unity of the finite and the Infinite; but in reference to this stage itself, the Essence was defined simply as the Infinite. This latter forms the basis, and the finite was merely added to it; and just for this reason the determination assumed a natural aspect, and was accordingly the Religion of Nature, because the form required natural existence in order to show itself in a definite actual shape. The Religion of Nature already proved also the inadequacy of what is immediately external to express what is internal. In the conception of the Immeasurable it passed beyond the immediate identity of the natural and the Absolute, and also beyond that of immediate Being and Essence. But the external form when stretched out to the Immeasurable snaps, as it were, natural Being vanishes, and begins to exist for itself as the Universal. Infinitude is not yet, however, immanent determination, and, in order to represent it, use is still made of natural forms which are external and inadequate.   In proportion as the Natural is posited as existing negatively in the Immeasurable, is it also positive looked at in its finite existence, as opposed to the Infinite. Or, to put it otherwise, the Immeasurable, which, in proportion as everything disappears within it, is in like proportion also powerless, is the contradiction of Power and powerlessness.   In contrast to this, we have now the Essence itself defined as the unity of the Infinite and the finite, as true Power, as infinitude which is concrete in itself, *i.e.*, as the unity of the finite and the Infinite. It is this, accordingly, that we have in the determination of wisdom which is the Power which determines itself within itself, and this determination is the finite aspect, and thus the Divine is known as what is concrete in itself, inherently infinite form.   This form is the aspect of the finite as potential, but posited here under the aspect of the Infinite.   In the concrete ideality of the Essence the contradiction referred to as existing in the Immeasurable is done away with, since the Essence is a manifestation of itself for itself, and not an abstract being-for-self.   Posited as Power, it is the absolute negativity which differentiates itself, but in such a way that the differences are done away with, and are only a semblance.   That is powerful which has the soul, the Idea of the " Other," which the Other is in its immediacy only. Whatever *thinks* that which the " Others " only *are*, constitutes their Power.   The Essence (not a particular Essence or *one* higher Essence)—*i.e.*, the Universe as absolute Power—is satisfied in itself and is Totality, since all other determinations are taken up into and absorbed in it.   In order to be, it does not have recourse to natural objects, but has a determinate character of its own within itself, and is the totality of its appearance or semblance.

Since thus the determination of pure thought belongs to the determining or characterisation of the Essence itself, it follows that further advance in characterisation is not connected with the natural mode or aspect of things, but takes place within the Essence itself. If, accordingly, we are to find three stages here, then they constitute an advance within the metaphysical notion itself. They are moments in the Essence, different forms of the notion for the religious self-consciousness which occupies this standpoint. At an earlier stage the advance was merely in the external form, here the advance is within the notion itself. Now, the Divine Essence is actual Essence, Essence for itself, and the differences are its own reflection of itself into itself. We thus get three conceptions. The first is that of Unity, the second that of Necessity, the third that of Conformability to an End, though of conformability which is finite and external.

We have (*a.*) Unity, absolute Power, negativity, which is posited as reflected into itself, as existing absolutely for self, or as absolute subjectivity, so that here, in this particular form of essential being, the sense element is directly abolished. It is Power which is actual, for itself, and has within it nothing belonging to sense, for this latter is the finite, which has not yet been taken up into, is not yet absorbed by, the Infinite. Here, however, it is in process of being absorbed. This subjectivity, which is actual, which exists for itself, is accordingly the One.

We have (*b.*) Necessity. The One is this absolute Power, and everything is posited in it as merely negative. This constitutes the conception or notion of the One. But when we express it thus, development is not as yet postulated. The One is nothing more than the form of simplicity, and necessity then comes to be the process of unity itself. It is the unity as inner movement, and is no longer the One, the unit, but the unity. The movement which constitutes the Notion is the unity, the absolute necessity.

We have (*c.*) Conformability to an End. In absolute necessity is posited or made explicit the movement which the One is only implicitly. It is the process, and it is the process of contingent things, for it is contingent things which are thus posited and negated. In necessity, however, it is only the transition, the coming and going of things, which is posited. But now it must be further posited that these things exist and appear as distinguished from this unity of theirs, from this process of necessity which belongs to them. They must appear, at all events, momentarily as existing, and at the same time as belonging to the power out of which they do not pass. They are thus means in general, and the unity consists in this, that it maintains itself within this process which belongs to it, and produces itself in these means. This is the unity of necessity itself, but thought of as distinguished from what moves itself, and within which it maintains itself, so that it has the element of Being only as something negative. Unity is thus End in general.

These three points stand in the following relation to each other. Since the Essence is absolute negativity, it is pure identity with itself, the One; it is at the same time the negativity of the unity, which, however, is in a relation to the unity, and owing to this interpenetration of both shows itself as necessity. In the third place, the One returns into itself out of the isolation of its difference, a unity, nevertheless, which, as being this self-absorption of the Form into itself, has a finite content, and in this way, by developing into the difference of the Form as totality, gives us the conception of conformability to an end, a conformability which is, however, finite.

When it is said that in this are contained the three metaphysical notions or conceptions of the three religions, it is not to be supposed that each of these conceptions belongs to one religion only. On the contrary, each of these three determinations or characteristics belongs to all three. Where One is the Essence, there too is necessity though only implicit, not in its determinate quality ; and so, too, if the One determines Himself in accordance with ends, then He is wise. Necessity is One also, and conformability to an end is present here also, only it lies outside of necessity. If conformability to an end is the fundamental characteristic, we have along with this the presence of the Power to carry out the ends, and the end itself is Fate. The point of difference simply is as to which of these determinations of the object is to be regarded as the Essence, and whether this latter is the One, or Necessity, or Power with its ends. The point of difference is simply as to which of them is to pass as the fundamental determination of the Essence for each religion.

What we have now to consider more definitely is the form in which these determinations appear as they have been connected with the proofs of the existence of God.

(a.) *The Conception of the One.*

Here we have not got to do with the proposition, God is only one; for it is implied in these words that the One is only a predicate of God; we have the subject, God, and a predicate outside of which He may have others in addition to this. That God is only One is a proposition which it is not difficult to prove. Being passes over into Essence, and this reflected into itself is what has been frequently called an Ens, or Individuum. When we say, God is the One, we mean something different from what was expressed formerly in the words, The Absolute Being is *One*, τὸ ἕν. Parmenides expressed it thus: Being alone is, or the One only is. This One, however, is only the abstract Infinite, not the Infinite as reflected into itself, and is thus rather the Immeasurable and Powerless, for it is the Infinite only as compared with actual existence in its infinitely manifold forms, and its existence is necessarily dependent on this relation. Power at first conceived of as the One is in reality the Universal posited as Power. The abstract One is the one side, and over against it is the manifoldness of the essence of the world. The concrete One, on the other hand, is individuality, the Universal, what is reflected into itself, the other side of which itself comprises all being in itself, so that it has returned into its own unity.

Reflection accordingly conceives of the unity of God as a characteristic quality, and seeks to demonstrate it. This, however, does not supply the form in which to express a proof of the existence of God. The One is distinguished from the substratum, and the point is simply to exhibit the characteristic of Being as One. Reflection lights upon this idea because One is just reflection into self.

Accordingly this characteristic or determination that God is only One has reference, to begin with, only to the Many with which it is contrasted, and so far also to the other Form, which will be dealt with as the second Form belonging to this stage. The disproof of the determination which comes later is thus given here in advance. This second form in itself and in the determination of its notion is undoubtedly more concrete; but as definite or determined Being in and for itself when it appears as Necessity is only something that *ought* to be, an ideal, and because it is only what ought to be is thus multiplicity, it has not as yet absolute reflection-into-self, and it is wanting in the characteristic of being One. Doubtless the characteristic of the One is also as yet one-sided, since it is only the abstract form in an actual state, for itself, and is not the developed form in the shape of content.

The development of the necessity of this characteristic of the One, the rising up to this one Subject as the One, is carried out thus. Being as One is conceived of as predicate, while God is presupposed as subject, and it is then shown that the characteristic of multiplicity is opposed to the presupposition of this subject. The relation belonging to the Many can thus be considered as consisting in their reference to each other; they are then thought of as coming into contact with each other, and getting into conflict with themselves. This conflict is, however, the appearance of the contradiction itself in an immediate way, for the different gods have to maintain themselves in accordance with their own nature or quality, and it is here that their finitude comes to light. In so far as God is presupposed as being the Universal or the Essence,·that finitude which is involved in the multiplicity is inadequate to express what is contained in that presupposition.

In the case of finite things we are accustomed to think that substances may be in conflict without losing their independence. It would seem, then, that it is only their superficial elements which they send out to engage in the conflict, while they keep their real selves in the background. In accordance with this a distinction is made between the inner nature of the subject and its relations, between the substance considered in reference to others and the substance as passive, without, prejudice to its aforesaid activity. This distinction is as yet un-proved. What the many are so far as content and power are concerned, they are only in contrast with something else ; their Being, as reflected into self, is simply some-thing devoid of content. If they are thus, so far as form also is concerned, independent, they are, nevertheless, finite so far as the content is concerned, and this succumbs to the same process of dialectic as that to which finite Being has to yield. In face of the presupposition of ab-solute Power, of the universal negativity of all that has Being, the multiplicity of such formal finite things accord-ingly directly disappears. It is directly involved in the presupposition of the Universal, that form and content cannot be so separated that a quality can attach to the one which is wanting to the other. Thus the gods by means of their qualities directly cancel each other.

Multiplicity is, however, in this case taken also in the sense of pure difference which does not come in contact with itself. Thus we speak of a multiplicity of worlds

which do not come into conflict and are not in contradiction with each other. Ordinary thought obstinately
clings to this idea by maintaining that the truth of such
a presupposition cannot be controverted because no contradiction is involved in it. It is, however, really one
of the ordinary bad forms of Reflection to say that it is
possible to form an idea of anything. It is certainly
possible to form to oneself an idea of everything, and to
conceive of it as possible; but that does not mean anything at all. If it be asked wherein the difference consists, and if the answer is that the one is as powerful as
the other, and that no one of them is to have qualities
which the other also has not, then the difference is an
empty phrase. The difference must necessarily directly
advance till it becomes a definite or determined difference,
and in that case, so far as our reflection is concerned,
there is wanting to the one what is peculiar to the other,
but *only* in so far as our reflection is concerned. Thus
the stone, in so far as we reflect upon it, is not so perfect
as the plant, yet there is no defect in the stone considered
in itself; it neither feels nor knows anything of its defect.
Thus the difference spoken of is only an idea in our mind,
in our reflection.

It is in this way, therefore, that Reflection reasons, and
its reasoning is correct, but all the same it is likewise
inadequate. The Universal, the Essence, is presupposed
under the form of Power, and it is asked if the predicate
of the One attaches to it. The determination of the One
is nevertheless already in harmony with the presupposition, for absolute Power is directly contained in the
determination of individuality, of oneness, or the One.
The proof is thus quite correct but superfluous, and what
is overlooked is that the absolute Power itself is already
contained in the definition or determination of the One.
To prove predicates of God is really not the business of
the Notion, nor is God in this way to be known philo-
sophically.

But as a matter of fact, the true meaning of this notion is not contained in the proposition that God is *One*, but rather in the statement that the One is *God*, so that the One exhausts the meaning of this Divine Essence, and is not a predicate. Nor is it a characteristic along with other characteristics, but, on the contrary, it is one which fully expresses the Essence in the sense of absolute Power as subjectivity, as reflected into itself. God is thus just this movement of the subject from itself and back to itself, the self-determination of itself as the One in such a way that subject and predicate are the same, are this movement within each other, so that there is nothing left which comes between them. This notion is not adapted to be expressed in the form of a mediation in which the notion will appear as a proof of the existence of God, for it is the Infinite, the absolute negativity from which we start in order to reach the determination of the One. The One is merely the determination which is attached to it, and which expresses the thought that this is subjectivity reflected into itself. The movement proceeds, so to speak, only within the potential Being of the Infinite. It is, therefore, not in the form of mediation that we have to consider it here. We certainly might say there is an advance from the Infinite to subjectivity determined within itself, but the beginning is the Infinite, and this Infinite, moreover, as the absolute negativity, is the Subject reflected into itself, in which all that is manifold is done away with and absorbed. If we wished to look at the mediation more closely, we would start from one thought and conceive of the Notion in and for itself as Thought, and from this we would go on to the Other, to Being. But here we cannot start from the Notion, for a beginning in this form gives a different proof of the existence of God, and one which belongs to the Christian religion, and not to the religion under consideration. The One is not yet thought of as Notion, not yet thought of as Notion for us; what is true, posited concretely in itself, such as we have in the Christian religion, is not as yet present here.

Since the Absolute is thus defined as the One and as Power, self-consciousness is merely a semblance of the Absolute. It is certainly something for which the Absolute manifests itself, and to which it stands in a positive relation, for the reflection of Power into itself directly gives repulsion, and this is self-consciousness, and thus personality. Self-consciousness begins here to have a certain value, but still it has only an abstract determination, so that self-consciousness in its concrete form knows itself merely as a semblance of existence. It is in bondage, has no extended sphere in itself, no room in which to act; heart and mind are hemmed in; what feeling it has consists only in feeling the Lord; it has its existence and finds its happiness only within this narrow enclosure. Even if, as is the case here, the element of difference comes to light, still it is held fast; it does not really break away, and is not set free. Self-consciousness concentrates itself only in this one point, and though it knows itself as essentially existing—for it is not killed as in Brāhma—it is at the same time the non-essential element in the Essence.

(b.) Necessity is something which is self-posited as mediation, and is here accordingly a mediation for self-consciousness. Necessity is movement, implicit process, implying that the accidental element in things and in the world is definitely characterised as accidental, and thus raises itself to and disappears in necessity. When in any religion the absolute Essence is conceived of, or known, or revered as Necessity, then this process is present. It might seem as if we had seen this transition already in the advance of the finite to the Infinite in the fact that the truth of the finite was the Infinite, the absorption of the finite in itself into the Infinite, and that in the same way the accidental also returns into necessity. Whether we regard the determination of the

advance of the finite to the Infinite or of the accidental
to Necessity, the distinction, so far as the advance is
concerned, does not seem at all to be an essential one.
As a matter of fact, both have the same fundamental
determination, so that, from one point of view, this is
correct; but if we regard the matter from another point
of view, the difference or distinction is more concrete
than that of the earlier form of the process. That is to
say, if we begin from the finite, then the matter stands
thus; but the first beginning is that it has real worth,
that it exists as Being, or, in other words, we take it to
begin with in an affirmative, positive form. Its end is
indeed involved in it, but at the same time it still possesses immediate Being. " Accidental " already suggests
something more concrete, for what is accidental can either
be or not be. The Real is accidental, for it may quite
as well be possibility, the Being of which has the value
of Not-Being. Thus there is posited in the accidental
the negation of itself, and it is accordingly a transition
from Being into Nothing. Like the finite, it is inherently
negative; but since it is also Not-Being, so too is it the
transition from Not-Being to Being. The characteristic
or determination of contingency is thus much richer and
more concrete than that of the finite. The truth of contingency is necessity, and this is determinate existence,
which has arisen by mediation with itself through its Not-
Being. Reality is a definite form of existence of this sort,
in the case of which the process is shut in within itself, and
which by means of itself comes into harmony with itself.

In connection with Necessity we have, however, to
make the following distinctions :—

1. External necessity is in a peculiar sense contingent
necessity. When an effect is dependent on causes, then
it is necessary ; when one or another set of circumstances
concurs, then one or another result must follow. Only
circumstances which occasion this are immediate ; and
since, regarded from this standpoint, immediate Being has

merely the value of possibility, the circumstances are such
as may or may not be, and so the necessity is relative,
and is related thus to the circumstances which constitute
the beginning, and which are accordingly immediate and
contingent.   This is external necessity, which has no
higher value than that possessed by contingency.   It is
possible to demonstrate external necessity in such a way
as to show that this or the other thing is necessary, but
the circumstances always remain contingent; they can
exist, but they can also not exist.   A tile may fall from
the roof and kill a man, but the falling down of the tile,
the concurrence, may be or may not be; it is contingent.
In this external necessity it is the result only which is
necessary; the circumstances are contingent.   These two,
the conditioning causes and the results, are for this reason
different.   The one is determined as contingent, the other
as necessary; this is the difference considered abstractly,
but there is also a concrete difference.   Something results
quite different from what was posited; and since the
forms are different, so too the content of the two sides is
different.   The tile falls accidentally; the person who is
killed, the particular concrete subject, his death, and that
act of falling down, are entirely heterogeneous, have a
perfectly different content; something appears as result
which is entirely different from what was posited.   When
life is considered according to the conditions of external
necessity as a result of soil, heat, light, air, moisture, &c.,
as a product of these conditions, what is implied is that
the matter is being looked at from the point of view of
external necessity.   This latter has to be carefully distinguished from the true inner necessity.

2. The inner necessity consists just in this, that
everything of the nature of cause, occasion, occasioning
circumstance, is presupposed and definitely distinguished,
and the result belongs to One.   The necessity puts together the two elements into one unity.   All that takes
place in this necessity takes place in such a way that

nothing results from the presupposed condition, which is
different from these, but rather the process is of such a
kind that whatever is presupposed appears also in the
result, coincides with itself, finds itself; or, to put it
otherwise, the two moments of immediate existence, and
of its being posited, are posited as one moment. In
external necessity contingency is substantial or immediate existence. What is, is not as being something
posited, the conditions do not belong to the unity, they
are immediate, and the result is only something posited,
is not Being. The effect is what is posited, the cause
is what is underived. In the true necessity these are
a unity; the circumstances exist, but they not only *are*,
they are also *posited* by means of the unity, are, as a
matter of fact, contingent, but are this in themselves; in
that they cancel themselves the negation of their Being
is the unity of necessity, so that their Being is one
which is implicitly negated. The result is, accordingly,
not only result, or only something posited, but it is just
because of what thus takes place that the result comes
to have Being. Necessity is thus the positing of the
conditions, they are themselves posited by means of the
unity; the result is also something posited, and is this
indeed by means of reflection, by means of the process,
by means of the reflection of the unity into itself; this
unity is therefore the Being of the result. Thus whatever takes place within necessity simply comes into harmony with itself. The unity projects itself outward,
disperses itself in circumstances which appear as if they
were contingent; the unity of itself projects its conditions as if they were innocent of any connection with
it—as if they were, so to speak, ordinary stones which
appear in an immediate way, and rouse no suspicion of
their being anything else. In the second stage they are
posited, they do not belong to themselves, but to an
" Other," to their result. They are thus broken up in
themselves, and the manifestation of their nature as

posited is their self-abrogation, the production of an
" Other," the result, namely, which, however, appears as
an " Other " only as opposed to their existence in a scattered form. The content, however, is one ; the result is
what they implicitly are, only the mode and manner
of their appearance are altered. The result is the sum
of what is contained in the circumstances, and the manifestation of this in a definite form. It is Life which thus
projects its own conditions, means of stimulus, impulses,
though in that form they do not look as if they were
Life, for the inner element, what is implicit, appears
first in the result. Necessity is thus the Process which
implies that the result and the preliminary condition are
different only as regards their form.

If we now consider this form and how necessity has
come to get the definite shape of a Proof of the existence of God, we see that the content is the true Notion.
Necessity is the truth of the contingent world. The
more detailed development of this thought belongs to
Logic. The notion of God is the absolute necessity ;
this is a necessary and essential standpoint, not indeed
the highest or the really true one, but one from which
the higher proceeds, and which is a condition of the higher
notion which itself presupposes it. Thus the Absolute is
necessity. The notion of absolute necessity does not yet
correspond to the Idea which we must have of God, but
which, however, is to be presupposed in the form of a
pictorial or general idea. The higher notion or grasp
has to grasp, to comprehend itself. There is here a defect
in this Proof of the existence of God. So far as the
form of the Proof is concerned in reference to absolute
necessity, we find it to be the well-known Cosmological
Proof, which is expressed simply thus : contingent things
presuppose an absolutely necessary Cause, but contingent
things exist, I and the World are such, therefore there is
an absolutely necessary Cause.

The defective element in this Proof is easily seen.

The major proposition runs thus : Contingent things presuppose an absolutely necessary Cause; this proposition,
taken in a general sense, is quite correct, and expresses
the connection between what is contingent and what is
necessary, and, in order to obviate captious criticisms
which would otherwise be made, one does not require to
say they presuppose an absolutely necessary Cause, for
this expresses a relation between finite things; but we
can say they presuppose the absolutely necessary in such
a way that this is conceived of as Subject. The proposition, accordingly, further contains a contradiction in
reference to external necessity. Contingent things have
causes ; they are necessary, that by means of which they
exist in this form may itself be contingent only, and so
we are referred back from the cause to contingent things
in endless progression. The proposition cuts short this
style of reasoning, and is perfectly justified in doing
so. What is only contingently necessary would be no
necessity at all, and the real necessity stands in contrast
to that implied in this proposition. The connection is in
a general way correctly expressed too, contingent things
presuppose absolute necessity; but the mode of the connection is incomplete, the union being defined as something presupposed or demanded. This is a connection
belonging to untutored reflection, and implies that contingent things are placed on one side and necessity on
the other, and thus while a transition is made from the
one to the other, both sides are firmly opposed to each
other. Owing to the fixity of Being in this form, contingent things become the conditions of the Being of
necessity. This is still more plainly expressed in the
minor proposition : There are contingent things, *consequently* there is an absolutely necessary Cause. Since
the connection is thus constituted in such a way that
one form of Being conditions the other, it would seem
to be implied in this that contingent things condition
absolute necessity ; the one conditions the other, and

thus necessity appears as if it were something whose existence is presupposed as dependent on or conditioned by contingent things. Absolute necessity is in this way put in a position of dependence, so that contingent things remain outside of it.

The true connection is as follows. Contingent things exist, but their Being has the value merely of possibility; they are and pass away; they are themselves simply pre-posited, or have hypothetical existence through the process of unity. Their first moment consists in their becoming posited with the semblance of immediate existence; their second moment consists in their being negated, in their being therefore conceived of essentially as appearance. In the Process they are essential moments, and so it may be said that they are the essential condition of absolute necessity. In the finite world it is true we start from some such immediate form of Being, but in the true world external necessity is simply the appearance referred to, and what is immediate is merely something posited, de-pendent on something else. It is this which constitutes the defect in mediations of this kind which pass for proofs of the existence of God. The really true content consists in this, that the Absolute must come to be recognised as absolute necessity.

3. Finally, absolute necessity actually is and contains in itself Freedom; for it consists just in this, that it comes together with, comes into harmony with itself; it is absolutely for itself, is not dependent on another; its action is free, is simply the act of meeting with or coinciding with itself, its process consists simply in its finding itself; but this is just freedom. Implicitly, neces-sity is free; it is only by an illusion that the distinction is made between it and what results from it. We see this in the case of punishment. Punishment comes upon a man as an evil, as force, as the exercise of power which is foreign to him, and in which he does not find himself. It appears as external necessity, as something external

which falls upon him, and something different from what he has done results from it; punishment follows on his action, but it is something different from, other than, what he willed himself. If, however, a man comes to recognise punishment as just, then it is the consequence and the law of his own act of will which is bound up with his act itself. It is the rationality of his act which comes to him under the semblance of an "other;" he has not to submit to any kind of force; he bears his own deed, feels himself to be free in it, it is his own which comes to him, justice, the rational element in what he has done. It is only, however, implicitly that necessity contains freedom, and this is an essential circumstance. It is only formal freedom, subjective freedom, and this means that necessity has not as yet any content in itself.

Just because necessity is the simple act of coming together with itself, is it freedom. We require in connection with it movement, circumstances, &c. This belongs to mediation, but when we say, This is necessary, then this is a unity; whatever is necessary, *is;* this is the simple expression, the result, in which the process has come together or coincided with itself. It expresses simple relation to itself, the act of finding itself; necessity is what is freest; it is not determined or limited by anything; all mediations are once more taken up into it and done away with. Necessity is the mediation which freely yields itself up; it is implicitly freedom. The feeling which finds expression in submitting to necessity, as it existed among the Greeks, and as it still exists amongst the Mohammedans, certainly contains freedom in it, but it is only potential or formal freedom: in presence of the necessity here, no content, no purpose, nothing definite has any value, and it is in this that its defect lies.

Necessity, according to the higher conception and notion of it, real necessity, is thus just freedom as such, it is the Notion as such; or, more definitely characterised, it is the

End.   Necessity, in short, is without content, or, to put it
otherwise, the difference contained in it is not yet posited ;
it is the process which we have seen, simple Becoming,
which only *is to* contain differences, and therefore what
is contained in it, though it is certainly difference, is
difference which is not as yet posited.   It is something
which coincides with itself though only through mediation, and in this way difference in general is posited.
It is, to begin with, only abstract self-determination ; the
determinateness or specialisation is merely something
which *is to be.*   In order that the determinateness be
real, it is necessary that the specialisation and the difference should, in the act of coinciding with self, be
posited as being *able* to hold out against the transition
which goes on in the process, as maintaining themselves
in the necessity.   To posit is to give determinateness,
and this determinateness, accordingly, is what coincides
with itself ; it is the content which maintains itself.
This act of coinciding, thus characterised as content
which maintains itself, is End.

In this specialisation or determinateness which takes
place in the process of coinciding or coming together,
there are two forms of determinateness to be noticed.
The determinateness appears as content which maintains itself going through the process without undergoing
alteration, and in the act of transition remaining equal
to itself.   Accordingly, so far as the determinateness is
that of Form, it appears here in the shape of subject
and object.   The content is, to begin with, subjectivity,
and the process means that it realises itself in the form
of objectivity.   This realised end is end, the content
remains what it was ; it is subjective, but at the same
time objective as well.

(*c.*) We have thus arrived at the idea of conformity to
an end ; it is in the end that the definite existence of
the notion in general begins, the Free existing as free
Being which is at home with itself, what maintains itself,

or, to put it more definitely, the Subject. The Subject
determines itself within itself; this determination, regarded from one point of view, is content, and the
Subject is free in it, is at home with itself, is free from
the content, it is its own content, and the content has
value only in so far as the Subject permits. This is the
Notion taken generally.

The Subject, however, also gives realisation to the
Notion. The particularity thus acquired is at first
simple, it is held within the Notion in the form of
Being which is at home with itself, and which has returned back into itself. This subjectivity, although it
is totality, is still at the same time one-sided—subjective
merely, only one moment of the entire form. The characteristic here is that the content is posited only in the
form of the equality of what coincides with itself. This
form thus defined as that which coincides with itself is
the simple form of identity with self, and the Subject is
the totality of Being as thus at home with itself. But
so far as the Subject is concerned, that specialisation
whereby it has an end is opposed to totality, and the
Subject accordingly seeks to do away with this form and
to realise the end. The realised end, however, remains
attached to the Subject; the latter possesses its own self
in it, has objectified itself, set itself free from its singleness or simplicity, while at the same time maintaining
itself in its manifoldness. This is the conception or
notion of conformity to an end.

The world has now to be regarded as being in
conformity to an end. We had previously the characterisation that things are contingent, but the higher
characterisation is the teleological view of the world, the
thought of its conformity to an end. It is possible to
accept the first of these characterisations and yet to be
in doubt as to whether we ought to consider things as
being in conformity to an end, whether some of them
are to be regarded as ends to which other things are

related as means, and it may be maintained that what appears as an end may have been merely produced mechanically under external conditions.

It is here, in fact, that characterisation of a permanent sort begins. The end maintains itself in the process; it begins and ends, it is something permanent, something exempted from the process, and which has its basis in the subject. The contrasted points of view may, accordingly, be put thus. Are we to keep to the point of view from which things are regarded as determined by other things, *i.e.*, by the element of contingency in them, by external necessity, or to that from which they are regarded as determined by the end? It has been already remarked that external necessity stands in contrast to the end, is something which is posited by, whose existence depends on, an " Other ; " the concurrence of circumstances is the producing factor, something different is the result; the end, on the other hand, is what remains, what gives the impulse, what is active, what realises itself. The conceptions of external necessity and conformity to an end are mutually opposed.

We saw that external necessity returns back into the absolute necessity which is its Truth, that this is implicitly freedom, and that whatever is implicit must be posited. This characteristic appears as subjectivity and objectivity, and thus we get the idea of End. We must therefore say, that in so far as things exist for us in immediate consciousness, in reflected consciousness, they are to be characterised as in conformity to an end, as having an end in themselves. The teleological view of things is an essential one; but this way of regarding things is at once seen to have in it a distinction, that between inner and outer necessity, and the inner again can itself, in accordance with its content, be a finite conformity to an end, and thus it comes to be once more included within the relation of external conformity to an end.

1. *External Conformity to an End.*—Suppose an end has

been posited in any kind of way and has to be realised, then in so far as the subject together with its ends is something finite, is an immediate definite form of existence, the further characteristic of realisation lies *outside* of it. It is, looked at from one point of view, immediate, and in that case the subject, together with its ends, is immediate, and the aspect under which realisation presents itself is an external one, *i.e.*, the realisation appears as material, as something which has been got outside, and serves simply to realise the end. It is, in fact, merely a means in reference to the end, and it is the latter which firmly maintains itself and is permanent. Being as an " Other," Being in the aspect of reality, the material, is, as compared with the fixed end, something which has no independence of its own, has no actual Being, but is simply a means with no soul in it. The end is outside of it and is first impressed upon it by the activity of the subject, which realises itself in the material. External conformity to an end has thus an objectivity outside of it which has no independence, and in contrast to which the subject, together with its ends, is what is permanent. The material has no power to offer resistance, but is simply a means for the end which realises itself in it, and in the same way the realised end is itself merely an external form in the material, for this latter is something which has been immediately got, and is therefore dependent, though it is independent as well. In their union, therefore, both of them, means and end, remain external to one another. Wood and stones are means, but the realised end is equally wood and stones which have received a certain form ; but all the same the material is still something external to the end.

2. *Inner Conformity to an End.*—This is the conformity which has its means in itself. Thus what has life is an end for itself, it makes itself into an end, and here the end is also the means. What has life is marked by this simple inwardness, which realises itself in its parts or

members; it is an articulated organism, an organism with differentiated members. Since the subject produces itself within itself, it has as its aim to have its means within itself. Each is a part or member and maintains itself, and is the means whereby the others are produced and maintained ; it is consumed and consumes ; it is this form, and not the material particles, which remains and maintains itself in this process. Life is thus an end in itself.

But it now further appears that the end, which is end for itself, stands at the same time in relation to external conformity to an end. Organic life has relations to inorganic Nature, and finds in it the means through which it maintains itself, and these means exist independently so far as this organic life is concerned. Thus inner conformity to an end has also relations to a conformity which is outside. Life can assimilate the means, but they have already been found for it, they have not come into existence through Life itself. Its own organs can produce the life but not the means.

We are here in the region of finite conformity to an end ; absolute conformity we shall get to later on.

The teleological way of looking at the world thus contains the different forms of the end in general. There are fixed ends and means, and even the end which has the end in itself is merely finite, dependent, standing in need of help in respect to the means. This conformity to an end is so far finite, and finitude in these relations to externality is, to begin with, the means, the material ; the end cannot continue to exist apart from these means, nor, on the other hand, can it exist unless these means are powerless in reference to the end.

3. The next element of truth in this relation of means and end is to be found in that universal Power or Force through which the means potentially exist for the end. From the standpoint of conformity to an end, things which are ends have the power of realising themselves, but they

have not the power of positing the means. Both the
end and the material appear as indifferent to each other,
both appear as having an immediate definite existence,
the means being something found for the end. Their
potentiality, accordingly, is necessarily the power which
posits the end, and brings the end, which has its end in
itself, into a unity with the means; and in order that the
finitude of the relation may be done away with—the
finitude being what we have so far been dealing with—
we must proceed to the point at which the Totality or
whole of the process in its inner conformity to an end,
comes into view. What is living has ends in itself;
it has means and material within its own existence; it
exists as the power or force of the means and its material.
This we find present at first only in the living individual
existence. It has in its organs the means, and is therefore its own material too. These means are pervaded
and penetrated by the end, they do not exist independently for themselves, they cannot exist apart from the
soul, apart from the living unity of the body to which
they belong. This fact must now take on the form of
what is universal, *i.e.*, the means and materials which
appear as accidental forms of existence as contrasted with
what the end implicitly is, have actually to be brought
under the sway of the Power in them, and to have their
soul only in the end, spite of their apparently indifferent
independent existence. The universal idea here is Power,
which exerts its power in accordance with ends, universal
Power. In so far as the end, which is an end in itself,
exists, and inorganic Nature is outside of it, this latter
as a matter of fact belongs to the Power which shows
its power in accordance with ends, so that those forms of
existence which appear immediately exist only for the
end. There are, it may be said, things which are implicitly ends, and things which appear as means, but this
characterisation cannot be maintained, for the first mentioned may in their turn be relatively means, while the

last mentioned may, on the contrary, exist in a permanent form. This second class, that of those things which appear as existing independently, is implicitly posited, not by means of the Power of the end, but by means of a higher essentially existing Power which conforms them to the end.

This is the general conception or notion of Power which acts in accordance with ends. The truth of the world consists in this Power; it is the Power of Wisdom, the absolutely universal Power, and since it is the world which is its manifestation, the truth of the world is the completely realised essential existence of the manifestation of a wise Power.

We have now more particularly to consider the proof of the existence of God which is based on this thought. Two points call for notice. The wise Power, namely, is the absolute Process in itself; it is the power of producing effects, of being active. This wise Power has by its very nature to posit a world which has ends in itself; its nature is to manifest itself, to pass into actual definite existence. This actual existence is, speaking generally, the positing of the difference, of the manifoldness which attaches to external existence. We thus get the element of difference in a more important and more essential specialised form. Power produces what it does produce in its character as wisdom, what is produced is the difference; this means that the one is implicitly an end and the other a means for the first; it is merely something in conformity with an end, contingent, and not an end in itself. This differentiation, namely, that the one is the means of the other, is the one side. The other side in this mediation consists in this, that the mutual relation between these two sides is Power, or, to express it differently, it is just this which characterises those on the one side as ends and the others as means, and is thus the maintenance or preservation of the ends. This aspect of the differentiation is Creation; it proceeds from the Notion; the wise

Power produces effects, makes distinctions, and thus is Creation.

It is to be noticed that this part of the mediation does not belong to the proof of the existence of God, for this part of the mediation begins with the conception or notion of wise Power. We have not here as yet reached the point at which the proof starts from the Notion, but that at which it starts from definite existence.

1. It is at this point that we first get the conception of Creation strictly so called; it is not to be found in any of the discussions which have gone before. We had first infinitude, then Power as the Essence of God. In the Infinite we have simply the negative of the finite; and in the same way in necessity finite existence is something which merely goes back whence it came; things disappear in it as accidental. What is is only in so far as it is a result. In so far as it is, all that can be asserted of it is only the fact that it is; nothing can be said of how it is; it can be in the particular way in which it is, but it might be otherwise as well, right or wrong, happy or unhappy. In necessity we get no further than formal affirmation; we do not get to the content; here there is nothing which is abiding, there is nothing which would be an absolute end. It is in Creation that we first come upon the positing and the being posited of affirmative forms of existence, not only as abstract, as things which only are, but as having content as well. It is just for this reason that Creation is only rightly in its place here. It is not the action of Power as Power, but of Power as Power that is wise, for Power first determines itself as wisdom; what appears as finite is thus already contained in it, and the determinations here get affirmation, *i.e.*, the finite existences, the things created get true affirmation. There are ends which are valid, and necessity is reduced to the condition of a moment in reference to the ends. The end is what persists in the Power, as

opposed to it and through it. Necessity is there on be-
half of the end, its process is the maintenance and the
realisation of the end ; the end stands above it, and necessity is thus posited as one *side* only of the process, so
that one part only of what is created is subjected to this
Power, and appears accordingly as contingent. It is from
the notion or conception of a wise Power that the act of
positing, along with the difference referred to, proceeds.

2. By means of the conception alluded to we get two
aspects of this truth; on the one hand we have ends,
and on the other what is contingent. The second step
accordingly is the mediation between the ends and what
is contingent. They are, as a matter of fact, different; life
and what has not life, each exists immediately for itself,
they have an equal right to be—they are; the Being of
the one has no more justification than that of the other.
The ends are living ; they are thus individuals existing as
so many immediate single points which stand off from
each other, and in reference to which the other exists for
itself and to which it can offer resistance. The mediation
or reconciliation between these two consists in this, that
the two do not exist for themselves in a similar way.
The one class consists of ends, the other of what has
merely material independent Being, and has no higher
signification even when it is living.

It is this second characteristic or mediation which has
been put into the special form of the Proof of the existence of God known as the Physico-Theological.

What has life is in fact Power, though at first it is
this only implicitly ; in its organs it is the living Soul
which is the Power, though this power does not yet hold
sway over the inorganic, which also exists and is infinitely
manifold. We thus have, on the one hand, what is as
yet Quality, what is, to begin with, immediate Being, and
the living things in a condition of indifference to each
other. They use the material which also exists in this
definite particular form which they themselves come to

have, and the other side is first given when the living things exist as power exercised over the material. It is by regarding the matter from this point of view that Understanding has constructed that Proof which is called the Physico-Theological.

In definite existence there are, in short, elements of two kinds which are indifferent to each other, and a third element is required through which the end can realise itself. Immediate existence is composed of elements which are indifferent to each other. Here it is the Good which is the ruling principle, and this means that each determination is so related to itself as to be indifferent towards what is other than it—that they are, in fact, different, though this does not mean that they are opposed to each other, for such opposition is not present in immediate existence. It is this inwardness, this potentiality, which forms the notion or conception of wise Power, and it is thus to this quality that the Proof after its fashion attaches itself. The Teleological Proof consists of the following moments as set forth by Kant, moments which he has specially taken up and criticised, and which he regarded as discredited. In the world are to be found clear traces or indications of a wise arrangement in accordance with ends. The world is full of life, spiritual life and natural life. These living things are implicitly organised, and so far as these organs are concerned it is possible to regard the parts as unrelated. It is true that the life in them is their harmony, but the fact of their existing in harmony does not seem to be based on their actual existence. Then, again, living things are related to what is external to them, and each form of life is related to its own part of inorganic nature. Plants require a particular climate or a particular soil, animals are of particular species—things, in fact, have their particular natures. Life is merely productive, and does not pass over into the Other along with which it forms part of a process. On the contrary, it continues to be·

itself while constantly altering and reconstructing the process. Thus what strikes any one who begins to reflect, is the element of harmonious relation in the world existing between the organic and the inorganic, and how existing things seem to be arranged with special reference to Man. For, at first, Man has before him things which have an independent existence, things which exist solely for themselves, but which, all the same, are in harmonious relation with his existence. What is really wonderful is that those very things which at first seem totally unrelated are just the things which really exist for one another, and therefore what produces wonder is the opposite of that indifference or absence of relation, namely, conformity to an end. We are thus in presence of a principle which is entirely different from that involved in unrelated existence.

This first principle is, so far as existing things are concerned, merely accidental. Nature, things, could not of themselves work harmoniously through so many forms of existence towards a contemplated end, and for this reason a rational arranging principle has to be forthcoming, and this the things themselves are not.

That things exist in conformity to an end is not a truth which is involved in or posited by the things themselves. Life certainly is so active that it makes use of inorganic nature, maintains itself by means of its act of assimilation, negates it, identifies itself with the inorganic and yet preserves itself in it. Its activity is certainly that particular activity of the subject which constitutes itself the centre point and uses the Other as a means, but the second characteristic is external to the things. Men, it is true, make use of things, they assimilate them, but the fact that there are such things which they can use is not involved in man's existence, is not posited by men. The fact of their being externally unrelated or indifferent to each other so far as their existence is concerned, as well as the fact of their existence, are not involved in or posited by the end. This indifference of things to each other does not express their true relation, but is merely an illusion. The true character of the relation is the teleological characterisation of conformity to an end, and it is in this, accordingly, that we have the absence of indifference in the relation between existing things. This expresses the essential relation, the relation which is valid and true. The Proof points to the necessity of having one supreme principle of order or regulating essence, for we infer from the unity of the world that the cause is one.

Kant, in opposition to this, says that this argument shows us God merely as an architect and not as a creator, and that it is concerned merely with the contingent elements of forms and not with the substance. It is, in fact, only the suitability of means to end which is demanded, the *quality* of objects in relation to each other in so far as it is posited by or depends for its existence on some Power. This quality, says Kant, is merely form, and the Power which posits would be a Cause producing forms merely, and not a Power creating matter. The distinction upon which this criticism rests has no meaning. There can be no positing of the form by the Power without the positing of the matter. If we have once got into the region of the Notion, we have got far past the distinction of form and matter, and must know that absolute form is something *real*, that therefore form is something, and that apart from matter it is nothing. When the word form is used in this connection it expresses a particular quality. The essential form, however, is the end, the Notion itself which realises itself; the form in the sense in which it is the Notion is the substantial element itself, the Soul; what can be distinguished from it as matter is something which is formal and entirely secondary, or it is merely a formal characterisation in the Notion.

Kant says further that the syllogism starts from the

world and from an arrangement and conformity to an
end which have been reached merely by observation, and
which express a merely contingent existence—what is
said about existence is undoubtedly correct, the contingent
is reached by observation—and goes on to infer the existence of a Cause proportionate to these, which works in
accordance with an end.   This remark is quite correct.
We say that the arrangement in accordance with an end
which we observe cannot have sprung up of itself ; it
demands the existence of a Power acting in accordance
with ends ; it is the content of this Cause, though we
cannot know anything more of this wisdom than what
we learn of it from observation.   All observation gives
nothing more than a relation ; but no one can reason
from Power to Almighty Power, from wisdom and unity,
to an all-wise and absolute Unity, and so the physico-
theological Proof gives us only a great Power, a great
Unity.   The content desired, however, is God, absolute
Power, Wisdom ;· but this is not involved in what is contained in observation, a leap is made from what is great
to what is absolute.   This is a point thoroughly well
established ; the content from which the start is made is
not that of God.

It is from conformity to an end that we start, and this
category is got at empirically ; these are finite contingent
things, and they are also ordered in conformity to an end.
What, then, is the character of this conformity ?   It is,
of course, finite.   The ends are finite, particular, and
are accordingly contingent also ; and it is here that the
element of inadequacy which attaches to this physico-
theological Proof comes in, a defect which is felt at once,
and which raises a suspicion against this style of argument.   Man uses plants, animals, light, air, water ; and
so too do animals and plants.   The end is thus an
entirely limited one ; animals and plants are at one time
ends and at another means—they eat and are eaten.
This physico-theological way of looking at things is apt

to lead to trivialities and to direct attention to small
details. It may satisfy those who wish for edification,
and the heart may be impressed by looking at things in
this fashion. It is another thing, however, if we have
to get to know God by this means, and if we mean to
speak of absolute wisdom. A bronto-theology, a testa-
cean-theology, &c., have been discovered in this way. The
content, the active working of God, are here simply such
finite ends as may be shown to be present in existence
generally. Absolutely higher ends would be found in
morality, in freedom ; moral good would have to be an
end for itself in order that an absolute end of such a
nature might also be attained in the world. But here
we are in the region of actions in accordance with ends
in general, while it is finite, limited ends which present
themselves in observation. The Power which works in
accordance with ends is merely the life-force, and is not
yet Spirit, the personality of God. When it is said that
the Good is the end, then it may be asked, What is good ?
If it is further said that happiness comes to men in proportion to their moral worth, that the end is that the
good man should be happy and the bad man unhappy,
then, as a matter of fact, we see in the world what forms
a most cruel contrast to this, and we find just as many
incitements to morality as there are sources of tempta-
tion. In short, perception and observation, considered in
this aspect, do indeed give us conformity to an end, but
in an equal degree do they give what is *not* in conformity
to an end, and in the long-run it comes to be a matter of
calculating which of the two elements predominates. It
is, accordingly, some such finite end, speaking generally,
which constitutes the content of the idea of the wisdom
of God.

The defect of the proof consists in.this, that the idea
of conformity to an end or of wisdom is defined in a
general way merely, and for this reason attention is
directed to those observations and to the knowledge

gained by sense-perception, in connection with which accordingly relative ends of this sort present themselves.

Even if God is conceived of as a Power working actively in accordance with ends, still this does not give what is sought after when we speak of God. A Power which works in accordance with ends is, in fact, the life-force of Nature, and not yet Spirit. The conception of the life-force expresses something which is an end for itself, an actually existing end and activity in accordance therewith. In its content, accordingly, as thus expressed, we have nothing beyond what is involved in the conception of living Nature.

So far as the form of this Proof is concerned, we have in it, speaking generally, that of the syllogism of the Understanding. There are existing things characterised by a teleological arrangement, *i.e.*, there are in a general way relations between things in conformity with ends, and in addition to this there is the definite existence of these objects which have the character of means, of something accidental so far as the ends are concerned. These objects, however, are at the same time *not* contingent when standing in this relation to one another, but rather it is implied in the notion or conception of the end, in the conception of the life-force, that not only have the ends been posited, but the objects too, which are means. This is quite correct, but the argument is further developed as follows. The arrangement of things in accordance with an end is composed, so far as its inner, its essential nature is concerned, of a Power which constitutes the connection or positing of the two, and by means of which they come to suit each other. Now, it is argued, if there are such things, here again it is the Being of these things which constitutes the starting-point. The transition, however, on the other hand, contains the moment of Not-Being. The means do not exist; they exist only in so far as they have been negatively posited, and so far as they exist they have merely a contingent existence in connection with the end. What, however, is demanded by the argument is, that they should not be forms of existence standing in a relation of indifference to the end. When, therefore, it is said that such things do actually exist, it is necessary to add to this the moment that their Being is not their *own* Being, but Being which has been degraded to a means. On the other hand, when it is said ends do actually exist, they certainly do; but since there is a Power which arranges them in a certain way, the existence of the ends in common with that of the means is posited as well. It is not the Being of the ends which, as positive Being, has the power of making the mediation the transition, but rather it is just in this transition that their Being is changed into a Being which has been posited or made dependent on something else.

The minor proposition here, however, does not get farther than the Being of things, instead of taking their Not-Being also into consideration. The general content of this form of proof is this : The world is arranged in accordance with an end, leaving out of consideration more definite ends. Conformity to an end is the notion not only in finite things, but expresses also the absolute essential character of the Notion, *i.e.*, the divine Notion, the essential characterisation or determination of God. God is Power, self-determination, and this means that He determines Himself in accordance with ends. The main defect in the argument is that it starts from perception, from phenomena. These supply a conformity to ends which is finite merely, while the pure end is the universal and absolute end.

We shall now pass on to the concrete or more definite form of religion, to the concrete determination of God. The notion or general conception is that of Power which works actively in accordance with ends. In the region of religion we occupy a different standpoint, that of consciousness or the self-consciousness of Spirit. Here we have the Notion no longer in the form merely of life-force, but as it determines itself in consciousness. We now have religion as consciousness of Spirit, which is a universal Power working in accordance with ends. In the object of religion it is the idea of Spirit in general which is present, but the point to determine is, which moment of Thought or Spirit is actively present. The content is not yet Spirit in and for itself; the object of the idea does not yet express the content of Spirit, this content being here a Power which works in accordance with ends. Since religion is defined as consciousness, here it is to be defined as self-consciousness. Here we have divine self-consciousness in general, both in its objective form as determination of the object, and also in its subjective form as determination of the finite spirit.

Consciousness, Spirit, determines itself here ás self-consciousness. That is implied in what has gone before; how it is so implied has now to be briefly indicated. In power, which is wisdom, the determinateness is posited as ideal in such a way that it pertains to the notion. The determinateness appears as determinate Being, Being for an Other. Along with consciousness difference is posited first as difference in reference to the self. Here it is posited as the individual difference of the self; it is relation to self, and consciousness is thus self-conscious-ness. God is posited as self-consciousness in so· far as consciousness and its connection with the object are thought of essentially as self-consciousness. Definite existence, the objectivity of God, the Other, is something ideal or spiritual. God is thus essentially for Spirit, for Thought in general, and this fact that He as Spirit is for Spirit is at all events one aspect of the relation. It may constitute the Totality of the relation when it means that God is worshipped in spirit and in truth, but it is essentially, at all events, one characteristic. We have further seen that the Notion must be characterised as end. The end must not, however, merely preserve this

form, remain shut up within itself and belong to itself;
on the contrary, it has to be realised. The question now
comes to be, supposing that wisdom has to act, that the
end has to be realised, what is to serve as the material
or sphere for this? This can be nothing else than Spirit
in general, or, to put it more definitely, Man. He is the
object of the Power which determines itself, which acts
in accordance with this determination, namely, wisdom.
Man, or finite consciousness, is Spirit in the character of
finitude. The act of realisation is a positing of the Notion
of a kind which is different from the mode in which the
absolute Notion realises itself, and consequently it assumes
the mode of finitude, which, however, is at the same time
spiritual. Spirit is only for Spirit; it is here characterised as self-consciousness, and the Other, in which it
realises itself, is the finite spirit, and there too it is equally
self-consciousness. This sphere or universal reality is
itself something spiritual. It must be a sphere in which
Spirit at the same time actually exists or is for itself.
Man is thus conceived of as an essential end, as the
sphere of divine power or wisdom.

Finally, Man thus stands to God in an affirmative
relation, for the fundamental determination is that he is
self-consciousness. Man, who constitutes this aspect of
reality, is accordingly self-consciousness; he is consciousness of the absolute Essence as being his own, consequently the freedom of consciousness is posited in God,
and thus Man is here at home with himself. This
moment of consciousness is an essential one, it is a fundamental determination, though not as yet the complete
expression of the relation. Man exists for himself as a
self-constituted end, his consciousness is free in God, it
is justified in God, exists essentially for self, and is directed
towards God. This is the principle in a general form,
while the definite forms are the particular religions, those
of Sublimity, of Beauty, and of Utility òr Conformity to
an End.

C.

DIVISION OF THE SUBJECT.

We have on the one side power pure and simple and abstract wisdom, and on the other a contingent end to be carried out. Both are united, and wisdom is unlimited; but for this reason it is indeterminate, and because of this the end as real is contingent or finite. The mediation of the two sides to concrete unity, which is of such a kind that the notion of wisdom is itself the content of its end, already constitutes the transition to a higher stage. The main determination here is expressed by the question, What is wisdom? what is the end? It is an end which is inadequate to the power.

(*a.*) The subjectivity which is inherently power has no connection with sense; the natural or immediate element is in it negated; it is only for Spirit, for Thought. This Power, which exists for itself, is essentially One. That which we have called reality, Nature, is only something posited, negated, and passes away into independent self-existent Being, where there is no Many, no One and the Other. Thus the One is purely exclusive, having no Other beside it, and not suffering anything alongside of it which might have independence. This One is the wisdom of The All; everything is posited by means of it, but is for it merely something external and accidental. This is the sublimity of the One, of this Power, and of Power which is wise. Since, on the other hand, it takes on the form of definite existence, namely, self-consciousness, and as Being exists for an Other, the end also is only one, though it is none the less sublime, and still it is a limited end which is not yet determined by means of multiplicity, and is thus an infinitely limited end. Both of these aspects correspond with one another, the infinitude of the Power and the limited character of its actual end. On the one hand there is sublimity, and on the other the opposite, an infinite limitedness or restrictedness. This is the first form in reference to the end. The One has what is infinite alongside of it, while, however, setting up for being the One.

So far as the relation between Nature and Spirit is concerned, the Religion of Sublimity means that the sensuous, the finite, the natural, what is spiritually and physically natural, has not yet been taken up into free subjectivity or transfigured within it. The characteristic of this stage is that free subjectivity is elevated to the condition of pure Thought, a form which is more adequate to express the content than the sensuous is. Here the natural element is dominated by this free subjectivity, in which the Other is merely ideal, and has no true lasting existence as against free subjectivity. Spirit is what raises itself, what is raised above the natural, above finitude. This is the Religion of Sublimity.

The Sublime is not, however, the Measureless, which, in order to determine itself and to take on a definite form, can make use only of what is immediately present and of silly distortions of it, and has to do this in order to produce a conformity with its inner nature. Sublimity, on the other hand, can do without immediate existence and its modes, and does not, like the other, get into a condition of poverty which forces it to lay hold of these modes in order to represent itself, but pronounces these to be a mere show or illusion.

(*b*.) The other characteristic or determination is that the natural or finite is transfigured in Spirit, in the freedom of Spirit. Its transfiguration consists in this, that it is a symbol of the spiritual in such a way that in this transfiguration of the physical-natural or spiritual-natural, the natural itself stands over against the spiritual as finite, as the other side of that essentiality, of that substantiality which we call God. This last is free subjectivity, in connection with which the finite is posited merely as a symbol, in which God, Spirit, appears. This is the mode of present individuality, of Beauty. In respect of the determination of the end, this mode means that the end is not one only, but that there are many ends, and that the infinitely limited end is elevated to the condition of a real end. Here the real end is no longer exclusive, but allows much—all, in fact, the right of existence alongside of it, and a genial tolerance is here the fundamental characteristic. There are subjects of various sorts which have a valid existence alongside of each other, many unities from which definite existence gets the means it employs, and thus existence gets a certain friendly character attached to it. Just because there are many particular ends, multiplicity does not disdain to exhibit itself in immediate determinate existence. The multiplicity, the kind or variety, possesses universality in itself. The end permits the different kinds of things to have a valid existence alongside of itself; it is on terms of friendship with particularity and shows itself in it, and in its character, as particular end, it permits the means to have a valid existence alongside of itself, and manifests itself in it. It is at this point that the determination or category of Beauty comes in. Beauty is end existing potentially, which allies itself with immediate existence, and in this way establishes its own validity. Above the Beautiful and the particular end there floats the Universal in the form of a Power devoid of anything subjective, devoid of wisdom, indeterminate in itself, and this accordingly is Fate—cold necessity. Necessity is, indeed, that particular development of the Essence which allows its phenomenal manifestation or appearance to unfold itself in the form of independent realities, while the moments of this outward manifestation show themselves in the shape of distinct or differentiated forms. Implicitly, however, these moments are identical, and their existence is accordingly not to be taken seriously. It is only Destiny, the inner identity of the differences, which is to be taken seriously.

(c.) The third form of religion is equally represented

by a finite particular end, which in its particularity represents itself as universality, and expands itself so as to reach universality, but which is all the same still empirical and external. It is not the true universality of the Notion, but one which, comprising the world and the peoples of the world within itself, extends them so as to reach universality, while it at the same time loses its determinate character, and has for its end the cold abstract Power, and is in itself devoid of an end.

In external existence these three moments are represented by the Jewish, the Greek, and the Roman religions. Power, as subjectivity, determines itself as wisdom acting in accordance with an end; this end is, to begin with, still undetermined; particular ends come into existence, and finally an empirical universal end appears.

These religions correspond in reverse order to those preceding them. The Jewish religion corresponds to the Persian, the element of difference common to the two being that, regarded from this standpoint, the determinateness represents the inner nature of the Essence which is the end of self-determination. At an earlier stage, however, in the religions which precede, the determinateness had a natural character. In the Persian religion this was represented by light, this element being in its nature universal, simple, and physical. This was accordingly the final stage reached, taking the natural as a starting-point, Nature being thus comprehended in a unity which was similar to that of Thought. Here, in the Jewish religion, particularity is represented by a simple abstract end, namely, power, which is really only wisdom. Regarding the question from the second standpoint, we have in the Greek religion many particular ends and one Power above them; in the Hindu religion there are in the same way the many natural realities, and above them Brāhma, the self-thinking One. Considering the matter from the third standpoint, we have an empirical universal end which is itself the selfless, all-destroying Destiny, not true subjectivity, and corresponding to this we have power as individual empirical self-consciousness. Thus, too, in the Chinese religion there appears an individual existence which represents itself as the Universal pure and simple, as determining everything as God. The first mode of natural existence is self-consciousness, individual, natural. The natural, in its character as something single or individual, is what actually exists as, and is determined as, self-consciousness. Here, accordingly, the arrangement is the reverse of what we have in the Religion of Nature. In the present instance, what is primary is Thought, which is concrete in itself, simple subjectivity, which then advances so as to get determination within itself. In the other case, in the Religion of Nature, it was the natural immediate self-consciousness which was the primary element, and which finally embodied itself in the pictorial conception of light.

I.

THE RELIGION OF SUBLIMITY.

What this religion has in common with that of Beauty is the ideality it ascribes to the natural, which it brings into subjection to the spiritual, and further that in it God is consciously known as conscious Spirit, as Spirit whose determinations are rational and moral. God, however, in the Religion of Beauty has still a particular nature or content, or, to put it otherwise, He is merely moral Power in the manifested form of Beauty, and therefore in a manifestation which still takes place in a sensuous material, in the region of sensuous matter, the matter of the idea or ordinary conception: the region in which the manifestation takes places is not yet that of Thought. The necessity for rising higher to the Religion of Sublimity is to be found in the fact that the particular spiritual and moral forces are taken out of their state of particularity and included within a spiritual unity. The truth of the Particular is the universal unity, which is concrete in itself in so far as it has the Particular within itself, and yet has this in itself in such a way that in its essence it is subjectivity.

The region for the play of this manifestation of reason, which, as subjectivity, is, so far as its content is concerned, universal, and is, so far as its form is concerned, free— the region in which pure subjectivity shows itself, is that of pure Thought. This pure subjectivity has been freed from the natural, and consequently from what is sensuous, whether this is found in the external world of sense or is a sensuous idea. It is the spiritual subjective unity, and it is this which first rightly gets from us the name God.

This subjective unity is not substance, but subjective unity; it is absolute Power, while the natural is merely something posited, ideal, and not independent. It does not manifest itself in any natural material, but in Thought. Thought is the mode of its definite existence or manifestation.

There is absolute power in the Hindu religion also, but the main point is that it be concretely determined within itself, and thus be the absolute wisdom. The rational characteristics of freedom, the moral characteristics, are united so as to form one characteristic, one End, and thus the characteristic of this subjectivity is holiness. Morality thus characterises itself as holiness.

The higher truth of the subjectivity of God is not the determination or characteristic of the Beautiful, in which the constituent element, the absolute content, is separated into particulars, but the characteristic of holiness; and the relation between these two determinations is similar to that between the animals and man: the animals have a particular character, but it is the character of universality which is the human moral rationality of freedom, and the unity of this rationality, a unity which has an essential independent existence, is the true subjectivity, the subjectivity which determines itself within itself. This is wisdom and holiness. The content of the Greek gods, the moral Powers, are not holy, because they are particular and limited.

A.

THE GENERAL NATURE OF THE CONCEPTION.

The Absolute, God, is defined as the one subjectivity, pure subjectivity, and, as a consequence, as subjectivity which is universal in itself, or the reverse. This subjectivity, which is universal in itself, is clearly One only. The unity of God consists in this, that the consciousness of God is the consciousness of Him as One. The point here is not to show that the unity exists·implicitly, that the unity lies at the basis of things, as is the case in the Indo-Chinese religion ; for God is not posited as infinite subjectivity when His unity is merely implicit, and He is not known and does not exist for consciousness as subjectivity. God in the present case is, on the contrary, consciously known as a personal One, not as One, as in Pantheism. Thus the immediate natural mode of conceiving of God disappears, the mode, for instance, which appears in the Persian religion, in which He is thought of as light. Religion is conceived of as the religion of Spirit, but only so far as its basis is concerned, only as it exists in the region that specially belongs to it, that of Thought. This unity of God contains itself One Power, a Power which consequently is absolute, and within this all externality, and consequently all that belongs to the world of sense, that takes on the form of sense, or is a picture, disappears.

God is here without form. He does not exist in any external sensuous form. There is no image of Him. He does not exist for the sensuous idea, but, on the contrary, He exists only for thought. The infinite subjectivity is the subjectivity which thinks, and, being thinking subjectivity, it exists only for thought.

(*a.*) God is defined as absolute power, which is wisdom. Power in its form as wisdom is, to begin with, reflected into itself as subject. This reflection into self, this self-determination of power, is the self-determination which is entirely abstract and universal, which does not yet particularise itself within itself, the determinate character being only determinateness in general. It is owing to this subjectivity which makes no distinction within itself that God is defined as One. Within this One all particularity has vanished. It is implied in this that natural things, the things which have a determinate particular character and constitute the world, have no longer any valid independent existence in their condition of immediacy. Independence is represented by One only. All else is merely something posited, dependent for its being on something else, something which is kept from existing by the One, for the One is abstract subjectivity, and all else is unsubstantial as compared with it.

(*b.*) The next point is the determination of the end followed out by the absolute Power. From one point of view, God is Himself His end. He is wisdom. And it is, to begin with, required of this determination that it be equal to the power. It is itself, however, merely a general end, or, to put it otherwise, wisdom is merely abstract, is merely called wisdom.

(*c.*) The determinateness, however, must not remain merely a determination within the Notion, but receive the form of reality also. This form is, to begin with, an immediate one. The end of God is, in fact, merely the first reality, and accordingly is a wholly single or individual end. The next step is that the end, the determinateness, should on its part be raised to the condition of concrete universality. We certainly have here pure subjectivity on the one side, but the determinateness is not yet equalised with it. This first end is thus limited, but Man, self-consciousness, is the sphere in which it shows itself. The end must, as being a divine end, be universal, inherently and potentially universal; it must contain universality in itself. The end is thus merely human, and as yet naturally the family, which widens out into a nation. A definite nation becomes here the end set before itself by wisdom.

That God should be thus characterised as One seems to us a thought which is familiar, and not striking and important, because we are accustomed to this figurative idea of Him. The idea is formal, too, but of infinite importance, and it is not to be wondered at that the Jewish people put such a high value upon it, for the thought that God is one is the root of subjectivity, of the intellectual world, the way to truth. The essential character of absolute truth is contained in it; still it is not yet truth as truth, for development is a necessary quality of this latter, but it is the *beginning* of truth and the formal principle of the absolute harmony of the Absolute with itself. The One is pure power, and all that is particular is posited in Him as negative, and not as belonging to Him as such, but as inadequate to express Him, as unworthy of Him. In the religion of Nature we saw the determinateness under the aspect of natural existence, as, for example, light, and the self-consciousness of the Absolute appeared in this manifold manner. In the infinite Power, on the other hand, all this externality is annihilated. There is, therefore, an essence without form or representation which does not exist for the Other in any natural mode, but only for thought, for Spirit. This definition of the One is that formal definition of unity which forms the basis of the conception of God as Spirit, and, so far as self-consciousness is concerned, it is the root of its concrete, true content.

But it is, to begin with, nothing more than the root merely. For the point to be determined is not how many spiritual predicates—as, for example, wisdom, goodness, mercy, are to be ascribed to the One, but what He does and really is. What we are concerned with is, the actual determination and reality. It must, therefore, be determined whether or not the action expresses the mode in which Spirit appears. If the activity is not of the kind which develops the nature of Spirit, then the subject may certainly pass for being Spirit so far as ordinary thought is concerned, but it is not itself true Spirit. The fundamental characteristic of activity here, however, is, to begin with, Power, which does not assume an outward form implying that the reality is its own reality, but rather its attitude to reality is still essentially a negative one.

B.

THE CONCRETE GENERAL IDEA OR POPULAR CONCEPTION.

(a.) *The Determination of the Divine Particularisation.*

First Determination.—In the divine act of judgment, God is wisdom ; God's self-determination, His differentiation, or, to put it more definitely, His act of Creation, is contained in it. Spirit is simply what mediates self within self, what is active. This activity implies a distinguishing from self, an act of judgment, which, in its original meaning, is separation or division. The world is something posited by Spirit ; it is made out of its nothing. The negative element in the world, however, is the affirmative element, the Creator, namely, in whom what is natural exists as the non-existent. The world, therefore, in its nothingness has sprung from the absolute fulness of the power of the Good. It has been created from its own nothingness, which, as being its Other, God is. Wisdom means that an end is present in the world, and determines it. This subjectivity, however, is what comes first, and is accordingly abstract to begin with, and consequently the particularisation of God is not yet posited as being within Himself, but rather His act of judgment or separation means that He posits something, and what is thus posited and gets a definite character exists at first in the form of an immediate Other. The higher conception is certainly that of God's act of Creation within Himself, by which He is beginning and end in Himself, and thus has the moment of movement, which is here still outside of Him, in Himself, in His inner nature.

When wisdom is not abstract but concrete, and God is thought of as self-determining in such a way that He creates Himself within Himself, and preserves what is created within Himself, so that it is produced and known as permanently contained within Himself as His Son, then God is known as concrete God, truly known as Spirit.

Since, however, wisdom is as yet abstract, the act of separation, what is posited, is something which has Being, the separation or judgment has still the form of immediacy, but it has this only in so far as it is form, for God creates absolutely out of nothing. He alone is Being, what is positive. He is, however, at the same time the positing of His power. The necessity by which God is the positing of His power is the birthplace of all that is created. This necessity is the material out of which God creates; it is God Himself, and He therefore does not create out of anything material, for He is the Self, and not the immediate or material. He is not One as against an Other already existing, but is Himself the Other in the form of determinateness, which, however, because He is only One, exists outside of Him as His negative movement. The positing of Nature necessarily belongs to the notion or conception of spiritual life, of the Self, and is the sinking of intelligence into sleep. Since power is conceived of as absolute negativity, the Essence, *i.e.*, what is identical with itself, is at first in a state of repose, of eternal calm and seclusion. But this very solitude in its own self is merely a moment of Power, and not its totality. Power is in its very nature a negative relation to self, a mediation within self; and since it is negatively related to self, the abolition or annulling of abstract identity is the positing of difference, determinateness, *i.e.*, it is the creation of the world. The element of nothing, out of which the world is created, is the absence of all difference, and it is in connection with this quality that Power, Essence, is first thought of. If, accordingly, it is asked where God got the material, the answer is, just in that simple relation to self. Matter is what is formless, what is identical with itself. This is merely a moment of the Essence, and is thus something different from absolute Power, and is accordingly what we call matter. The creation of the world, therefore, means the negative relation of the Power to itself, in so far as it is to begin with something which is defined as merely identical with self.

The creation by God is something very different from the act of proceeding from God, or from the idea of the world proceeding out of God. All peoples have had theogonies, or, what comes to the same thing, cosmogonies. In these the fundamental category is always procession, not the fact of something being created. It is out of Brahmā that the gods proceed, while in the cosmogonies of the Greeks, the highest, the most spiritual gods are those which have finally proceeded from some source, which have been the last so to proceed. This poor category of procession now disappears, for the Good, Absolute Power, is a Subject.

This procession does not express the true character of what is created. What thus proceeds is what exists, what actually is, and in such a way that the Ground or Essence from which it proceeds is thought of as the unessential element which has disappeared in something higher. What proceeds out of God is not thought of as something created, but as something independent, self-subsistent, not as something which has no inherent in-

dependence. This, therefore, is the form taken by the
Divine self-determination, the mode of particularisation.
It cannot blunder, for wisdom is necessary to the very
idea of it. It is not, however, any kind of particularisation of God in Himself, otherwise God would be
known as Spirit. The particularisation, just because
God is One, attaches to the other aspect of existence.
This particularisation is, to begin with, the Divine act of
characterisation in general, and is thus Creation. This
positing of the world is not transitory, but, on the contrary, what proceeds out of God preserves the character
of something posited, of the creature, in fact. Thus what
is created has upon it the mark of something which has
no independence. This is the fundamental characteristic,
and one which remains attached to it because God is
conceived of as Subject, as infinite Power. Here Power
exists only for the One, and thus it follows that what is
particular is merely something negative, something posited,
as compared with the subject.

Second Determination. — This determination means
that God is hypothetically Subject. If He is not, then
Creation is a vague popular conception which readily
suggests the mechanical and technical methods of production used by man, and this is an idea which we must
keep out of our minds. God is the First: His act of
creation is an eternal creating, in which He is not a
result, but that which originates. When He is conceived
of in a higher way, namely, as Spirit, He is the self-
creating, and does not proceed out of Himself, being both
beginning and result. Here, however, God is not conceived of as Spirit. Human production, technical production, is an external process. The Subject, what is First,
becomes active, and connects itself with something other
than itself, and thus comes to stand in an external relation to the material which has to be manipulated, which
offers resistance and has to be overcome. Both actually
exist as objects which have a mutual relation to each

other. God, on the other hand, creates absolutely out of nothing, since there is nothing which was before Him.

The mode of production, therefore, in connection with which He is Subject, is intuitive, is *infinite activity.* In the case of human production, I am consciousness, I have an end, and know what it is, and I have, too, accordingly the material, and know that my relation to it is a relation to an " Other." Intuitive production, on the contrary, the production of Nature, belongs to the conception of Life. It is an inward act, inner activity, which has no reference to something actually existing. It is life-force, the eternal production of Nature, and Nature, speaking generally, is something posited, something created.

God is in reference to the world the totality of His determinateness, of His negation, and in reference to the totality of immediate Being, He is what is pre-supposed, the subject which remains absolutely first. Here the fundamental characteristic of God is subjectivity, which relates itself to itself, and as inherently existing permanent subjectivity it is what is first.

The derivative character of the Greek gods, who represent the spiritual element, is something which belongs to their finitude. It is this which gives them their conditional character, in accordance with which their own nature is considered as dependent on something previously existing, as is the case with the finite spirit of Nature.

This subjectivity, however, is the absolutely First, the Beginner of things, its conditional character being done away with ; but it is only something which begins, and this does not mean that the subjectivity is characterised as result and as concrete Spirit.

If what was created by the absolute Subject were itself, then the difference would in that case be done away with and absorbed in this difference. The first Subject would be the last, something which resulted from itself. But this is a characteristic we have not yet got, and all we can say is that this absolute Subject is something which begins merely—that is first or primary.

The third determination of God in relation to the world. —This is expressed by what we call the attributes of God. These represent His determinate character, *i.e.*, inasmuch as we have seen that there is a particularisation of God, God's self-determination, and that this self-determination is the creation of the world, it follows that along with this there is posited the fact of a relation on the part of God to the world, or to put it otherwise, the attributes are the determinate element itself, only known in the Notion of God.

The One is something which has got determinate character, which is known as being, as not returning into God, the Other is God's being made determinate as a determinate quality of God. It is this that we are in the habit of calling by the name of attributes, God's relations to the world, and to say that we know only this relation of God to the world and do not know God Himself, is to use an unfortunate expression. It is just this which is His own determinate character, and it is this consequently which is represented by His own attributes.

It is only when things are represented in an external way and from the point of view of the senses, that anything can be said *to be*, and to be for self, in such a way that its relations to other things, its attributes, are distinguished from its existence, for it is just these which constitute its own peculiar nature. The manner in which a man stands related to others is just his nature. The acid is nothing else than the particular character of its relation to the base—that is the nature of the acid itself. If we understand the relation in which an object stands to other things, we understand the nature of the object itself.

These distinctions, therefore, are of a very inferior character, since they directly coincide as being the product of an understanding which does not know them, and is not aware what it possesses in these distinctions. This determinateness as something external, immediate, as a determinateness of God Himself, is His absolute power, which is wisdom, the definite moments of which are goodness and righteousness.

Goodness consists in the fact that the world is: Being does not belong to it, as Being is here reduced to the condition of a moment, and is only a Being which has been posited or created. This act of dividing, of differentiation, represents the eternal goodness of God. What is thus distinguished from God has no right to be; it is external to the One, something manifold, and because of this, something limited, finite, whose essential character is not to be, but the goodness of God consists just in the fact that it is. Inasmuch as it is something which has been posited, it also passes away, is only appearance. God only is Being, the truly real; Being which excludes any of its elements, Being outside of God, has no right of existence.

God can be a Creator in the true sense only in so far as He is subjectivity, for as such He is free, and His determinate character, His self-determination, is set free. It is only what is free that can have its determinations standing over against itself as free and can give them freedom. This differentiation, whose totality is represented by the world, this Being, is The Good.

The Being of the world, however, is only the Being of Power, or, to put it otherwise, the positive reality and independence or self-existence of the world is not its own self-existence, but the self-existence of Power. The world accordingly must, in relation to the Power, be thought of as something incomplete in itself. The one side is represented by the manifoldness of the differences, the infinite realm of definite existence, the other side accordingly by the substantiality of the world, though this quality does not attach to the world itself, but is rather the identity of the Essence with itself. The world does not maintain itself independently; on the contrary, its Being-for-self, its real existence, is the

Power which maintains itself in the differences, inasmuch as it remains Being-for-self, and thus represents the Being of the world. The world is thus divided within itself; regarded from one side it is dependent, selfless difference, and regarded from the other side it is its own Being.

The manifestation of the nothingness, of the ideality of this finite existence, of the fact that Being is here not true independence—this manifestation in the form of Power, is Righteousness, and in this justice is done to finite things. Goodness and righteousness are not moments of Substance. These characteristics exist in Substance in a state of being, and they also are immediately present in it as not being, as becoming.

Here the One is not thought of as Substance, but as the personal One, as Subject, and here the determination of the end is the determinateness of the Notion itself. The world *has* to be, and so, too, it *has* to change, to pass away. Here righteousness is thought of as determination of the Subject in its self-differentiation from these determinations which belong to it, from this world which is its own world.

Creation, preservation, passing away are, in the ordinary conception of them, separated in time, but in the Notion they are essentially moments only of one process, namely, of the process of Power. The identity of Power with itself is thus the Nothing out of which the world has been created, being both the subsistence of the world and the cancelling and absorbing of this subsistence or independent existence. This identity of Power which presents itself in the Being of things, too, is both the Being of things and their Not-Being. In so far as goodness is concerned, the world exists only as having no justification for its existence in itself, as upheld and maintained in a contingent way, and in this fact is, at the same time, contained its negativity, which owes its existence to righteousness.

The characteristics indicated are certainly characteristics of the Notion itself, but the subject which possesses them has not its real nature in them. The fundamental characteristics are the One and Power, and the Notion, the inmost nature of the subject, is posited as still existing independently of the attributes. If they really belonged to it, then they would themselves be Totality, for the Notion is the absolute goodness, it shares with itself its own characteristics. In the case of their belonging to the Notion, it would be further implied that they themselves were the whole Notion, and thus it would be for the first time truly real; in which case, however, the Notion would be posited as Idea and the subject as Spirit, in which goodness and righteousness would be totalities.

But although goodness and righteousness contain the element of difference, they are not thought of as being the abiding character of Power. Power, on the contrary, is by its very nature what is without definite character, what is undetermined, *i.e.*, it shows itself essentially powerful as against these very differences; its goodness passes over into righteousness, and *vice versâ*. Each being posited for itself excludes the other, while the very nature of Power consists in this, that it simply does away with or cancels the determinateness.

Righteousness is the moment of negation, *i.e.*, it makes manifest the nothingness of things. Righteousness thus understood is a characteristic, just as origination and passing away are in Siva. It simply expresses the general aspect of the process, the aspect of contingency, the nothingness of which is made plain. It does not express negation as an infinite return into self, which would be the characteristic of Spirit. Negation is here nothing more than righteousness.

(*b.*) *The Form of the World.*

The world thus regarded is prosaic; it exists essentially as a collection of things. In the East, and in Greek life particularly, a feeling of delight arises from the friendly and joyous character of the relation in which Man stands to Nature, since Man, in so far as he is related to Nature, is related to the Divine. By taking up this generous attitude he spiritualises what is natural, makes it into something Divine, gives it a soul.

This unity of the Divine and the natural, this identity of the ideal and the real, is an abstract characterisation, and is easily reached. The true identity is that which is found in infinite subjectivity, which is not conceived of as neutralisation, as a kind of mutual blunting of the characteristics of the two elements, but as infinite subjectivity, which determines itself, and sets its determinations free in the form of a world. At this stage these determinations thus set free are, in their character as things, at the same time unsubstantial or dependent, and this is indeed their true nature. They are not gods, but natural objects.

These particular moral Powers, which the higher Greek gods essentially are, possess independence only in form, because their content, owing to its particular character, is unsubstantial. This is a false form; the Being of these unsubstantial things, which are immediate regarded from the present standpoint, is really conceived of as something formal, as something unsubstantial, which comes to have Being not in the shape of absolute divine Being, but Being which is abstract, one-sided, and since it gets the character of abstract Being, it has attached to it the categories of Being, and being finite, the categories of the Understanding.

We are in the presence of prosaic things when the world thus exists for us, in the presence of external things, existing in accordance with the manifold connection of the Understanding as expressed by ground and consequence, quality, quantity, and all such-like categories of the Understanding.

Nature is here undeified, natural things have no substantiality or independence in themselves, and the Divine is only in the One. It might well seem to be a matter for regret that Nature should in any religion be undeified, and should get the character of what has no divine element in it. We are wont rather to extol the unity of the ideal and the real, the unity of Nature and God, and where natural things are considered to be freely determined as substantial and divine, it is the custom to call this the identity of ideality and reality. This is certainly the Idea, but such a determination of identity is so far very formal, it is cheaply got, and it is to be found everywhere. The main point is the further determination of this identity, and the true one is to be found only in what is spiritual, in God, who in a real way determines Himself, so that the moments of His Notion are at the same time themselves present as totality. Natural things, so far as their particular existence is concerned, have, as a matter of fact, an implicit existence ; looked at through their Notion, their relation to Spirit, to the Notion, is an external one, and so too Spirit as finite, and appearing as this particular form of life, is itself external. Life, it is true, is essentially something inward, but the totality referred to, in so far as it is merely life, is external relatively to the absolute inwardness of Spirit ; abstract self-consciousness is equally finite. Natural things, the sphere of finite things, purely abstract Being, represent something which in its nature is external to itself. It is here at this stage that things get the character of externality ; they appear in accordance with their Notion in their true nature. If regret be felt that such a position is assigned to Nature, it must at the same time be granted that this beautiful union of Nature and God holds good for fancy only, not for reason. Even those who object so strongly to the undeifying of Nature, and extol that identity, will all the same certainly find it very difficult to believe in a Ganga, a cow, a monkey, a sea, &c., as God. It is here, on the contrary, that a foundation is laid for a more rational way of looking at things and at their connection.

This, however, is not as yet the place at which to give to this form of conscious thought theoretic completeness and make it knowledge. In order to do this, there must exist a concrete interest for things, and the Essence must be conceived of not merely as universal, but also as determinate Notion. The definite theoretic view of things cannot exist alongside of the popular idea of abstract wisdom and of one limited end.

The relation of God to the world in general is thus defined as His immediate manifestation in it in a particular, individual way, for a definite end in a limited sphere, and it is at this point that the definite conception of miracles comes in. In the earlier religions there are no miracles ; in the religion of India everything has been in a deranged state from the very start. The idea of miracle comes in first in connection with the thought of opposition to the order of Nature, to the laws of Nature even when these have not as yet been discovered, but when there is only the consciousness of a natural connection between things of a general character. It is here we first meet with the miraculous, and the idea which is formed of it is that God manifests Himself in some individual thing, and does this at the same time in opposition to the essential character of this thing.

The true miracle in Nature is the manifestation of Spirit, and the true manifestation of Spirit is fundamentally the Spirit of Man and his consciousness of the rationality of Nature, his consciousness that in these scattered elements, and in these manifold contingent things, conformity to law and reason are essentially present. In this religion, however, the world appears as a complexity of natural things which affect each other in a natural way, and stand in an intelligible connection with each other, and the necessity for miracles is present so long as that connection is not conceived of as the

objective nature of things, *i.e.*, so long as God's manifestation in them is not thought of as eternal universal laws
of Nature, and so long as His activity is not thought of
as essentially universal. The rational connection which
is first reached at this stage is only objective connection,
and what it means is that the individual thing as such
exists in its finiteness for itself, and is consequently in
an external relation.

Miracle is still conceived of as an accidental manifestation of God; the universal absolute relation of God to
the natural world is, on the other hand, sublimity. We
cannot call the infinite Subject conceived of in itself and
in its relation to itself, sublime, for so thought of, it is in
its essential nature absolute and holy. The idea of sublimity first comes in in connection with the manifestation
and relation of this Subject to the world, and when the
world is thought of as a manifestation of the Subject, though
as a manifestation which is not affirmative, or as one which,
while it is indeed affirmative, has yet its main characteristic
in this, that what is natural, what is of the world, is negated
as inadequate to express the Subject, and is known as such.

Sublimity is therefore this particular appearing and
manifestation of God in the world, and it may be defined
thus. This act of manifestation shows itself at the same
time as sublime, as raised above this manifestation in
reality. In the Religion of Beauty there is a reconciliation of the signification with the material, of the sensuous
mode and Being for an "Other." The spiritual manifests itself entirely in this external way. This external
mode is a symbol of what is inner, and this inner something is completely known in its external form.

The sublimity of the manifestation, on the other hand,
directly destroys reality, the matter and material which
belong to it. In His manifestation God directly distinguishes Himself from it, so that it is expressly known to
be inadequate to manifest Him. The One has not therefore His complete Being and essential existence in the

externality of the manifestation as the gods of the Religion of Beauty have, and the inadequacy of the manifestation is not something of which there is no consciousness, but, on the contrary, it is expressly posited along with consciousness as inadequacy.

It is not accordingly enough to constitute sublimity that the content, the Notion, be higher than the outward Form, even if this latter be exaggerated and stretched beyond its natural measure, but what manifests itself must also be the Power which is above the outward form. In the religion of India the representations of the Divine are devoid of measure, and yet they are not sublime but are rather a distortion, or, it may be, they are not distorted, as, for instance, the cow and the ape, which express the entire power of Nature, yet the signification and the outward form are not proportionate to each other; they are not sublime, however, for indeed it is this want of mutual proportion which is the greatest defect. It is accordingly necessary that the Power be at the same time put above the outward form.

Man in a state of natural consciousness can have natural things present before him, but his spirit does not suit with such a content. The mere act of looking around gives nothing sublime, but rather the glance towards heaven which is above and beyond what lies around. This sublimity is in a special sense the character of God in relation to natural things. The Old Testament Scriptures are extolled because of the presence in them of this sublimity. " And God said, Let there be light, and there was light." Here we have one of the sublimest passages. The Word represents the greatest possible absence of effort, and this breathing is here at the same time light, the world of light, the infinite pouring forth of light; and thus light is degraded to the rank of a word, to something so transitory as a word. God is further represented as using the wind and the lightning as servants and messengers, Nature is so obedient to Him. It

is said, "From Thy breath the worlds proceed; before
Thy threatenings they flee away; if Thou openest Thine
hand, they are filled with good; if Thou hidest Thy face,
they are troubled; if Thou holdest in Thy breath, they
pass away into dust; if Thou sendest it forth, they
spring up again." Sublimity consists in this, that Nature
is represented as thus entirely negated, in subjection,
transitory.

C.

THE END GOD WORKS OUT IN THE WORLD.

First Determination.—The determination of the end
appears here as the essential one that God is wise, to
begin with—wise in Nature generally. Nature is His
creature, and He lets His power be known in it, though
not His power only, but His wisdom as well. This
wisdom reveals itself in what it produces by the presence
of arrangement in accordance with an end.

This end has rather the character of something indeterminate, superficial; the conformity to an end is rather
of an external kind, "Thou givest to the beast its food."
The true end and the true realisation of the end are not
present within Nature as such, but rather they are essentially to be found in consciousness. He manifests Himself
in Nature, but His essential appearing is that He appears
in consciousness, in His reflection or reappearance, in
such a way that in self-consciousness it reappears that
His end is just to be known by consciousness, and that
He is an end for consciousness.

Sublimity, to begin with, gives only the general idea
of power, and not as yet that of an end. The end is not
only the One, the truth rather being that only God Himself can be His end, and this means that His Notion becomes objective for Him, and that He possesses Himself
in the realisation. This is the universal end in general.
If, accordingly, turning our attention to the world, to

Nature, we here seek to regard it as the end of God, then we see that it is His power only that is manifested in it, it is only His power that becomes objective to Him in it, and wisdom is as yet quite abstract. When we speak of an end, it must not be thought of as simply power; it must have a really determinate character. Spirit is, in fact, the region in which it can be present, and since God is end in Spirit as consciousness, in Spirit which is posited over against Him, and here, therefore, in the finite spirit as such, His end in the finite spirit is His representation, His recognition. God here has the finite spirit over against Him. Being-other, or other-ness, is not as yet posited as having absolutely returned into itself. The finite spirit is essentially consciousness. God must, therefore, be an object of consciousness as being the Essence, *i.e.*, in such a way as to be acknow-ledged and extolled. It is the glory of God which is, to begin with, His end. God's reflex presence in self-con-sciousness, taken generally, is not yet known. God is only recognised, but if He is also to be really known or cognised, then it is necessary that He, as Spirit, should posit differences in Himself. Here He has as yet only the abstract characterisations referred to.

Thus at this stage the thought that religion, as such, is the end, is an essential characteristic, which means that God becomes consciously known in self-consciousness, that He is object in it, and has an affirmative relation to it. He is God as being infinite power and subjectivity in Himself. The second point is that He manifests Himself, and that this should be essentially in another spirit, which, as finite, stands in an objective relation to Him. Thus the characteristic which comes in here is the acknowledgment and exaltation of God, the glory of God, His universal glory, for not only the Jewish nation, but the whole earth, all peoples, all nations are to praise the Lord. This end, namely, that He should be recog-nised, known, honoured by consciousness, may, to start

with, be called the theoretic end. Its more definite form
is that of the practical end, the peculiarly real end, which
realises itself in the world, but always in the spiritual
world.

Second Determination.—This essential end is the moral
end, morality, signifying that Man, in what he does, has
present to his mind what is in accordance with law,
what is right. This element of law of what is right is
the Divine element, and in so far as it belongs to the
world, and is present in finite consciousness, it is something which has been posited by God.

God is the Universal. The man who guides himself
and his will in accordance with this universal is the free
man, and thus represents the universal will, and not his
own particular morality. The doing of what is right is
here the fundamental characteristic, walking before God,
freedom from selfish ends, the righteousness which has
worth before God.

Man does what is thus declared to be right in reference to God with a view to the glory of God. This
right-doing has its seat in the will, in the inner nature of
man ; and, in contrast to this exercise of will in reference
to God, we have the natural state of existence, of Man,
and of what acts.

Just as we saw that in Nature there was a broken up
or disjointed state of things, that God existed independently while Nature had Being, but was yet something
in subjection, so too we see exactly the same distinction
in the human spirit ; we have right-doing as such, then,
again the natural existence of Man. This, however, is
equally something determined by means of the spiritual
relation of the will, just as Nature in general is something posited by the absolute Spirit.

The natural existence of Man, his outward worldly
existence, is placed in direct relation to what is inward.
If this will of his is a substantial, essential will, action
is right action ; and so, too, Man's external existence

ought to be in keeping with this something which is inward and right. It can go well with Man only according to his works, and he must not only conduct himself morally in a general way, respect the laws of his country, and sacrifice himself for his country, happen what may, but there arises a definite demand that it should also go well with whoever does right.

An essential point here is that real existence, definite Being in an external form, be made to correspond with, brought into subjection to, and determined in accordance with, what is inner and right. This essential condition enters here in consequence of, and on the basis of, the fundamental relation of God to the natural finite world.

There is here an end, and one which must be carried out, namely, this difference, which must at the same time come to be in a state of harmony, so as to show that natural existence governs itself, and bears witness to what is essential, to what is spiritual. So far as Man is concerned, he must be determined, governed, by what is truly inward, by right-doing.

In this way the well-being of Man is divinely guaranteed, but it is so guaranteed only in so far as it is in conformity with the Divine, the moral, divine law. This is the band of necessity, which, however, is no longer blind, as we shall see it is in other religions, where it is only the empty indeterminate necessity from which the Notion is absent, so that the Concrete is outside of it. The gods, the moral Powers, are subject to necessity, but the necessity is not characterised by the presence in it of what is moral and right.

Here necessity is concrete, in the sense that what has essential Being, Being in and for itself, gives laws, wills the Right, the Good, and as a consequence of this, this Being has an affirmative definite Being which is adequate to it, an existence which is a state of well-being or welfare. It is this kind of harmony of which Man is conscious in this sphere of thought.

It is on this that is founded the belief that it must, nay, that it ought, to go well with him. He is an end for God, and he is this as being a whole. And yet he, as constituting a whole, is himself something differentiated or distinct, since he has the power of willing and an external existence. The conscious subject now knows that God is the bond of this necessity, that He is this unity which brings about a state of well-being proportionate to the well-doing, and that this connection exists, for the divine universal will is at the same time the will which is determined in itself, and has consequently the power to bring about that connection.

The consciousness that these are thus joined together constitutes that faith, that confidence, which is a fundamental and praiseworthy trait of the Jewish people. The Old Testament Scriptures, the Psalms especially, are full of this confidence.

This, too, is the line of thought which is represented in the Book of Job, the only book the connection of which with the standpoint of the Jewish people is not sufficiently recognised. Job extols his innocence, finds his destiny unjust, he is discontented, *i.e.*, there is in him a contradiction—the consciousness of the righteousness which is absolute, and the want of correspondence between his condition and this righteousness. It is recognised as being an end which God has that He makes things go well with the good man.

What the argument points to is that this discontent, this despondency, ought to be brought under the control of pure and absolute confidence. Job asks, " What doth God give me as a reward from on high ? Should it not be the unrighteous man who is rejected thus ? " His friends answer in the same sense, only they put it in the reverse way, " Because thou art unhappy, therefore we conclude that thou art not righteous." God does this in order that He may protect man from the sin of pride.

God Himself at last speaks : " Who is this that talks

thus without understanding ? Where wast thou when I laid the foundations of the earth ? " Then comes a very beautiful and magnificent description of God's power, and Job says, " I know it; he is a man without knowledge who thinks he may hide his counsel." This subjection is what is finally reached ; on the one hand, there is the demand that it should go well with the righteous, and on the other, even the feeling of discontent when this is not the case, has to be given up. It is this resignation, this acknowledgment of God's power, which restores to Job his property and the happiness he had before. It is on this acknowledgment of God's power that there follows the re-establishment of his happiness. Still, at the same time, this good fortune is not regarded as something which can be demanded by finite man as a right, independent of the power of God.

This confidence in God, this unity, and the consciousness of this harmony of the power, and at the same time of the wisdom and righteousness of God, is based on the thought that God is determined within Himself as end, and has an end.

We have further to consider in this connection this fact, that Spirit becomes inward, the movement of Spirit within itself. Man must do right. That is the one absolute command, and this doing of what is right has its seat in his will. Man is by this means thrown back upon his inner nature, and he must occupy himself in thus considering his inner life, and finding out whether it is righteous, whether or not his will is good.

This examination into and anxiety about what is wrong, the crying of the soul after God, this descent into the depths of the spirit, this yearning of the spirit after what is right, after what is in conformity with the will of God, is something specially characteristic of this form of religion.

This end further appears as being at the same time limited. The end is, that men should know and acknow-

ledge God, that what they do they should do for the
glory of God; that what they will should be in accordance with God's will, and that their will should be a true
will. This end has, at the same time, a limitation attached
to it, and we have to consider in how far this limitation
belongs to the essential nature of God, to what extent
the conception, the ordinary idea of God itself, still contains this limitation.

If the ordinary or popular idea of God is limited,
those further realisations of the divine conception in
human consciousness are limited also. What is always
most essential, but is also most difficult, is to understand the presence of the limitation in One, and to
recognise that it is at the same time a limitation of the
Idea, and in such a way that this latter does not yet
appear as the absolute Idea.

God, as the one who determines Himself in His freedom and according to His freedom in such a way that
what is spiritual is free, is wisdom; but this wisdom,
this end, is at first merely end and wisdom in general.
The wisdom of God, His self-determination, have not yet
received their development. This development within
the Idea of God is first found in the religion in which the
nature of God is entirely revealed.

The defect of this Idea is that though God is the One,
He is this in Himself only in the determinateness of His
unity, and is not what eternally develops itself within
itself. There is not as yet any developed determination.
What we call wisdom is so far something abstract—
abstract universality.

The real end which we have is the first end. It exists
as an end of God in Spirit as actual, and thus it must
have universality in itself, it must be a divine and true
end in itself, and one which has substantial universality. A substantial end in Spirit means that the
spiritual individuals know themselves to be one, and act
towards each other as one and are in unity. The end is

a moral one, and it finds its sphere in real freedom. It is that part of thought in which what is practical comes into play, an end in actual consciousness. It is, however, a first end, and the morality connected with it is of the immediate natural kind. The end is thus the family and the connection of the family. It is this one particular family exclusive of all others.

The real immediate first end of divine wisdom is thus still quite limited, quite particular, just because it is the first end. God is absolute wisdom, but He is this in the sense of being entirely abstract wisdom, or, to put it otherwise, the end in the divine notion is one which is as yet purely general, and is consequently an end devoid of content. This indeterminate end thus devoid of content, changes in actual existence into immediate particularity, into the most perfect limitation; or, in other words, the state of potentiality in which wisdom still exists is itself immediacy, naturalness.

God's real end is thus the family, and in fact this particular family, for the idea of many single families already gives proof of the extension of the thought of singleness by means of reflection. We have here a noteworthy, and absolutely rigid contrast—in fact, the most rigid possible contrast. God is, on the one hand, the God of heaven and of earth, absolute wisdom, universal power, and the end aimed at by this God is at the same time so limited that it concerns only one family, only this one people. All peoples, it is true, *ought* also to acknowledge Him and praise His name, but His *actual* work and that which has been really accomplished consists of this particular people only, regarded in their general condition and definite existence, in their inner and outer, political and moral actually existing condition. God is thus only the God of Abraham, of Isaac, and of Jacob, the God who has brought us out of Egypt. Since God is only One, He is present also only in one universal spirit, in one family, in one world. The families as families come first, those which were brought out of Egypt are the nation, and here it is the heads of the family who constitute the definite element of the end. Universality is thus still something natural, and the end is accordingly only human, and is therefore the family. Religion is thus patriarchal, and it is accordingly the family which expands into the people. A nation means a people, because, to begin with, it has its origin in Nature. This is the limited end, and in reference to all others it is exclusively the divine end.

The five Books of Moses start with the creation of the world, and immediately after we come upon the Fall, which has to do with the nature of man as man. This universal element present in the creation of the world, and next that fall of man, and of man in his generic character, are ideas which have had no influence on the form subsequently taken by the Jewish religion. We have merely this prophecy, the universal element in which did not become a truth for the Israelitish people. God is only the God of this people, not the God of men, and this people is God's people.

It may be further remarked, with the view of making more generally intelligible the connection between the universal wisdom of God in itself and the completely limited nature of the real end, that when man wills the universal good, and has this as his end, he has made his arbitrary will the principle of his resolves and his acts. For this universal good, this universal end, does not contain within itself the Other, the Particular. When, however, it is necessary to act, then this real end demands something determinate, and this determinateness lies outside of the Notion, since the latter has no such determinateness in itself, but is still abstract, and the particular end is for this reason not yet sanctified, because it has not yet been taken up into the universal end of the Good.

In politics, if it is only universal laws which are to hold sway, then the governing element is force, the arbitrary will of the individual. The law is real only in so far as it is made particular, for it is through its being made particular that the universal first becomes something living.

The other peoples are shut out from this single real end. The People has its own peculiar nationality, and consists of certain families and the members of these. This privilege of belonging to the People, and consequently of standing to God in this relation, rests on birth. This naturally demands a special constitution, special laws, ceremonies, and worship.

The peculiarity connected with the end is further developed so as to include the possession of a special district. This district or soil must be divided amongst the different families, and is inalienable, so that the excluding of other peoples results in gaining this wholly empirical and external Present. This exclusion is, in the first instance, not polemical, but, on the other hand, it is the special possession which is the reality, the individual enjoyment of this individual people, and the relation of the individual people to the almighty, all-wise God. It is not polemical, *i.e.*, the other peoples *can* also be brought into this relation to adore God in this way. They *ought to* glorify the Lord, but that they should come to do this is not a real end. The obligation is only ideal and not practical. This real end appears first in Mohammedanism, where the particular end is raised to the rank of a general one, and thus becomes fanatical.

Fanaticism, it is true, is found amongst the Jews as well, but it comes into play only in so far as their possession, their religion, is attacked, and it comes into play then because it is only this one end which is by its very nature exclusive and will tolerate no accommodation to anything different, no fellowship, no intercourse with it.

Third Determination.—Man is exalted above all else in the whole creation. He is something which knows, perceives, thinks. He is thus the image of God in a

sense quite other than that in which the same is true of the
world. What is experienced in religion is God, He who is
thought, and it is only in thought that God is worshipped.

In the religion of the Parsis we had dualism, and the
idea of contrast implied in this we have in the Jewish
religion as well. The contrast or opposition does not,
however, occur in God, but is found in the spirit which
is His " Other." God is Spirit, and what He has produced,
namely, the world, is also Spirit, and it is in this latter
that He is in Himself the " Other " of His essence.
What is involved in finitude is, that in it difference
appears as division. In the world God is at home with
Himself; it is good, for the Nothing or non-existence
which belongs to it, and out of which the world has been
created, is the Absolute itself. The world, however, as
representing this first act of judgment, of separation, on
God's part, does not get the length of being absolute
contrast. It is only Spirit which is capable of being
this absolute contrast, and it is this which gives it its
depth. The contrast or opposition exists within the
other spirit, which is consequently the finite spirit. This
is the place where the contest between good and evil
goes on, and it is the place, too, in which this fight must
be fought out. All these characteristics arise out of the
nature of the Notion. This opposition is a difficult point,
for it constitutes the contradiction, which may be stated
thus: the Good is not contradictory in virtue of its own
nature, but rather it is by means of evil that contradiction first enters, and it occurs only in evil. But then
the question arises: How has evil come into the world ?
At this stage such a question has both meaning and
interest. In the religion of the Parsis this question
cannot occasion any difficulty, for there the Evil exists
quite as much as the Good. Both have sprung from
something which is devoid of all definite character. Here,
on the other hand, where God is power and the one
Subject, and where everything depends for its existence

solely on Him, evil is a contradiction, for God is certainly
the absolute Good. An old pictorial representation of
this, namely, the Fall, has been preserved in the Bible.
This well-known account of how evil came into the
world is in the form of a myth, and appears at the same
time in the guise of a parable. Of course when a speculative idea, something true, is thus represented in a sensuous
figure, in the form of something which has actually
happened, it can hardly miss having certain traits about
it which don't fittingly express the truth itself. You find
the same thing in Plato when he speaks in pictorial
language of the Ideas, for there, too, the inadequacy of
the picture to express the truth is apparent. This is
how the narrative runs :—After the creation of Adam and
Eve in Paradise, God forbade the first human beings to
eat of a certain tree. The serpent, however, misleads
them, and gets them to eat of it by saying, "You will
become like God." God then imposes a severe penalty
on them, but at the same time says, "See, Adam is
become as one of us, for he knows what is good and evil."
Looked at from this particular side, man, according to
God's declaration, has become God, but regarded from the
other side, this means that God has cut off man's chance
of reaching Him by this path, inasmuch as He drives
him out of Paradise. This simple story may, to begin
with, be taken as embodying something like the following
meaning. God laid down a command, and man, impelled
by a boundless feeling of pride which led him to wish
to be equal to God (a thought which came to him from
the outside), transgresses this command, and for his
miserable silly pride it was ordained that he should be
severely punished. God laid down that command formally only, with the view of putting him in circumstances in which his obedience might be proved.

According to this explanation, everything takes place
in accordance with the ordinary finite laws of cause and
effect. God, undoubtedly, forbids evil, but such a pro-

hibition is something wholly different from the prohibition to eat of a certain tree. What God wills or does not will must represent His true eternal nature. Such a prohibition is further thought of as having been imposed only on a single individual, and man justly rebels against being punished for guilt that is not his own—he will only answer for what he has done himself.

On the other hand, in the story, regarded as a whole, there is a deep philosophical meaning. It is Adam, or man in general, who appears in this narrative. What is here related concerns the nature of man himself, and it is not a formal childish command which God lays on him, for the tree of which Adam is not to eat is called the tree of the knowledge of good and evil, and thus the idea of a tree with an outward definite form disappears. Man eats of it, and he attains to the knowledge of good and evil. The difficulty, however, is that it is said God forbade man to reach this knowledge, for it is just this knowledge which constitutes the character of Spirit. Spirit is Spirit only through consciousness, and it is just in this knowledge that consciousness in its highest form is found. How, then, could this prohibition have been given? Cognition, knowledge, represents this two-sided dangerous gift. Spirit is free, and to this freedom good as well as evil is referred, and it thus contains the power of arbitrary choice to do what is evil. This is the negative side attaching to the affirmative side of freedom referred to. Man, it is said, was in a state of innocence; this is, in fact, the condition of the natural consciousness, but it must be done away with as soon as the consciousness of Spirit actually appears. That represents eternal history, and the nature of man. He is at first natural and innocent, and incapable, consequently, of having moral acts attributed to him. In the child there is no freedom, and yet it belongs to the essential character of man that he should once more reach innocence. What is his final destiny is here represented as his primitive condition—the harmony between man and the Good. The defect in this pictorial representation is that this unity is described as a condition of immediate Being. It is necessary to pass out of this condition of original natural- ness, but the state of separation or disunion which then arises has to pass into a state of reconciliation again. Here this idea of reconciliation is represented by the thought that man ought not to have passed beyond that first condition. In the whole of this pictorial account, what is inward is expressed in terms of what is outward, and what is necessary in terms of what is contingent. The serpent says that Adam will become like God, and God confirms the truth of this, and adds His testimony that it is this knowledge which constitutes likeness to God. This is the profound idea lodged in the narrative.

But further, a punishment is next inflicted on man. He is driven out of Paradise, and God says, "Cursed be the ground for thy sake, in sorrow shalt thou eat what it brings forth to thee; thorns and thistles shall it bear to thee, and thou shalt eat the herb of the field. In the sweat of thy face shalt thou eat thy bread, and thou shalt return unto the ground, for out of it wast thou taken; for dust thou art, and unto dust shalt thou return."

We have to recognise that here we have the conse- quences of finitude; but, on the other hand, the greatness of man just consists in the fact that he eats his bread in the sweat of his brow, and that through his own activity, his work, and the exercise of his understanding, he wins sustenance for himself. Animals have the happy lot, if you like to call it so, of being supplied by Nature with what they need. Man, on the other hand, elevates what is necessary to this natural life to the rank of something connected with his freedom. This is just the employment of his freedom, though it is not the highest form in which he employs it, for that consists rather in knowing and willing the Good. The fact that man regarded from the natural side is also free, is involved in his nature, and is

not to be considered as in itself punishment. The
sorrow of the natural life is essentially connected with
the greatness of the character and destiny of man. For
him who is not yet acquainted with the loftier nature of
Spirit, it is a sad thought that man must die, and this
natural sorrow is, as it were, for him what is final. The
lofty nature and destiny of Spirit, however, just consists
in the fact that it is eternal and immortal ; still, this
greatness of man, this greatness of consciousness, is not
yet contained in this narrative, for it is said : God said,
" And now, lest he put forth his hand and take also of the
tree of life, and eat and live ·for ever " (iii. 22). Then
further (v. 19), " Till thou return unto the ground whence
thou wast taken." The consciousness of the immortality
of Spirit is not yet present in this religion.

In the entire narrative of the Fall these grand features
are present in what has the appearance of being an illo-
gical form, owing to the pictorial style in which the whole
is presented to us. The advance out of the merely natural
·life, and the necessity for the entrance of the consciousness of good and evil, constitute the lofty thought to
which God Himself here gives utterance. What is defective in the account is that death is described in such a
way as to leave the impression that there is no place for
consolation in regard to it. The fundamental note of the
account is that man ought not to be natural, and in
this is contained the thought expressed in true theology,
that man is by nature evil. Evil consists in resting in
this natural state ; man must advance out of this state
by exercising his freedom, his will. The further development of this thought accordingly involves that Spirit
should once more attain to absolute unity within itself,
to a state of reconciliation, and freedom is just what contains this turning back of Spirit into itself, this reconciliation with itself. Here, however, this conversion or
turning back has not yet taken place ; the difference has
not yet been taken up into God, *i.e.*, has not yet reached

a state of reconciliation. The abstraction of evil has not yet disappeared.

It has to be observed further that this story ceased to have a living interest for the Jewish people, and that it did not receive any further development in the Books of the Hebrews. If we except some allusions in the later apocryphal books, it is not mentioned, speaking generally, in the others. For a long time it lay unworked, and it was in Christianity that it was first to attain its true significance. Still it cannot at all be said that man's conflict within himself is something which did not exist amongst the Jewish people. On the contrary, it consti- tutes an essential characteristic of the religious spirit amongst the Hebrews, but it was not conceived of in the speculative sense as implying that it arises from the nature of man himself, being represented rather as con- tingent, as taking place in single individuals. In contrast to the sinner and the man who is in conflict with him- self, we get the picture of the righteous man, in whom evil and the conflict with it are represented as not being an essential moment in his life, but rather righteousness is thought of as consisting in the doing of God's will, and in being steadfast in the service of Jehovah by observing the moral commandments connected alike with the pre- cepts of ritual and the requirements of state law. Still the conflict of man within himself is apparent every- where, especially in the Psalms of David. Sorrow cries out of the innermost depths of the soul conscious of its sinfulness, and as a consequence we find the most sorrowful prayers for pardon and reconciliation. This deep sorrow is thus undoubtedly present, but it appears rather as belonging to the single individual than as something which is known to be an eternal moment of Spirit.

These are the principal moments of the religion of the One, so far as they concern particularisation and the determination of an end on the part of the One. This latter determination brings us to worship.

D.

WORSHIP.

God has essentially a relation to self-consciousness, since it is the finite spirit which constitutes the sphere in which His end appears. We have now to consider the religious sentiment or feeling of religion as seen in this self-consciousness. The mediation which it needs, in so far as it is feeling, is the positing of the identity, which is potentially posited, and is thus the mediating movement. This feeling represents the most inward movement of self-consciousness.

1. Self-consciousness brings itself into relation with the One, and is thus, to begin with, intuition, pure thought of the pure Essence as pure power and absolute Being, alongside of which nothing else of equal value can be put. This pure thought, therefore, as reflection into self, as self-consciousness, is self-consciousness with the character of infinite Being for self, or freedom, but freedom devoid of all concrete content. This self-consciousness is thus as yet distinct from real consciousness, and nothing of all the concrete characteristics of spiritual and natural life, of the fulness of consciousness, of the impulses, inclinations, and of all that belongs to the realm of spiritual relations, nothing of all this has as yet been taken up into the consciousness of freedom. The reality of life has still a place outside of the consciousness of freedom, and this last is not yet rational, it is still abstract, and no full, concrete, divine consciousness is as yet in existence.

Since, therefore, self-consciousness exists only as consciousness, while, however, in the way of an object for the simplicity of thought there exists as yet no corresponding object, and since the determinateness of consciousness has not yet been taken up into it, the Ego is an object for itself only in its abstract state of unity with itself only as immediate particularity. Self-consciousness is accordingly devoid of expansion and extension, devoid of all concrete specification, and God as infinite power is also without determinate character in Himself, and there is no third thing, no definite form of existence in which they might meet. So far it is a condition of unmediated relation, and the two contrasted elements —the relation to the One in pure thought and intuition, and abstract return into self, Being for self,—are immediately united. Since, then, self-consciousness, as distinguished from its object, which is pure thought and can only be grasped in thought, is empty, formal self-consciousness, naked and devoid of specific character in itself, and since, further, all real concrete specification belongs to power only, in this absolute contrast the pure freedom of self-consciousness is turned into absolute absence of freedom, or, in other words, self-consciousness is the self-consciousness of a servant in relation to a master. The fear of the Lord is the fundamental characteristic of the relation which here exists.

I have a general feeling of fear produced by the idea of a Power above me, which negates my value as a person, whether that value appears in an outward or in an inward way as something belonging to me. I am without fear when, on the one hand, in virtue of possessing an invulnerable independence, I disregard the force above me, and know myself to be power as against it in such a way that it has no influence over me; and, on the other hand, I am without fear too when I disregard those interests which this Power is in a position to destroy, and in this way remain uninjured even when I am injured. Fear has commonly a bad meaning attached to it, as if it implied that the person who experiences fear did not wish to represent himself as power, and was not capable of doing so. But the fear here spoken of is not the fear of what is finite or of finite force. The finite is contingent power, which, apart from any fear felt, can seize and injure me; but, on the other hand, the fear

here spoken of is the fear of the Unseen, of the Absolute,
the counterpart of my consciousness, the consciousness of
the self which is infinite as opposed to me the finite self.
Before the consciousness of this Absolute, as being the
one single purely negative Power, special forces of any
kind disappear, everything which has the mark of 'the
earthly nature upon it simply perishes. This fear, in
the form of this absolute negativity of oneself, is the
elevation of consciousness to the pure thought of the
absolute power of the One. And this fear of the Lord
is the beginning of wisdom, which consists in not allow-
ing the particular, the finite by itself, to have a valid
existence as something independent. What has a valid
existence can have this only as a moment in the organisation of the One, and the One is the abrogation of all that
is finite. This wise fear is the one essential moment of
freedom, and consists in being freed from all that is particular, in breaking away from all accidental interests,
and in general, in the feeling on man's part of the
negativity of all that is particular. It is accordingly
not a particular fear of any particular thing, but, on the
contrary, it consists in the positing of this particular fear
as a thing of nought; it is deliverance from fear. Thus
fear is not the feeling of dependence, but rather it is the
stripping oneself of dependence of every kind; it is pure
surrender of self to the absolute Self, in contrast to which
and into which the particular self melts away and disappears.

In this way, however, the subject is only in the infinite
One. Absolute negativity, however, is relation to self,
affirmation; by means of absolute fear the Self accordingly exists, and exists in its self-surrender, in the
absolutely positive. Fear in this way changes into
absolute confidence, infinite faith. At another stage
confidence can take the form of a state in which the
individual relies upon himself. This is the stoical freedom in chains. Here, however, freedom does not as yet

take on this form of subjectivity, but rather self-consciousness has to sink itself in the One, while this latter,
again, represented as the Other, is the principle of
repulsion, in which self-consciousness regains its self-
certainty.   This process can be conceived of under the
following form.

The state of servitude is, in fact, self-consciousness,
reflection into self and freedom, which, however, is devoid
of all general extension and rationality, and finds its
determinateness, its content, in the immediate sensuous
self-consciousness.   It is the " I " as this particular individual, in immediate particularity, which is accordingly
end and content.   In the relation in which he stands to
his Lord the servant finds his absolute, essential self-
consciousness, and in view of Him he annihilates everything in himself.   It is, however, just because of this
that he regains his position as existing absolutely for
himself, and his particularity or individuality just because it has been taken up into that intuition of the
Absolute and is made to form its concrete side, is, owing
to this relation, absolutely justified.   The fear in which
the servant regards himself as nothing, gains for him the
restoration of his justification.   But because the servile
consciousness rests obstinately on its particularity, and
because its particularity has been taken up into the
unity immediately, it is exclusive, and God is—-

2. The exclusive Lord and God of the Jewish people.
It need not surprise us that an Oriental nation should
limit religion to itself, and that this religion should appear as absolutely connected with its nationality, for we
see this in Eastern countries in general.   The Greeks
and the Romans were the first to adopt foreign forms of
worship, and all kinds of religion were introduced amongst
the latter, and did not rank as national.   In Oriental
countries, however, religion is essentially closely connected with nationality.   The Chinese, the Persians, have
their State religion, which is for them only.   Amongst

the Hindus birth determines for every individual even
his rank and his relation to Brāhma, and accordingly
they do not in any way demand that others should adopt
their religion; in fact, amongst the Hindus, such a demand has no meaning whatever, since, according to their
ideas, all the various peoples of the earth belong to their
religion, and foreign nations are reckoned collectively as
belonging to a particular caste. Still this exclusiveness
is rightly regarded as more striking in the case of the
Jewish people, for such strong attachment to nationality
is in complete contradiction with the idea that God is to
be conceived of only in universal thought, and not in one
particular characterisation. Amongst the Persians God
is The Good. That is also a universal characteristic;
but it is itself still in the condition of immediacy, consequently God is identical with light, and that is a form of
particularity. The Jewish God exists only for Thought,
and that stands in contrast with the idea of the limitation of God to the nation. It is true that amongst the
Jewish people, too, consciousness rises to the thought of
universality, and this thought is given expression to in
several places. Psalm cxvii. 1 : "O praise the Lord, all
ye nations, praise him, all ye peoples. For his grace
and truth are great toward us to all eternity." The
glory of God is to be made manifest amongst all peoples,
and it is in the later prophets particularly that this
universality makes its appearance as a higher demand.
Isaiah makes God even say, "Of the heathen who shall
honour Jehovah will I make priests and Levites;" and
a similar idea is expressed also in the words, "In every
nation he that feareth God and worketh righteousness is
accepted with Him." All this, however, comes later.
According to the dominant fundamental idea, the Jewish
people are the chosen people, and the universality is thus
reduced to particularity. But as we have already seen
above in the development of the Divine end how the
limitation attached to this is based on the limitation

which is still involved in the characterisation of God, so now this limitation is explained for us from the nature of the servile consciousness; and we see too, now, how this particularity arises from the subjective side. This honouring and recognition of Jehovah is something which is peculiar to them, those servants, and they have themselves the consciousness that it is peculiar to them.

This harmonises, too, with the history of the people. The Jewish God is the God of Abraham, of Isaac, and of Jacob, the God who brought the Jews out of Egypt, and there is not the slightest trace of the thought that God may have done other things as well, and that He has acted in an affirmative way amongst other peoples too. Here, therefore, it is from the subjective side, from the side of worship, that the idea of particularity comes in, and in any case it can be said that God is the God of those who honour Him, for it is God's nature to be known in the subjective spirit, and to know Himself there. This is a moment which essentially belongs to the idea of God. The act of knowing, of acknowledging, belongs essentially to this characterisation or determination. This often comes out in what is for us a distorted way, when, for instance, God is said to be mightier and stronger than the other gods, exactly as if there were gods besides Him; for the Jews, however, these are false gods.

There is this particular nation which honours Him, and so He is the God of this nation, its Lord, in fact. It is He who is known as the Creator of heaven and earth, He has set bounds and limits for everything and bestowed on everything its peculiar nature, and so too He has given to man his proper place and his rights. This expresses the characterisation according to which He as Lord gives His people laws, laws which have to do with the entire sphere of their actions, both the universal laws, the Ten Commandments—which are the universal, ethical, legal, fundamental, characteristics of lawgiving

and morality, and which are not held to be laws given
by reason, but rather laws written down by God—and
also all the rest of the State laws and regulations.
Moses is called the lawgiver of the Jews, but he was
not to the Jews what Lycurgus and Solon were to the
Greeks, for these two gave as men their own laws. He
only made the laws of Jehovah known ; it was Jehovah
Himself who, according to the story, engraved them on
the stone. Attached to the most trifling regulations, the
arrangement of the tabernacle, the usages in connection
with sacrifices, and everything relating to all other kinds
of ceremonial, you find in the Bible the formula " Jehovah
saith." All law is given by the Lord, and is thus entirely
positive commandment. There is in it a formal, absolute authority. The particular elements in the political
system are not, speaking generally, developed out of the
universal end, nor is it left to man to give it its special
character, for the Unity does not permit human caprice,
human reason, to exist alongside of it, and political change
is in every instance called a falling away from God ; but,
on the other hand, the particular laws, as being something
given by God, are regarded as eternally established. And
here the eternal laws of what is right, of morality, are
placed in the same rank and stated in an equally positive
form with the most trifling regulations. This constitutes
a strong contrast to the conception which we have of God.
Worship is now the service of God; the good man, the
righteous man, is he who performs this service, by keeping
and observing both the moral commandments and also the
ceremonial laws. This is the service of the Lord.

The people of God is accordingly a people adopted by
covenant and contract on the conditions of fear and
service. That is to say, the self-conscious community
is no longer an original and immediate unity in union
with the Essence, as is the case in the Religion of Nature.
The external form of the Essence in the Religion of
Nature is only a pictorial representation of Nature, an

outer covering which does not truly separate the two sides of what constitutes the religious relation, and is therefore only an unessential separation of the two, only a superficial distinction. The present standpoint, on the contrary, is based in the first instance on absolute reflection into self as abstract Being-for-self, and it is here accordingly that the mediation of the relation between self-consciousness and its absolute Essence comes in. The self-consciousness does not, however, represent man as man in the sense of universality. The religious relation is something special, which, regarded from the point of view of man, may be called contingent, for all that is finite is external to Absolute Power, and contains in it no positive character. This particularity of the religious relation is not, however, a particularity amongst others, but is rather a separate, infinite preference. Because of the character which thus attaches to the relation, the latter finds expression in the thought that this people has been adopted on the condition of its having the fundamental feeling of its dependence, *i.e.*, of its servitude. This relation between the infinite Power and what has independent Being is accordingly not one which is posited essentially and originally, or has come into existence only through the love of God to man, but rather this unity has been established in an external way through a contract. And, in fact, this adoption of the People is something which has taken place once for all, and occupies the place of what in revealed religion in its completed form is known as redemption and reconciliation.

Closely connected with the representation of God as the Lord is the fact that the Jewish people gave themselves wholly up to His service. It is this which explains, too, that marvellous steadfastness which was not a fanaticism of conversion like Mohammedanism, which is already purified from the idea of nationality and recognises believers only, but a fanaticism of stubbornness. It rests entirely on the abstraction of one Lord; the idea of vacillation comes into the mind only when various interests and points of view exist alongside of each other, and in such a struggle it is possible to take one side or the other, but in this state of concentration of thought on one Lord, the mind is completely held fast to one side. The consequence of this is that in view of the existence of this firm bond there is no freedom. Thought is simply bound on to this unity, which is the absolute authority. Many further consequences follow from this. Amongst the Greeks, too, it is true, certain institutions were held to have divine authority, but they had been established by men; the Jews, on the other hand, made no such distinction between the divine and the human. It was owing, too, to this absence of the idea of freedom that they did not believe in immortality, for even though it is perhaps possible to point to certain traces of belief in it, still those passages in which they occur are always of a very general character, and had not the slightest influence on the religious and moral points of view from which things were regarded. The immortality of the soul is not as yet an admitted truth, and there is accordingly no higher end than the service of Jehovah, and so far as man himself is concerned, his aim is to maintain himself and his family in life as long as possible. Temporal possessions, in fact, are consequent upon service, not something eternal, not eternal blessedness. The conscious perception of the unity of the soul with the Absolute, or of the reception of the soul into the bosom of the Absolute, has not yet arisen. Man has as yet no inner space, no inner extension, no soul of such an extent as to lead it to wish for satisfaction within itself, but rather it is the temporal which gives it fulness and reality. According to the Law, each family receives a property which must not be alienated, and in this way the family is to be provided for. The aim of life consequently was mainly the preservation of this bit of land.

This expresses the essential character of the family, together with the land which belongs to it and from which it derives its subsistence. The possession of a country is what self-consciousness of this kind receives from its God. It is consequently that very confidence before referred to which is the absolutely limited constitutive element of the individual family existence. Just because man in the absolutely negative condition of self-surrender exists in what is purely positive, and consequently is once more in a condition of immediacy, confidence, as expressing the surrender of finite interests, turns into the surrender of the surrender, and thus comes to represent in turn the realised finite individual, his happiness and possessions. These possessions and this people are identical, inseparable. God's people possess Canaan. God has made a covenant with Abraham, the one side of which is constituted by this possession, and it is the affirmative in this sphere of empirical particular interests. Both are inseparable, the special possession and the confidence, the piety. The possession consequently gets an infinitely absolute authorisation, a divine authorisation; and yet at the same time the title to the possession does not take the form of a juridical right, of a property; this latter, as being different from possession, is not applicable here. Property has its source in personality, in this very freedom of the single individual. Man is essentially a holder of property in so far as he is a person, but the possession, as expressing the empirical aspect of property, is entirely free to take any form, this being left to chance. *What* I possess is a matter of accident, a matter of indifference; when I am recognised as a holder of property, I am a free subjectivity and the possession is a matter of indifference. Here, on the contrary, this definite possession as such is identical with the feeling of confidence, and it is consequently this possession to which an absolute title attaches. The idea of *property* does not come in here, ánd so the idea of free-will does not appear either. God, the absolute Idea, and then property, and possession, represent three different stages. Here the uniting middle term, property, drops away, and the possession is taken up into the divine will in an immediate form. It is this empirical individual possession which is to have value as such and as thus authorised, and it is taken out of the reach of the free act of designation on the part of the individual, who cannot sell it but can only pledge it for some time, and always only until the year of Jubilee.

The other side, namely, the negative relation, corresponds to the affirmative side. The recognition of Power as constituting the negative side must also be defined empirically or externally in reference to property. Particular acts of conduct, real ways of acting, must in the same way have their negative side as the acknowledgment of the Lord. There must be a service, not simply fear, but an act of surrender in particular things. This is the other side of the covenant, which, on the one hand, has possession as its effect, but, on the other, demands service also, so that just as this particular country is attached to this particular nation, the nation itself is bound by the obligation of rendering the service required by the Law. These laws, looked at from one side, are family laws, have reference to family conditions, and have a moral content; but looked at from the other side, the main point about them is that what is inherently moral in them is regarded as something which has been laid down in a purely positive way, and so naturally we have joined on to this a large number of external accidental regulations which are simply to be observed. The irrationality of the service corresponds to the irrationality of the possession, and we thus have an abstract obedience which does not require any inwardness in respect of any definite character belonging to it, since its justification for existing is an abstract one. Just because God is absolute

H

power, all actions are of an indeterminate character, and for this reason they get their determinate character in an entirely external and arbitrary way. The keeping of the commandment which demands service, obedience to God, is the condition upon which the nation continues in the state in which it is. This is the other aspect of the covenant. It is possible for individuals, or for the whole nation, to fall away by self-will from the laws, but this is a falling away merely from definite commandments and from ceremonial service, and not a falling away from what is original or fundamental, for this latter is something which has the authority of what ought to be. Accordingly the penalty attached to disobedience is not an absolute penalty, but is merely external misfortune, namely, the loss of the possession, or its diminution and curtailment. The penalties which are threatened are of an external earthly sort, and have reference to the undisturbed possession of the land. Just as the obedience demanded is not of a spiritual and moral sort, but is merely the definite blind obedience of men who are not morally free, so also the penalties have an external character. The laws, the commands, are to be followed and observed merely as if by slaves or servants.

If we consider those penalties which are threatened in the form of frightful curses, the thorough mastery which this nation attained to in the matter of cursing is worthy of notice; and yet these curses have reference only to what is external, and not to what is inward and moral. In the third Book of Moses, in the twenty-sixth chapter, we read :—

"If ye shall despise My statutes, and will not do all My commandments, and break My Covenant, I will visit you with terror, consumption, and the burning ague, that shall consume the eyes and cause sorrow of heart. Ye shall sow your seed in vain, and your enemies shall eat it; and they that hate you shall reign over you, and ye shall flee when none pursueth you. And if ye will not yet for all this hearken unto Me, then I will punish you seven times more for your sins. And I will make your heaven as iron, and your earth as brass; and your toil and labour shall be lost, so that your land shall not yield her increase, and the trees shall not yield their fruits.

" And if ye walk contrary to Me, and will not hearken unto Me, I will bring seven times more plagues upon you, according to your sins. I will also send wild beasts among you, which shall eat your children, and tear your cattle, and make you few in number; and your highways shall be desolate. And if ye will not be reformed by Me by these things, but will walk contrary to Me, then will I punish you yet seven times for your sins. And I will bring a sword upon you that shall avenge the quarrel of My covenant. And though ye are gathered together within your cities, yet will I send the pestilence among you, and will deliver you into the hand of the enemy. Then will I break the staff of your bread, so that ten women shall bake in one oven, and they shall deliver you your bread again by weight; and when ye eat, ye shall not be satisfied.

" And if ye will not for all this hearken unto Me, then I will walk contrary unto you also in fury, and will chastise you yet seven times, so that ye shall eat the flesh of your sons and daughters. And I will destroy your high places, and cut down your images, and cast your carcases upon your idols, and My soul shall abhor you, and I will make your cities waste, and bring your sanctuaries unto desolation; and I will not smell the savour of your sweet odours. And I will bring the land into desolation, so that your enemies which dwell therein shall be astonished at it. And I will scatter you among the heathen, and will draw out a sword after you."

We have already seen that amongst the Jews the place of evil is in the subjective spirit, and 'that the Lord is not engaged in a conflict with evil, but that He punishes evil. Evil accordingly appears as an external accident, and this is how it is represented in the story of the Fall, according to which it enters in from the outside, in that man is deceived by the serpent.

God punishes evil as something which ought not to be. It is good only that ought to be, since it is what the Lord has enjoined. There is here as yet no freedom, and there is not even freedom to find out what the divine and eternal law is. The characteristics of the Good, which are undoubtedly the characteristics of reason as well, derive their worth from the fact that they are rules laid down by the Lord, and the Lord punishes any transgression of these; this is the wrath of God. The relation in which the Lord here stands to the Good expresses merely the idea of something that ought to be. What He ordains is what ought to be, is law. To the Lord belongs the exercise of penal righteousness; the conflict between good and evil occurs within the subject as being finite. An element of contradiction is thus present in finite consciousness, and consequently there enters in a feeling of contrition, of sorrow, caused by the fact that the Good is only something which ought to be.

3. The third aspect of worship or cultus is reconciliation. It has reference essentially only to the particular faults of separate individuals, and is brought about by means of sacrifice.

Here sacrifice is not intended simply to signify that the offerer is symbolically renouncing his finitude, and preserving his unity with God, but it signifies more definitely the act of acknowledgment of the Lord, a testifying that He is feared; and it has the still further signification of being an act whereby what of the finite remains has been redeemed and ransomed. Man cannot look on Nature as something which he can use according to his own arbitrary desires; he cannot lay hold of it directly, but he must get whatever he wishes to have through the mediation of something foreign to himself. Everything is the Lord's, and must be bought back from

Him; and thus it is that the tithe is ordained, and that the first-born has to be redeemed.

The expiation for sins accordingly takes place in a peculiar way, namely, by bringing in the idea that the punishment which has been merited, the merited manifestation of the nullity of him who has lifted himself up in sinfulness, can be transferred to what is offered in sacrifice. This is sacrifice. The individual makes it plain that his standing before God has no worth. It is thus that the idea arises that the due manifestation of the sinner's nothingness is transferred to what is offered, since God acknowledges the sacrifice, and in this way gives the self a positive standing, or, in other words, a standing in itself.

The externality which thus attaches to the sacrifice arises from the fact that the expiation is thought of as being punishment, and not as purification as such; rather it is looked on as being an injury done to the evil will in this sense that the will is supposed to suffer damage. Closely connected with this idea is the fact that it is the blood specially which is offered up by being sprinkled on the altar. For if it is life which is to be yielded up as representing the highest of all earthly possessions, it follows that something must be surrendered to God which is really living, and the blood, in which the life of the animal is supposed to be, is given back to the Lord. We saw that amongst the Hindus the whole animal world was held in honour. Here again it is deprived of this honour, but the blood is still regarded as something inviolable and divine; it is held in respect, and must not be eaten by men. Man does not yet possess the feeling of his concrete freedom which leads him to regard life simply as life, as something inferior and subordinate to what is higher.

The Transition to the Stage which follows.

Speaking generally, we, as a matter of fact, find that here we are in the region of free subjectivity, but still the essential characteristic which belongs to free subjectivity has not yet been fully carried right through the totality of the religious consciousness in the Religion of Sublimity. God was characterised for Thought as substantial Power, and as the Creator, but in this character He is, to begin with, merely the Lord of His creatures. Power is thus the cause which differentiates itself, but it is something which merely puts forth its authority over, exercises its lordship over, that in which it thus differentiates itself.

A further stage of progress accordingly is reached, when it is seen that this " Other " is something free—free from external restraint, and God becomes the God of free men, who, even while rendering Him obedience, are actually free in their relation to Him. This standpoint, if we look at it in an abstract way, contains within it the following moments : God is a free, absolute Spirit, and manifests Himself by setting His " Other " over against Himself. What is thus posited by Him is His image, for the subject creates only itself, and that which it becomes by self-determination is again nothing else than itself. But in order that it may be really determined, or get a specific nature as Spirit, it must negate this " Other," and return to itself, for then only when it knows itself in the " Other " is it free. But if God knows Himself in the " Other," it follows that the " Other " has an actual independent existence, is for itself, and knows itself to be free.

This represents the release of the " Other " as being now something free and independent. Thus freedom is found first of all in the subject, and God is still characterised as Power, which is for itself, has real existence, and releases the subject. The differentiation or further characterisation which is thus reached seems, in accordance with what has been stated, to consist simply in this, that the creatures are no longer merely in a state of service, but rather find their freedom in the very act of rendering service. This moment of the freedom of subjects or persons for whom God is, and which is wanting in the standpoint of the Religion of Sublimity which we have been considering, we have already seen in a lower stage of thought, in the sphere of the Religion of Nature, in the Syrian religion, namely.

In the higher stage, to which we now pass, what in the lower was represented in a natural immediate way is transferred to the pure region of Spirit, and is ascribed to its inner mediation. In the religion of sorrow or pain we saw that God loses Himself, that He dies, and exists only by means of the negation of Himself. This act of mediation is the moment which is again to be taken up here. God dies, and from this death He rises again. That is the negation of Himself which we, on the one hand, conceive of as the " Other " of Himself, as the world ; and He Himself dies, which means that in this death He comes to Himself. In this way, however, the " Other " is represented as freely existing for itself, and accordingly the mediation and rising again belong to the other side, the side of what has been created.

Considered thus, it seems as if the conception of God Himself underwent no change, but that the change is only in the aspect in which the " Other " is regarded. That it is just here where freedom comes in, and that it is this side, namely, that of the " Other," which is free, is to be explained from the fact that in the finite, this otherness of God dies away, and so the Divine appears again in the finite in an actual way, or for itself. Thus what is of the world is known as something which has the Divine in it, and the Being-other or otherness which at first is characterised only as negation, is again negated, and is the negation of negation within itself

This is the kind of mediation which belongs to freedom.
Freedom is not pure negation, it is not merely an act of
flight and surrender. Freedom of that sort is not yet the
true affirmative freedom, but is negative freedom only.
It is the negation of what is in a merely natural state in
so far as this itself exists as something negative, which
first gives the affirmative determination of freedom.
Since the " Other," namely, the world, finite consciousness, with its servitude and contingent character, is
negated, it follows that in this act of mediation the determination of freedom is to be found. The elevation or
exaltation of Spirit is thus this particular elevation above
the state of mere naturalness, but it is an elevation in
which, if it is to become freedom, the subjective spirit
must also be free in its own nature, for itself. This
accordingly is at first seen only in the subject or individual. " God is the God of *free* men."

It is, however, equally true that any further determination or characterisation takes place quite as much within
the nature of God. God is Spirit, but He is Spirit in
any essential sense only in so far as He is known to be
the self-diremption of Himself, the producer of differentiation within Himself, the eternal act of creation, and in
such a way that this creation of an " Other " is a return
to Himself, a return to the knowledge of Himself. It is
thus that God is a God of free men. Since it belongs to
the essential character of God Himself that He should
be in His very nature the " Other " of Himself, and that
this " Other " is a determination or quality within His
own nature, so that He thereby returns to Himself and the
human element is reconciled to God, it follows that we thus
get the determination which is expressed by saying that
Humanity is itself in God. Thus man knows that what
is human is a moment of the Divine itself, and consequently he stands in a free relation to God. For that to
which he stands related as to his own essential being has
the essential characteristics of humanity in itself, and

thus, on the one hand, man is related, as it were, to the negation of his merely natural life, and, on the other hand, to a God in whom the human element is itself affirmative and an essential characteristic. Man thus, as occupying such a relation to God, is free. What exists in men as concrete individuals is represented as being something divine and substantial, and man in all that constitutes his essential nature, in all that has any value for him, is present in what is Divine. Out of his passions, says one of the ancients, man has made his gods, *i.e.*, out of his spiritual powers.

In these powers self-consciousness has its essential attributes for its object, and knows that in them it is free. It is not, however, particular individual subjectivity which has itself as its object in these essential characteristics, and which is conscious that the well-being of its particular nature is based on them. This is the case in the religion of the One where it is only this immediate definite existence, this particular natural existence of the particular subject or individual, which is the end, and where it is the individual, and not his universality, which constitutes what is essential; and where, further, the servant has his own selfish aims. Here, on the other hand, self-consciousness has for its object its specific nature, its unisality as manifested in the divine powers. Self-consciousness is consequently raised above the need of making any absolute claim to have its immediate individuality recognised, it is raised above the need of troubling about this, and it finds its essential satisfaction in a substantial objective Power. It is only the Moral, what is universal and rational, which is held to be in and for itself essential, and the freedom of self-consciousness consists of the essentiality of its true nature and its rationality. The sum and substance of the phase upon which the religious spirit has now entered may be expressed thus. God is in His own nature the mediation which man expresses. Man recognises himself in God

and God and man say of each other—That is spirit of
my spirit. Man is Spirit just as God is Spirit. He has
also, it is true, finitude and the element of separation in
him, but in religion he discards his finitude since his
knowledge is the knowledge of himself in God.

We accordingly now pass to the Religion of Humanity
and Freedom. The first form of this religion, however,
is itself infected with the element of immediacy and
naturalness, and thus we shall see the Human existing
in God under what are still natural conditions. The
inward element, the Idea, is indeed potentially what is
true, but it has not yet been raised above the state of
nature, which is the first and immediate form of its
existence. The human element in God expresses His
finitude only, and thus this religion, so far as its basis is
concerned, belongs to the class of finite religions. It is,
however, a religion of spirituality, because the mediation
which, as separated and divided up into its moments,
constituted the foregoing transition stages, is now put
together so as to form a totality, and constitutes the
foundation of this religion.

II.

THE RELIGION OF BEAUTY.

This Religion of Beauty, as has been already indicated,
is seen in a definitely existing form in the religion of
the Greeks, which, both in its inner and outer aspects,
presents us with an infinite amount of inexhaustible
material, beside which, owing to its sympathetic attrac-
tiveness, its grace, and charm, one would fain linger.
Here, however, we cannot enter into details, but must
confine ourselves to the essential characteristics of its
notion or conception.

We must thus (A.) indicate the notion or conception of
this sphere of religious thought; then (B.) consider the

outward form of the Divine in it; and (C.) its form of worship as the movement of self-consciousness in relation to its essential powers.

A.

THE GENERAL CONCEPTION OR NOTION.

The fundamental characteristic here is subjectivity as the self-determining Power. This subjectivity and wise power we have already met with under the form of the One who is as yet undetermined within Himself, and whose end, as it appears in the sphere of reality, is accordingly the most limited possible. The next stage, now, is that this subjectivity, this wise power or powerful wisdom, particularises itself within itself. This stage, just in consequence of this, is, on the one hand, the lowering of universality, of abstract unity and infinite power, to a condition of limitation within a circle of particularity, though, on the other hand, again, it at the same time involves the elevation of the limited individuality of the real end as against universality. In the region of the particular, what shows itself here is both of these movements, and this accordingly is the general characteristic of this stage. We have next to consider the fact that from one point of view, the determinate notion, the content of the self-determining Power, which is a particular content owing to its being in the element of subjectivity, makes itself subjective within itself. There actually are particular ends; they make themselves subjective, to begin with, on their own account, and so we get a definite sphere composed of a number of particular divine subjects. Subjectivity, as end, is self-determination, and hence it has particularisation in it—particularisation, in fact, as such, in the form of a world of concretely existing differences which exist as so many divine forms. Subjectivity in the Religion of Sublimity has already a definite end,

namely, the family, the nation. But this end is only
realised in so far as the service of the Lord is not
neglected. Through this latter requirement, which
implies the abrogation of the subjective spirit so far as
the determinate end is concerned, this end becomes a
universal one. Thus if, on the one hand, through the
breaking up of the one subjectivity into a multiplicity of
ends, subjectivity is lowered to the condition of particularity, on the other hand, the particularity is set over
against universality, and these differences in this way
here become divine, universal differences. This particularity of the ends is thus the coming together of the
abstract universality and the individuality of the end—
their happy mean. This particularity thus constitutes
the content of universal subjectivity, and in so far as it
is posited in this element it gives itself a subjective form
as a subject. With this we enter upon a really ethical
stage, for when we have the Divine penetrating the
determinate relations of Spirit in an actual form, determining itself in accordance with the substantial unity,
we have what is ethical. And at the same time the real
freedom of subjectivity also comes into existence, for the
definite content is something which the finite self-consciousness has in common with its God. Its God ceases
to be a " Beyond," and has a definite content which on
its determinate side is elevated to essentiality, and through
the abolition and absorption of the immediate individuality or singleness has become an essentially existing
content.

As regards the constituent element as such, the content that is, the substantial principle, as has been shown
in the context, is just rationality, the freedom of Spirit,
essential freedom. This freedom is not caprice, and
must be clearly distinguished from it; it is essential,
substantial freedom, the freedom which in its determinations determines itself. Since freedom, as self-determining, is the principle or basis of this relation, what we

have here is concrete rationality which contains essentially moral principles.

That freedom is just this, namely, the desiring or willing of nothing except itself, the desiring of nothing else than freedom, and that this is the true moral element from which moral determinations spring, or, in other words, that the formal element of self-determination changes round into the content, is a thought which cannot here be further followed up.

While morality constitutes the essential basis, still what comes first is morality in its immediacy. It is the rationality above referred to as absolutely universal or general, and thus still in its impersonal or substantial form. The rationality is not yet one subject, and has not yet left the virgin unity in which it is morality, and raised itself to the unity of the subject, or, in other words, has not plunged into itself.

Absolute necessity and the spiritual human embodiment are still separate. Determinateness, it is true, is posited in a general way, but this determinateness is, on the one hand, abstract, and on the other is left free to take on determinateness in manifold shapes, and is not yet taken back into that unity. That it should ever be so taken back would be due to the circumstance that the determinateness has developed into an infinite opposition or antithesis—as in the Religion of Sublimity— and has gone on increasing till it became infinite ; for it is only when it has reached this extreme that it becomes at the same time capable of attaining to unity in itself. The entire circle of the gods, as these take on a definite form, must itself be taken up into and placed within the sphere of necessity as in a pantheon. But it is only capable of this, and is only worthy of attaining this, when its manifoldness and diversity become generalised into *simple* difference. Not till this happens is it adequate to that element, and so immediately identical in itself. The different spirits must be conceived of as

Spirit in such a way that Spirit is made to stand out distinctly as representing their essentially universal nature.

2. Because the unity of necessity is not yet carried back to the ultimate point of infinite subjectivity, the spiritual and essentially moral determinations appear as disconnected or lying outside of one another; the content is the fullest possible, but its constituent parts are disconnected.

Ethics in general must be distinguished from morality and ethics as the Greeks understood them; and by ethics in general is meant the subjectivity of ethics, that subjectivity which can give account of its principles and has an ethical intention, an ethical design and aim.

Morality is here as yet the substantial Being, the true Being of what is moral, but not as yet the knowledge of it. So far as the objective import is concerned, this means that just because one subjectivity, the particular reflection into self, is not yet present—and just in virtue of this fact—the moral content has no connecting element in it, its basis being constituted by the Πάθη, the essentially spiritual powers, the universal powers of the moral life, and chiefly of the practical life, life in the State, and, in addition to this, justice, bravery, the family, oaths, agriculture, science, and so on.

Closely connected with the fact that what is moral has no inner connection as it appears in these particular forms, is that other want of connection, namely, that the natural appears as something opposed to these spiritual powers. The determination of immediacy, which has this disconnected condition as its consequence, involves the further idea that the natural forces, the sky, the earth, rivers, the division of time, appear as opposed to the spiritual forces.

3. The last form of determinateness is that of the antithesis between essential self-consciousness and the finite self-consciousness, between the essential spirit and

the finite spirit. In this determinateness the form of
the natural outward embodiment of subjectivity comes
into view, the natural outward form is imagined by self-
consciousness as something divine, and this divinity
accordingly stands over against self-consciousness.

B.

THE OUTWARD FORM OF THE DIVINE.

(a.) *The Conflict of the Spiritual and the Natural.*

Since the fundamental determination is spiritual subjectivity, the power of Nature cannot be considered as
being the essential power in its own right. Yet it is
one of the particular powers, and as the most immediate
is the first of those through whose abrogation the other
spiritual powers first originate. We have seen the nature
of the power of the One, and how His real and actual
sublimity first resulted from creation. This one fundamental principle, as the self of the Absolute, is wanting
here. Thus the starting-point here is within the sphere
of what is immediately natural, which cannot at this
stage appear as if created by the One. The unity in
which these particular forms of the powers of Nature
repose is' not spiritual, but is, on the contrary, an essentially natural unity, chaos, in fact.

"But first of all," sings Hesiod, "was Chaos" (Theog.
v. 116). Chaos is thus itself something posited, but
what the positing agent is we are not told. It is only
said that it came into being. For the fundamental principle here is not the self, but rather the selfless, the
necessity, of which it can only be said that it is. Chaos
is the moving unity of the immediate, but it itself is not
yet subject, particularity ; hence it is not said of it that
it begets, but as it only comes into being itself, so this
necessity comes into being in turn out of it, namely, the

wide extended earth, the shades of Tartaros, the night of
Erebos, as also Eros, adorned beyond all with beauty.
We see the totality of particularity originating here; the
earth, the positive element, the universal basis; Tartaros,
Erebos, Night, the negative element, and Eros, the uniting
and active element. The particular elements are now
themselves productive; the earth produces the heavens
out of itself, brings forth the hills without fructifying
love, the desolate Pontus, but when united with the sky
bears Oceanos and its rulers. She further brings forth
the Cyclopes, the forces of Nature as such, while the earlier
children, natural things, themselves exist as subjects. The
Earth and the Sky are thus the abstract powers which, by
fructifying themselves, cause the sphere of natural particular things to come into existence. The youngest child
is the inscrutable Cronos. Night, the second moment,
brings forth all that from the natural side has the moment
of negation within itself. Thirdly, these particular forms
unite in a reciprocal relation, and beget the positive and
negative. All these are conquered later on by the gods
of spiritual subjectivity; Hecate alone remains in the
form of Fate or Destiny as representing the natural side.

The primary power, that which rules over this circle
of natural forces, is the abstraction in general out of
which they have risen, Uranos; and inasmuch as he is
power only as positing his abstraction, so that this last is
alone what has valid worth, he drives away all his children. But the main offspring of Heaven is inscrutable
Time, the youngest child. This latter conquers Uranos
through the cunning of the Earth. Everything here is
in the form of a subjective end, and cunning is the negative of force. But inasmuch as the particular forces
make themselves free, and set up on their own account,
Uranos calls them by a name suggestive of punishment,
calls them Titans, whose wrong-doing is one day to be
avenged on them.

These particular natural forces are also personified, but

this personification is, so far as they are concerned, superficial only ; for the content of Helios, for example, or of
Oceanos. is something natural, and not superficial Power.
Thus, if Helios is represented in human fashion as active,
what we have is the empty form of personification.
Helios is not god of the sun, not the sun-god (the Greeks
never express themselves thus), and Oceanos is not the
god of the sea in such a way that the god and that over
which he rules are distinguished from each other ; on the
contrary, these powers are natural powers.

The first moment in this natural sphere is thus Chaos
posited together with its moments by abstract necessity ;
the second is the period of begetting under the rule of
Uranos, in which these abstract moments which have
proceeded out of chaos are the productive element ; the
third is the period of the sovereignty of Cronos, when
the particular natural powers, themselves just born, give
birth in turn to something else. In this way what is
posited is itself the positing factor, and the transition
to Spirit is made. This transition shows itself more
definitely in Cronos, in that he himself brings about
the downfall. He is sovereign pre-eminently through
the abrogation of the immediate divine forms. But he
himself is immediate, and thereby presents the contradiction of being, while in himself immediate, the abrogation of immediacy. He begets the spiritual gods
out of himself ; yet in so far as they are at first merely
natural, he does away with them, and swallows them up.
But his abrogation of the spiritual gods must itself be
abrogated, and this is accomplished in its turn through
cunning working against the natural force of Cronos.
Zeus, the god of spiritual subjectivity, lives. Thus over
against Cronos there appears his Other, and there arises,
in fact, the conflict between the natural powers and the
spiritual gods.

However much, then, this breaking up may take place,
representing a state of things in which the natural powers

make their appearance as independent, still the unity of
the spiritual and the natural—and this is what is essential—appears more and more clearly, and this unity is,
moreover, not the neutralisation of the two, but is, on the
contrary, that form in which the spiritual is not only the
predominant element, but is also the ruling and determining factor, and in which the natural is ideal and
brought into subjection.

The Greeks have expressed the consciousness of this
subjugation of the natural powers by the spiritual element
by telling how Zeus, through a war, founded the sovereignty of the spiritual gods, conquered the nature-power,
and hurled it from its throne. It is spiritual powers
accordingly that rule the world.

In this war of the gods we find the whole history
of the Greek gods and their nature expressed. With
the exception of this war, they have done nothing; and
even when they take up the cause of an individual, or
say that of Troy, this is no longer *their* history nor the
historical development of their nature. But the fact
that they, as representing the spiritual principle, attained
to mastery over the natural and conquered it, is what
constitutes their essential act, and forms the essential
element in the ideas of the Greeks regarding them.

The natural gods are thus subdued, driven from their
throne; the spiritual principle is victorious over the
religion of nature, and the natural forces are banished
to the borders of the world, beyond the world of self-
consciousness, but they have also retained their rights.
They are, while nature-powers, at the same time posited
as ideal, or as in subjection to the spiritual element,
so that they constitute *a* determination in what is spiritual, or in the spiritual gods themselves. This natural
moment is still present in these gods, but is in them
only as a kind of reminiscence of the nature element,
only as one of their aspects.

To these old gods, however, belong not only nature-powers, but also Dike, the Eumenides, the Erinyes; the Oath too and Styx are counted as amongst the ancient gods. They are distinguished from the later ones by this, that although they are what is spiritual, they are spiritual as a power existing only within itself, or as a rude undeveloped form of Spirit. The Erinyes are those who judge only inwardly, the oath is this particular certainty in my conscience, its truth lies, even if I take it outwardly, within myself. We may compare the oath with conscience.

Zeus, on the contrary, is the political god, the god of laws, of sovereignty, of laws definitely recognised, however, and not of the laws of conscience. Conscience has no legal authority in the State. If men appeal to conscience, one man may have one kind of conscience and another another, and thus it is positive law alone which has authority here. In order that conscience may be of the right kind, it is necessary that what it knows as right should be objective, should be in conformity with objective law, and should not merely dwell within. If conscience is right, then it is this as something recognised by the State, when the State has an ethical constitution.

Nemesis is likewise an ancient deity. It is merely the formal element which brings down what is lofty, what exalts itself; it is the merely levelling principle, envy, the putting down of what is distinguished or exalted, so that it may be on a level with other things. In *Dike* we have merely strict abstract justice. Orestes is prosecuted by the Eumenides and is acquitted by Athene, by the moral law, by the State. Moral law or justice is something different from bare strict justice; the new gods are the gods of moral law.

But the new gods have themselves in turn a double nature, and unite in themselves the natural and the spiritual. In the real view of the Greeks the natural element or nature-power was undoubtedly not the truly independent or self-sufficing element.   On the contrary, this latter was found only in spiritual subjectivity. Subjectivity as such which is full of content, the subjectivity which determines itself in accordance with ends, cannot have in it a merely natural content.   Greek imagination did not, accordingly, people Nature with gods after the fashion of the Hindus, for whom the form of God seems to spring out of all natural forms.   The Greek principle is rather subjective freedom, and hence the natural is clearly no longer worthy to constitute the content of the divine.   But, on the other hand again, this free subjectivity is not yet the absolutely free subjectivity, not the Idea, which would have truly realised itself as Spirit, *i.e.*, it is not yet universal infinite subjectivity.   We are only at the stage which leads to this. The content of free subjectivity is still particular; it is spiritual indeed, but since Spirit has not itself for its object, the particularity is still natural, and is even still presented as the one essential characteristic in the spiritual gods.

Thus Jupiter is the firmament, the atmosphere (in Latin we have still the expression *sub jove frigido*), what thunders; but besides being this natural principle, he is not only the father of gods and men, but also the political god, representing the law and morality of the State, that highest power on earth.   He is, moreover, in addition to this, a many-sided moral power, the god of hospitality in connection with the old customs at a time when the relationship of the different states was not as yet well defined, for hospitality had essentially reference to the moral relationship of citizens belonging to different states.

Poseidon is the sea, like Oceanos, Pontus; he restrains the wildness of the elements, but he is also included amongst the new gods.   Phœbus is the god who has knowledge, and, in accordance with analogy and substantial logical definition, he corresponds to the light and is the reflex or reminiscence of the sun-power.

The Lycian Apollo has a direct connection with light, and the ideas connected with him come from Asia Minor: in the East the natural element, light, gets greater prominence. Phœbus decrees the pestilence in the Greek camp, and this is immediately connected with the sun. Pestilence is the effect of the hot summer, of the heat of the sun. The representations, too, of Phœbus have attributes and symbols that are closely connected with the sun.

The same divinities that were at an earlier stage Titanic and natural appear afterwards possessed of a fundamental characteristic which is spiritual and which is the ruling one, and in fact there has been a dispute as to whether there was any natural element left at all in Apollo. In Homer Helios is undoubtedly the Sun, but is at the same time brightness as well, the spiritual element which irradiates and illumines everything. But even at a later period, Apollo still has something of his natural element left, for he was represented with a nimbus round his head.

This is what we find to be the case generally, though it may not be particularly noticeable in the case of the individual gods. Perfect consistency is, however, not to be found here. An element appears at one time in a stronger and more pronounced form, and at another in a weaker form. In the *Eumenides* of Æschylus the first scenes are laid before the temple of Apollo. There we have the summons to worship, and first of all the worshippers are invited to adore the oracle-giver (Γαῖα), the principle of Nature, then Θέμις, already a spiritual power, though, like Dike, belonging to the ancient gods; next comes Night and then Phœbus—the oracle has passed over to the new gods. Pindar too speaks of a similar succession in reference to the oracle. He makes Night the first oracle-giver, then comes Themis, and next Phœbus. We thus have here the transition from natural forms to the new gods. In the sphere of Poetry, where these doctrines originate, this is not to be taken historically as something so fixed as to preclude the possibility of there being any deviation from it.

Thus too the noise, the rustling of leaves, the light noise of suspended cymbals, which represent the first form in which the oracle was given, are mere natural sounds. It is not till a later period that a priestess appears who in human sounds, if not actually in clear and distinct sounds, gives forth the oracle. Similarly the Muses are first nymphs, springs, waves, the noise or murmuring of brooks. In every case the starting-point is some aspect of Nature, natural powers which are transformed into a god with a spiritual character. Such a transformation shows itself also in Diana. The Diana of Ephesus is still Asiatic, and is represented with many breasts and covered with images of animals. She has, in fact, as the basis of her character, natural life, the producing and nourishing power of Nature. On the other hand, Diana of the Greeks is the huntress who kills animals. She does not represent the idea of hunting generally, but the hunting of wild animals. And indeed by the bravery of spiritual subjectivity these animals, which in the earlier spheres of the religious spirit were thought of as having an absolute claim to exist, are subdued and killed.

Prometheus, who was also reckoned amongst the Titans, is an important and interesting figure. Prometheus is the power of Nature, but he is also the benefactor of men, for he taught them the first arts. He brought down fire from heaven for them; the power to kindle fire already implies a certain amount of civilisation; it means that man has already got beyond his primitive barbarism. The first beginnings of civilisation have thus been preserved in grateful remembrance in the myths. Prometheus also taught men to offer sacrifice in such a way that they too might have something of the offering. The animals, it was supposed, did not belong to men, but to a spiritual power, *i.e.*, men formerly ate no flesh. He, however, took the whole offering from Zeus, that is to say, he made two heaps, one of bones, over which he threw the skin of the animal, and another of the flesh, and Zeus laid hold of the first.

Sacrifice thus became a feast in which the gods had the entrails and the bones. This same Prometheus taught men to seize animals and use them as their means of sustenance; animals, it was formerly thought, should not be disturbed by men, and were held in high respect by them. Even in Homer mention is made of the sun-cattle of Helios, which were not to be interfered with by men. Amongst the Hindus and the Egyptians it was forbidden to slaughter animals. Prometheus taught men to eat flesh themselves and to leave to Jupiter only skin and bones.

But Prometheus is a Titan. He is chained to the Caucasus, and a vulture constantly gnaws at his liver, which always grows again—a pain which never ceases. What Prometheus taught men had reference only to such acquirements as conduce to the satisfaction of natural wants. In the mere satisfaction of these wants there is never any sense of satiety; on the contrary, the need is always growing and care is ever new. This is what is signified by this myth. In a passage in Plato it is said that Prometheus could not bring Politics to men, because the science of politics was preserved in the citadel of Zeus. The idea is thus here expressed that this science belonged to Zeus as his own peculiar property.

It is, indeed, gratefully mentioned that Prometheus makes life easier for men by introducing arts and handicrafts; but, spite of the fact that these are connected with the powers of the human mind, he still belongs to the Titans, for these arts are not in any sense laws, nor have they any moral force.

If the gods represent spiritual particularity looked at from the side of Substance, which breaks itself up so as to form them, as a consequence of this, on the other hand, the limitedness of the particular is advanced to substantial universality.   We thereby get the unity of the two ; we have the divine end made human, and the human end elevated to the divine.   This gives us the heroes, the demi-gods.   Specially significant in this respect is the figure of Hercules.   He has human individuality ; he has worked very hard, and by his virtue he has obtained heaven.   The heroes are thus not gods straight off; they have first by labour to put themselves into the rank of the Divine.   For the gods of spiritual individuality, although now at rest, are yet what they are only through their struggle with the Titans.   This potentiality or inherent nature of theirs gets an explicit form in the heroes.   Thus the spiritual individuality of the heroes is higher than that of the gods themselves ; they are actually what the gods are implicitly ; they represent the carrying into effect of what is implicit, and if they have also to struggle and work, this is a working off of the natural element which the gods still have in themselves.   The gods come out of the powers of Nature ; the heroes, again, come out of the gods.

Since the spiritual gods are thus the result reached through the overcoming of the powers of Nature, though they exist in the first instance only through these, they have their development or becoming in themselves, and manifest themselves as concrete unity.   The powers of Nature are contained in them as their basis, although this, their implicit nature, is likewise transfigured.   Hence, in the case of the gods, we have this reminiscence or echo of the natural elements, a feature which Hercules does not possess.   There are, indeed, several signs that the Greeks themselves were conscious of the presence of this difference.   In Æschylus, Prometheus says that he placed his consolation, his confidence, and satisfaction in the fact that a son would be born to Zeus who would hurl him from his throne.   This prophecy of the overthrow of the rule of Zeus, to be accomplished through the manifested unity of the divine and the human which belongs to the heroes, is expressed also by Aristophanes; for Bacchus says to Hercules, "When Zeus dies and goes, thou wilt succeed him."

(b.) *Formless Necessity.*

The unity which binds together the plurality of the particular gods is at first superficial only. Zeus rules them in fatherly, patriarchal fashion, which implies that the ruler does in the end what the others on the whole wish, while these give their assent to all that occurs. But this sovereignty is not serious. The higher absolute unity, in the form of absolute Power, stands over them as their pure and absolute power. This power is Fate or Destiny, simple necessity.

This unity, as being absolute necessity, has universal determinateness within it. It is the fulness of all determinations; but it is not developed in itself, the fact rather being that the content is divided in a particular way among the many gods who issue forth from this unity. It is itself empty and without content, despises all fellowship and outward embodiment, and rules in dread fashion over everything as blind, irrational, unintelligible power. It is unintelligible because it is the concrete alone of which we can form an intelligent conception; but this necessity is still abstract, and has not yet developed so as to have the conception of an end, has not yet reached definite determinations.

Necessity, accordingly, essentially relates itself to the world. For determinateness is a moment in necessity itself, and the concrete world is developed determinateness, the kingdom of finitude, of definite existence generally. Necessity has at first a merely abstract relation to the concrete world, and this relation is the external unity of the world, equality or uniformity simply, which is without any further determination in itself, and is

incomprehensible—Nemesis, in short. It brings down
what is high and exalted, and thus establishes equality.
But this equalising is not to be understood as meaning
that when what pushes itself forward or is too high is
brought down, what is low is, in its turn, raised up.
On the contrary, that which is low is as it was meant to
be ; it is the finite which has no particular claims, and
no kind of infinite value in itself to which it could appeal.
It is thus not *too* low. It has in it power, however,
to rise above the common lot and the ordinary limit of
finitude, and when it thus acts in opposition to uniformity it is again thrust down by Nemesis.

If we now directly consider the relation of the finite
self-consciousness to this necessity, we see that under
the pressure of its iron power it is to have only an
obedience without inward freedom. But *one* form of
freedom is at least present when we look at the matter
from the side of feeling. The Greek who has within
him the feeling of the necessity calms his soul with that.
It is so ; there is nothing to be done against it ; with
this I must content myself ; just in this feeling that I
must be content with it, that this even pleases me, we
have the freedom which is implied in the fact that it is
mine.

This mental attitude implies that man has this simple
necessity before him. In that he occupies the standpoint, " It is so," he has set all that is particular on
one side, has made a renunciation of and abstracts from
all particular ends and interests. The vexation, the
discontent which men feel consists just in this, that they
stick to a definite end, and will not give this up ; and
then if things do not fit in with this end, or, as may
happen, go quite contrary to it, they are dissatisfied.
There is then no harmony between what is actually present and what men wish to have, because they have the
" ought to be " within themselves—" That ought to be."

Thus discontent, division, are inherently present ; but

those who occupy the standpoint referred to cling to no aim, no interest, as against actually existing circumstances. Misfortune, discontent, is nothing but the contradiction implied in the fact that something is contrary to my will. If the particular interest is given up, then by this act I have retreated into this pure rest, into this pure Being, into this "is."

There is here no consolation for man, but then it is not necessary. He requires consolation when he desires compensation for some loss; but here he has renounced the inner root of worry and discontent, and has wholly given up what is lost, because he has the power which enables him to look into necessity. It is, accordingly, nothing but a false illusion to imagine that consciousness is annihilated when brought into relation to necessity— that it relates itself to something which is absolutely beyond its own world, and finds in it nothing having a relationship with itself. Necessity is not one person, and accordingly consciousness does not exist in it on its own account, for itself, or in other words, it is not an individual or selfish oneness in its immediacy. In relation to that which is one person it is independent, wishes to be independent, to be for itself, and to stand on its own basis. The servant or vassal, in performing his service, in his condition of subjection, has fear, and in doing any base act against his master he has a self-seeking design. But in relation to necessity the subject appears as something which does not exist independently, or as determined for itself, it has, on the contrary, surrendered itself, retains no end for itself, and the revering of necessity is just this indeterminate attitude of self-consciousness, this attitude which is wholly devoid of the element of opposition. What we now-a-days call fate is just the opposite of this attitude of self-consciousness. We speak of just, unjust, merited fate. We use the word fate by way of explanation, that is, as suggesting the reason of any condition in which individuals are, or of the fate of

individuals. Here there is an external union of cause
and effect by which an inherited evil, an ancient curse
that rests on his house, breaks out in the individual.
In such cases fate implies that there exists some sort of
reason, but a reason that is at the same time away
beyond the present, and fate is here nothing but a connection of causes and effects, of causes, which, so far as
the person is concerned upon whom the fate falls, should
be finite causes, and where there is nevertheless a hidden
connection between that which the sufferer is in himself
and that which befalls him as something unmerited.

   The perception of and reverent regard for necessity is,
on the other hand, the direct opposite of the foregoing.
In it that mediation and the superficial reasoning about
cause and effect are done away with.   We cannot speak
of a belief in necessity as if necessity were something
essentially existing, or were a connection of relations,
such as that of cause and effect, and as if it thus stood
opposed to consciousness in some objective outward form.
On the contrary, the expression " it is necessary " directly
presupposes the abandonment of all argumentative reasoning, and the shutting up of the spirit within simple
abstraction.   Noble and beautiful characters are produced
by this attitude on the part of the human spirit, which
has thus given up that which, as the saying goes, fate
wrests from us.   It produces a certain grandeur and
repose and that free nobility of soul which is also found
amongst the ancients.   This freedom is, however, only
of the abstract kind, which merely stands above the concrete and particular, but does not actually come to be in
harmony with what is definite, *i.e.*, it is pure thought,
Being, Being-within-self, the relinquishment of the particular.   In the higher forms of religion, on the contrary,
there exists the consolation that the absolute end and
aim will be reached even in misfortune, so that the negative changes round into the affirmative.   " The sufferings
of the present are the path to bliss."

Abstract necessity, as this abstraction of thought and of the return into self, is the one extreme; the other extreme is the singularity or individual existence of the particular divine powers.

(c.) *Posited necessity or the particular gods, their appearance and outward form.*

The divine particular powers belong to what is implicitly universal, to necessity, but they come out from it because it is not yet posited for itself as the Notion and determined as freedom. Rationality and the rational content are still in the form of immediacy, or, in other words, subjectivity is not posited as infinite subjectivity, and the individuality hence appears as external. The Notion is not yet revealed, and its definite existence as it here presents itself does not yet contain the content of necessity. But it is at the same time made plain that the freedom of the particular is merely the semblance of freedom, and that the particular powers are held within the unity and power of necessity.

Necessity is not in itself anything divine, or at least is not the divine in a general sense. We may indeed say that God is necessity, *i.e.*, it is one of His essential qualities, though it may be one which is still imperfect, but we cannot say that necessity is God. For necessity is not the Idea, but rather abstract Notion. But Nemesis, and still more these particular powers, are already divine in as far as the former has a relation to definitely existing reality, while these powers again are in themselves characterised as distinguished from necessity, and consequently as distinguished from one another, and are contained in necessity as the unity of the wholly universal and particular.

Accordingly, because particularity is not yet tempered by the Idea, and necessity is not the fully concrete measure of wisdom, unlimited contingency of content makes its appearance in the sphere of the particular gods.

(*a.*) *The contingency of form or outward embodiment.*—
The twelve principal gods of Olympus are not arranged
in accordance with the Notion, and they do not constitute
any system.   One moment of the Idea, it is true, plays a
leading part, to begin with, but it is not carried out in
detail.

The divine powers of necessity being separate from
it, are external and thus unmediated, merely immediate
objects, natural existing things, such as sun, sky, earth,
sea, mountains, men, kings, and so on.   But they are
also still held fast by necessity, and thus the natural
element in them is abrogated.   If no advance were made
beyond the thought that these powers were, in their
natural immediate form of existence, divine essentially
existing beings, this would be a reversion to the Religion
of Nature, in which light, or the sun, or some particular
king is as immediate, God, while the inner element, the
universal, has not yet reached that moment of the relation
which, nevertheless, necessity essentially and absolutely
contains in itself, since in the latter the immediate is
merely something posited and abrogated.

But even if it is abrogated and preserved, the element
of Nature is still a determinate characteristic of the particular powers, and because it is incorporated in self-conscious individuals it has become a fruitful source of
contingent determinations.   The determination of time,
the year, the division of the months, still hang so much
about the concrete gods that some, as Dupuis, for example,
have even tried to make them into calendar gods.   The
idea, too, of the productive power of Nature, of beginning
to be and ceasing to be, is seen to be operative within the
sphere of the spiritual gods in the many points of agreement still existing between these gods and Nature.   But
when thus lifted up into the self-conscious form of these
gods, those natural characteristics appear as contingent,
and are changed into characteristics of self-conscious
subjectivity, whereby they lose their original meaning.

The right to search for so-called philosophemes or philo-sophical ideas in the actions of these gods, must be freely granted. For instance, Zeus feasted with the gods for twelve days amongst the Ethiopians; Juno hung between heaven and earth, and so on. Ideas such as these, as also the endless number of amours ascribed to Zeus, have undoubtedly their primary source in an abstract concep-tion which had reference to natural relations, natural forces, and to the regular and essential element in these, and thus we have the right to search after the concep-tions aforesaid. These natural relations are, however, at the same time degraded to the rank of contingent things, since they have not retained their original purity, but are changed into forms which are in conformity with sub-jective human modes of thought. Free self-consciousness no longer concerns itself about such natural characteristics.

Another source of contingent determinations is the Spiritual itself, spiritual individuality and its historical development. The god is revealed to man in what befalls himself or in the fate of a state, and this becomes an event which is regarded as an action of the god, as revealing the goodwill or enmity of the god. We get an infinitely manifold, but at the same time a contingent content, when any event, such as good fortune or bad fortune, is elevated to being the action of a god, and serves to determine more definitely and in individual instances, the actions of the god. As the God of the Jews gave a particular land to the people and led their fathers out of Egypt, so a Greek god is conceived of as having done this or the other thing which happens to a people, and which they look on as divine or as a self-determination of the divine.

We have further to take into consideration also the locality in which, and the time at which, the conscious-ness of a god first began. This element of origin within defined limits, united with the joyousness of the Greek character, is the source of a number of delightful stories.

Finally, the free individuality of the gods is the main source of the manifold contingent content ascribed to them. They are, if not infinite, absolute spirituality, at least concrete subjective spirituality. As such, they do not possess an abstract content, and there is not only one quality in them, on the contrary, they unite in themselves several characteristics. Did they possess only one quality this would be merely an abstract inner element, or simply a certain signification, and they themselves would be merely allegories, *i.e.*, would be concrete in imagination merely. But in the concrete fulness of their individuality they are not tied down to the limited lines and modes of operation belonging to one exclusive quality. On the contrary, they can now go about freely in what are voluntary but are at the same time arbitrary and contingent directions.

So far we have considered the embodiment of the divine as it is based in the implicit or potential nature belonging to it, *i.e.*, in the individual nature of these deities, in their subjective spirituality, in their chance appearances in time and place, or as it occurs in the involuntary transformation of natural determinations into the manifestation of free subjectivity. This embodiment has now to be considered as it appears in its perfected form united with consciousness. This is the manifestation of the divine powers which is for " Other," that is, for subjective self-consciousness, and is known and embodied in the conception consciousness forms of it.

(β.) *The manifestation and conceiving of the divine.*— The actual form which the god attains to in his appearance and manifestation to the finite spirit, has two sides. The god, that is to say, appears in externality, and owing to this a division, a separation, takes place which determines itself in such a way that the manifestation has two sides, one of which pertains to the god and the other to the finite spirit. The side which pertains to the god is his self-revelation, his showing of himself. Looked at from this side, all that belongs to self-consciousness is passive reception. The mode of this manifestation is one which exists pre-eminently for Thought; what is eternal is taught, given, and its existence does not depend on the caprice of the individual. Dreams, the oracle, are manifestations of this kind. The Greeks embodied this idea in all kinds of forms. For instance, a divine image fallen from heaven, or a meteor, or thunder and lightning, are reckoned as a manifestation of the divine. Or it may be this manifestation, as the first and as yet inarticulate proclamation of the divine to the consciousness, is the rustling of the trees, the stillness of the woods in which Pan is present.

Since this stage is only the stage of freedom and rationality in their first form, the spiritual power either appears in outward guise—and this is the basis of that natural aspect which still attaches to this standpoint—or if the powers and laws that make themselves known to the inward thought of man are spiritual and moral, they are this to begin with *because* they are, and it is not known whence they come.

The manifestation is now the boundary-line of both sides, which separates them and at the same time relates them to each other. At bottom, however, the activity belongs to both sides, and the true comprehension of this undoubtedly constitutes a serious difficulty. This difficulty also appears again later on in connection with the idea of the grace of God. Grace enlightens the heart of man, it is the Spirit of God in man, so that man can be regarded in relation to its work in him as passive, and in such a way that it is not his own activity which is manifested in his actions. In the Notion, however, this double activity is to be conceived of as one. Here in the present stage, this unity of the Notion is not yet made explicit, and the side of productive activity, which belongs to the subject as well, appears as independent and separate in this way, namely, that the subject produces the manifestation of the divine *consciously* as *its own* work.

It is self-consciousness which grasps, interprets, gives form to what was, to begin with, abstract, whether it is inward or outward, and produces it in the form in which it is held to be God.

The manifestations in Nature or any particular immediate and external element, are not manifestations in the sense that the Essence is only to be regarded as a thought within our minds—as, for instance, when we speak of the forces of Nature and of its outward effects. Here it does not lie in the natural objects themselves, does not lie in the objectivity in them as such that they exist as manifestations of what is inward. As natural objects they exist only for our sense-perception, and for this they are not a manifestation of the universal. Thus it is not, for example, in light as such that thought, the universal, announces its presence. In the case of natural existence we must on the contrary first break through the husk behind which thought, that which is the inward element in things, hides itself.

What is necessary is that the natural, the external, should in itself and in its externality be directly exhibited as abrogated and taken up into something higher, and as being in its own nature manifestation, so that it has only meaning and significance as the outward expression and organ of thought and of the universal. Thought must be for sense-perception, that is, what is revealed is on the one hand the sensuous mode of truth, while on the other hand that which is perceived by the senses is at the same time thought, the universal. It is necessity that has to appear in a divine fashion, *i.e.*, in definite existence as necessity in immediate unity with this concrete existence. This is posited necessity, *i.e.*, definitely existing necessity, which exists as simple reflection into itself.

Imagination is now the organ with which self-consciousness gives outward form to the inwardly abstract or to the external, which is at first something having immediate Being, and posits it as concrete. In this process the natural loses its independence and is reduced to being the outward sign of the indwelling spirit, in such a way that this latter alone is essentially allowed to appear.

The freedom of Spirit here is not yet the infinite freedom of thought; the spiritual essences are not yet in the element of Thought. Did man exercise thought in such a way that pure thought constituted the basis, there would be for him only one God. Just as little, however, does man come upon his essential beings as present immediate natural forms; on the contrary, he brings them forward into existence for idea or figurative thought, and this bringing of them forward as representing the middle stage between pure thought and the immediate perception of Nature, is imagination or fancy.

In this way the gods are formed by human imagination, and they originate in a finite fashion, being produced by the poet, by the muse. They have this finitude essentially in themselves, because so far as the content is concerned they are finite, and in virtue of their individuality have no connection with each other. They are not discovered by the human mind as they are in their essentially existent rational content, but in so far as they are *gods*. They are made, invented, but are not fictitious. They certainly come forth out of the human imagination in contrast to what actually exists, but they do this as *essential* forms, and this product of the mind is at the same time recognised as being what is essential.

It is in this sense we are to understand the remark of Herodotus that Homer and Hesiod made their gods for the Greeks. The same might be said of every priest and wise " ancient " who was capable of understanding and explaining the presence in the natural of the divine and of the essentially existing powers.

When the Greeks heard the roaring of the sea at the funeral of Achilles, Nestor came forward and explained it as meaning that Thetis was taking part in the mourning. Thus, too, in the case of the pestilence, Calchas says that Apollo had brought it about because he was angry with the Greeks. This interpretation just means that an embodiment is given to natural phenomena, that they get the form of a divine act. What takes place within the mind is similarly explained. According to Homer, for instance, Achilles would like to draw his sword, but he calms himself and restrains his anger. This inward prudence is Pallas, who represses anger. In this interpretation originated those innumerable charming tales and the endless number of Greek myths which we possess.

From whatever side we consider the Greek principle, the sensuous and natural element is seen to force its way into it. The gods as they issue out of necessity are limited, and they have also still traces of the natural element in them, just because they reveal the fact that they have sprung from the struggle with the forces of Nature. The manifestation by which they announce themselves to self-consciousness is still external, and the imagination which gives shape and form to this manifestation does not yet elevate their starting-point into the region of pure thought. We have now to see how this natural moment is wholly transfigured into a beautiful form.

(γ.) *The beautiful form of the divine powers.*—In absolute necessity determinateness is reduced to the unity of immediacy, " it is so." But this means that the determinateness, the content, is rejected, and the stability and freedom of the feeling which keeps to this sensuous perception consists only in the fact that it abides firmly by the empty " is." But definitely existing necessity is for immediate perception, and indeed exists for it in its character as natural determinate existence which in its determinateness takes itself back into its simplicity, and actually exhibits in itself this act of withdrawal or taking of itself back. Determinate existence, which is only this process, is in the state of freedom, or, to put it otherwise, determinateness exists as negativity, as reflected into itself, and as sinking itself into simple necessity. This determinateness which relates itself to itself is subjectivity.

For this process of concretely existing necessity the reality is accordingly the spiritual, the human form. This is a sensuous and natural object and thus exists for immediate perception, and it is at the same time simple necessity, simple reference to self, in virtue of being which it plainly announces the presence of thought. In every instance of its contact with reality, of its externalisation, it is directly decomposed, dissolved, and merged in simple identity ; it is an externalisation, a manifestation, which is really the externalisation of Spirit.

This relationship is not easily grasped, namely, that the fundamental determination and the one side of the Notion is absolute necessity, while the side of reality in virtue of which the Notion is Idea, is the human form. The Notion must, above all, have actual reality. This determination accordingly is more directly involved in necessity itself, for it is not abstract Being, but what is actual and determinate, determinate in and for itself. Thus the determinateness, just because it is at the same time natural, external, reality, is further directly taken back into simple necessity, so that it is this necessity which exhibits itself in this variegated sensuous element. It is only when it is no longer necessity but Spirit, which constitutes the Divine, that the latter comes to be regarded as existing wholly in the element of thought. Here, however, the moment of external perceptibility still remains, in which, spite of its material character, simple necessity nevertheless exhibits itself. This is only the case when we have the human form, because it is the form of the spiritual, and only in it can reality be taken back for consciousness into the simplicity of necessity.

Life generally is this infinitude of free existence, and as what is living is it this subjectivity, which reacts against the immediate determinateness and posits it as identical with itself in feeling. But the life of the animal, that is, the actual existence and externalisation of its infinitude, has plainly a merely limited content, is sunk in merely particular conditions. The simplicity to which this determinateness is taken back is a limited and merely formal one, and the content is not adequate to this its form. For thinking man, on the other hand, the spiritual is expressed in his particular conditions also ; this expression of it lets us see that man even in any one limited condition is at the same time above it, transcends it, is free, and does not go outside of himself, continues to be at home with himself. We can very easily judge whether a man in the act of satisfying his wants behaves like an animal or like a man. The human element is a delicate fragrance which spreads itself over every action. Besides, man has not only this element of mere life, but has likewise an infinite range of higher ways of expressing himself, of higher deeds and ends, the constituent element of which is just the Infinite, the Universal. Thus man is that absolute reflection into self which we have in the conception of necessity. It properly belongs to physiology to get a knowledge of the human organism, of the human form as the only form truly adequate for Spirit, but as yet it has accomplished little in this regard. Aristotle long ago expressed the truth that it is only the human organisation which is the form of the spiritual, when he pointed it out as being the defect in the idea of the transmigration of souls, that according to this theory the bodily organisation of human beings was of a merely accidental kind.

The individual actual man still essentially has, however, in his immediate existence the element of immediate natural life, which makes its appearance as something temporary and fleeting, as that which has fallen away from universality. In accordance with this element of finitude, there emerges a discordance or want of harmony between that which man implicitly, in his real nature is, and what he actually is. The impress of simple necessity is not stamped on all the features and parts of the individual man. Empirical individuality and the expression of simple inwardness are mingled together, and the ideality of the natural, freedom and universality are, owing to the conditions of the merely natural life and because of a number of natural needs which come into play, obscured. Looked at from this point of view, from which an " Other " appears in man, the appearance of the outward form does not correspond with simple necessity, but the fact that on his existence in all its shapes and parts the stamp of universality, of simple necessity is impressed—which Goethe appropriately called *significance,* as representing the essential character of classic art—renders it necessary that the form should be planned only in Spirit, should be produced only out of it, and brought into existence only by its mediation, that it should in short be ideal and a work of art. This is something higher than a natural product. We are, no doubt, in the habit of saying that a natural product is the more excellent, just because it is made by God, while a work of art is made only by man, as if, forsooth, natural objects did not also owe their existence to immediate natural finite things, to seeds, air, water, light; as if the power of God lived only in Nature and not also in what is human, in the realm of the spiritual. If the real truth is that natural products only flourish under the conditions supplied by what for them are external and contingent circumstances, and under their influence, an influence which comes from without, then in the work of art it is the necessity which appears as the inward soul and as the notion of externality. That is to say, necessity does not here mean that objects are necessary in themselves and have necessity as their predicate, but that necessity

is the subject, that which manifests itself in its predicate, in external existence.

If in this process the manifestation belongs to the
subjective side, so that God appears as something made
by man, still that is merely *one* moment. For this
positing of God, the making of His existence dependent
on man, is, on the other hand, mediated by the abrogation
of the individual self, and thus it was possible for the
Greeks to see their god in the Zeus of Phidias. The
artist did not give them in an abstract way something
which was *his own* work, but presented to them the
appropriate and peculiar manifestation of the essential,
the outward form of actually existing necessity.

The form given to the god is thus the ideal form.
Previous to the time of the Greeks there was no true
ideality, nor was it possible for it to appear at any
subsequent time. The art of the Christian religion is
indeed beautiful, but ideality is not its ultimate principle.
We cannot get at the element of defect in the Greek
gods by saying that they are anthropopathic, a category of
finitude under which we may put the immoral element,
as, for example, the stories of the amours of Zeus, which
may have their origin in older myths based on what is
as yet the natural way of looking at things. The main
defect is not that there is too much of the anthropopathic
in these gods, but that there is too little. The manifestation and the aspect of the definite existence of the divine
do not yet advance so far as immediate actuality, in the
form of a definite individual, that is, as this definite man.
The truest, most proper form is necessarily this, that the
absolute Spirit which exists for itself should advance to
the point at which it shows itself as individual empirical
self-consciousness. This characteristic, consisting thus
in advance to the sensuous definite individual, is not
yet present here. The form made by man in which the
divinity appears has, it is true, a material side, but this
has still such pliability that it can be perfectly adapted

to the manifested content. It is only when separation in God advances to its ultimate limit and appears as man, as a particular empirical self-consciousness, that this sensuousness, this externality, is, so to speak, set free as sensuousness, that is to say, the conditionateness of externality and its want of suitability to express the Notion actually come to light in the god. Here matter, the sensuous, has not yet this form. On the contrary, it keeps true to its content. As the god, though spiritual, universal power, issues out of Nature, he must have the natural as the element of his embodiment, and it must be made plain that it is just the natural which is the mode of the expression of the divine. The god thus appears in stone, and the material is still held to be adequate to the expression of the god as god. It is only when the god appears and reveals himself as a definite individual that Spirit, the subjective knowledge of Spirit as Spirit, is seen to be the true manifestation of God, and it is not till then that sensuousness is set free, that is to say, it is no longer blended with the god, but shows itself to be inadequate as his form; the sensuousness, the immediate individuality, is nailed to the cross. In this process of inversion, it is also shown, however, that this self-alienation, or self-emptying of God in the human form, is only one side of the divine life, for this self-emptying, this manifestation, is taken back again in the One who then for the first time becomes Spirit for thought and for the Church. This single, existing, actual man is done away with and taken up into something higher, and appears as a moment, as one of the persons of God in God. Thus only is man as a definite individual man truly in God, and thus the manifestation of the divine is absolute, and its element is Spirit itself. The Jewish idea that God essentially exists for thought alone, and the sensuousness of the Greek form of beauty, are equally contained in this form of the divine, and as being taken up into something higher, are freed from the limitation attaching to them.

At this stage, in which the divine still requires the sensuous for its essential representation, it appears as a multiplicity of gods. In this multiplicity, it is true, necessity presents itself as simple reflection into self, but this simplicity is only form, for the matter in which it exhibits itself is still immediacy, the element of Nature, not the absolute matter, namely, Spirit. It is thus not Spirit as Spirit that is here represented ; the truth rather being that the spiritual existence goes ahead of the consciousness of the content, for this latter is not yet itself Spirit.

C.

WORSHIP OR CULTUS.

This is here a very big subject. Worship essentially means that the empirical consciousness elevates itself, and that man gives himself the consciousness and feeling of the indwelling of the divine within him, and of his unity with the divine. If the work of art is the self-revelation of God and the revelation of the productivity of man as the positing of this revelation by the abrogation of his particular knowledge and will, on the other hand, the work of art equally involves the fact that God and man are no longer beings alien to one another, but have been taken up into a higher unity. The positing or bringing out of what is implicit in the work of art is here accordingly worship, and this latter is hence the relationship whereby the external objectivity of God is, relatively to subjective knowledge, abrogated, and the identity of the two set forth. In this way the external divine existence, as something divorced from existence within the subjective spirit, is abrogated, and thus God is, as it were, called to mind within the sphere of subjectivity. The general character of this worship consists in this, that the subject has an essentially affirmative relationship to his god.

The moments of worship are as follows : (*a.*) Inner feeling or subjective attitude. The gods are duly recognised and revered; they are the substantial powers, the essential, real content of the natural and spiritual universe, the Universal. These universal powers, as exempt from contingency, are recognised by man just because he is thinking consciousness. Thus the world no longer exists for him in an external and contingent fashion, but in the true mode. We thus hold in respect duty, justice, knowledge, political life, life in the State, family relationships. They represent what is true, the inner bond which holds the world together, the substantial element in which the rest exists, the valid element, what alone holds its ground against the contingency and independence which act in opposition to it.

This content is the objective in the true sense, *i.e.*, what is absolutely and essentially valid and true, not in the external objective sense, but within subjectivity also. The substance of these powers is the moral element peculiar to men, *their* morality, their actual and valid power, their own substantiality and essentiality. The Greek people are hence the most human people ; with them everything human is affirmatively justified and developed, and the element of measure is present in it.

This religion is essentially a religion of humanity, that is, the concrete man, as regards what he actually is, as regards his needs, inclinations, passions, and habits, as regards his moral and political relations, and in reference to all that has value in these and is essential, is in his gods in presence of his own nature. Or, to put it otherwise, his god has within him the very content composed of the noble and the true, which is at the same time that of concrete man. This humanity of the gods is what was defective in the Greek view, but it is at the same time its attractive element. In this religion there is nothing incomprehensible, nothing which cannot be understood ; there is no kind of content in the god which is not known to man, or which he does not find and know in himself. The confidence of a man in the gods is at the same time his confidence in himself.

Pallas, who restrained the outbreak of wrath in the case of Achilles, is his own prudence. Athene is the town of Athens, and is also the spirit of this particular Athenian people; not an external spirit or protecting spirit, but the spirit who is living, present, actually alive in the people, a spirit immanent in the individual, and who in her essential nature is represented as Pallas.

The Erinyes are not the Furies represented in an outward way. On the contrary, they are meant to suggest that it is man's own act and his consciousness which torment and torture him, in so far as he knows this act to be something evil in himself. The Erinys is not only an external Fury who pursues the matricide Orestes, but suggests rather that it is the spirit of matricide which brandishes its torch over him. The Erinyes are the righteous ones, and just because of that they are the well-disposed, the Eumenides. This is not a euphemism, for they really are those who desire justice, and whoever outrages it has the Eumenides within himself. They represent what we call conscience.

In the *Œdipus at Colonos*, Œdipus says to his son, "The Eumenides of the father will pursue thee." Eros, love, is in the same way not merely the objective, the god, but is also as power the subjective feeling of man. Anacreon, for instance, describes a combat with Eros. "I also," he says, "will now love; long ago Eros bade me love, but I would not follow his command. Then Eros attacked me. Armed with breastplate and lance, I withstood him. Eros missed, but after that he forced his way into my heart." "But," thus he concludes, "what is the use of bow and arrow? the combat is within me." In thus recognising the power of the god, and in this reverential attitude, the subject is absolutely within the sphere of his own nature. The gods are his own emotions.

The knowledge the subject has of the gods is not a knowledge of them merely as abstractions away beyond the sphere of reality. On the contrary, it is a knowledge which includes the knowledge of the concrete subjectivity of man himself as something essential, for the gods are likewise within him. Here we have not that negative relation, where the relation of the subject to what is above it, even if it is the highest form of relation, is merely the sacrifice, the negation of its consciousness. The powers here are friendly and gracious to men, they dwell in man's own breast ; man gives them reality, and knows their reality to be at the same time his own. The breath of freedom pervades this whole world, and constitutes the fundamental principle for this attitude of mind.

But the consciousness of the infinite subjectivity of man is still wanting, the consciousness that moral relations and absolute right attach to man as such, that man, just because he is self-consciousness, possesses in this formal infinitude the rights as well as the duties of the human race. Freedom, morality, is the substantial element in man, and to know this as the substantial element, and to posit in it his own substantiality, is what constitutes the value and the dignity of man. But it is the formal subjectivity, self-consciousness as such, the inherently infinite individuality, and not the merely natural and immediate individuality, which contains the possibility of that value, *i.e.*, the real possibility, and the one on account of which the individual himself has infinite rights. Now, because in the natural morality of the untutored man the infinitude of formal subjectivity is not recognised, man as such does not attain to that absolute value according to which he has worth in and for himself, whatever be his inward qualifications, whether born in this or the other place, whether rich or poor, whether belonging to this people or to that. Freedom and morality have still a special, particular form, and the essential right of man is still affected by what is contingent, so that it is essentially at this stage that slavery is found to exist. It is still a matter of accident whether a man is a citizen of this particular State or not, whether he is free or is not free. And because, further, the infinite opposition is not yet present, and because the absolute reflection of self-consciousness into itself, that climax of subjectivity, is still wanting, morality as individual conviction and rational insight is not yet developed.

Nevertheless, in morality, individuality is in a general sense taken up into universal substantiality, and thus there here enters in—if at first only as a faint semblance, and not yet as the absolute demand of Spirit—the idea of the eternal nature of the subjective, individual spirit, the idea of immortality. The demand for the immortality of the soul could not make its appearance at any of the earlier stages already considered, either in the religion of Nature or in the religion of the One. In the former, the immediate unity of the spiritual and the natural is the fundamental idea, and Spirit is not yet self-conscious, or for itself. In the latter, Spirit is, it is true, self-conscious and exists for itself, but it is still unrealised ; its freedom is still abstract, and its Being is still a natural form of existence, the possession of a particular land and its welfare. But that is not Being as the determinate existence of Spirit within itself; it does not yet imply full satisfaction in the spiritual. The duration is only the duration of the race, of the family, of natural universality, in short. But here self-consciousness is complete and realised in itself; it is spiritual. Subjectivity is taken up into universal essentiality and is thus known as essentially Idea ; and here we meet with the conception of immortality. But this consciousness becomes more definite when morality appears on the scene; self-consciousness goes down into itself, and hence it will recognise that only as good, true, and right which it finds to be in harmony with itself and its thought. With Socrates and Plato accordingly the question of the immortality of the soul is the one expressly raised, while before their day this idea was considered more as a merely general one, and as one which had not absolute value in and for itself.

As infinite subjectivity, the absolute point of the unity of the Notion, is still wanting to self-consciousness, it is still wanting also to its essentialities, to what represents for it real existence. This unity is found within that which we have come to know as its necessity ; but this lies outside the circle of the particular, substantial, essential beings. The particular essential beings, like man as such, have no absolute justification, for any justification they have they possess only as a moment of necessity, and as rooted in this absolute unity which is reflected into itself. They are many, though of divine nature, and this their scattered and manifold character is at the same time a limitation, so that divine nature is not attributed to them in any really serious sense. Above the many substantial essential beings there floats the ultimate unity of absolute form—necessity, and self-consciousness, which is in relation to the gods, is at the same time freed by this necessity from them, so that their divinity is at one time taken in a serious sense and at another in an opposite sense.

This religion has, speaking generally, the character of absolute joyousness ; self-consciousness is free in relation to its essential beings, because they are its own, though at the same time it is not chained to them, since absolute necessity floats above them too, and they go back into it, just as consciousness with its particular ends and needs also sinks itself in it.

The feeling accordingly of subjective self-consciousness in relation to necessity is this sense of repose which abides in the region of calm, in this freedom, which is, however, still an abstract freedom. It is so far an escape, a flight, but it is at the same time freedom, inasmuch as man is not overcome, weighed down by outward misfortune.

Whoever has this consciousness of independence may be indeed outwardly worsted, but he is not conquered or overcome.

Necessity has its own sphere; it has reference only to the particular element of individuality in so far as a collision of spiritual powers is possible, and the individuals are affected by necessity and are brought into subjection to it. Those individuals are in a special way in subjection to necessity and have a tragic interest attaching to them, who raise themselves above the ordinary moral conditions, and who seek to accomplish something special for themselves. This is the case with the heroes who through their own acts of will are separated from others; they have interests which go beyond the ordinary peaceful circumstances in which the government and action of God proceed. They are those who will and act in a special way of their own; they stand above the Chorus, above the calm, steady, harmonious, ordinary moral course of life. This last is exempt from the influence of destiny, restricts itself to the ordinary sphere of life, and rouses none of the moral powers against it. The Chorus, the people, viewed in one aspect, has its particular side too; it is subject to the common lot of mortals, namely, to die, to suffer misfortune and such-like, but an issue of this kind is the common lot of mortal men, and represents the course of justice relatively to the finite. That the individual should suffer some accidental misfortune, that he should die, is something which belongs to the order of things.

In Homer, Achilles weeps over his early death, and his horse weeps over it too. That would be regarded in our day as a silly thing for a poet to mention. But Homer could attribute to his hero this foreknowledge, for it cannot alter anything in his life and actions; it simply *is* so for him, and otherwise he is what he is. The thought can indeed make him sad, but only momentarily; things are so, but this disturbs him no further;

he may indeed be sad, but he cannot be vexed or annoyed. Vexation is the sentiment of the modern world; the feeling of vexation or annoyance presupposes an end, a demand on the part of modern freewill, which considers itself warranted and justified in indulging this feeling if any such end should not be realised. Thus the modern man easily gets into the mood in which he loses heart with regard to everything else, and does not even seek to reach other things he might quite well have made his aim if otherwise unsuccessful All else that belongs to his nature and destiny he abandons, and in order to revenge himself destroys his own courage, his power of action, all those ends of destiny to which he might otherwise have quite well attained. This is vexation; it could not possibly have formed part of the character of the Greeks or of the ancients, the truth being that their grief regarding what is necessary is of a purely simple kind. The Greeks did not set before themselves any end as absolute, as essential, any end the attainment of which ought to be warranted; their grief is therefore a grief of resignation. It is simple sorrow, simple grief, which has for this reason the element of serenity in it. No absolute end is lost for the individual; here, too, he continues to be at home with himself, he can renounce that which is not realised. *It is so;* and this means that he has withdrawn himself into abstraction, and has not set his own Being in opposition to what is. The liberation here is the identity of the subjective will with that which *is;* the subject is free, but only in an abstract fashion.

The heroes, as was remarked, bring about an alteration in the course of simple necessity, in this way, namely, that an element of division comes in, and the higher, really interesting element of division, so far as Spirit is concerned, is that it is the moral powers themselves which appear as divided and as coming into collision.

The removal of this state of collision consists in this, that the moral powers which are in collision, in virtue

of their one-sidedness, divest themselves of the one-sidedness attaching to the assertion of independent validity,
and this discarding of the one-sidedness reveals itself outwardly in the fact that the individuals who have aimed
at the realisation in themselves of a single separate moral
power, perish.

Fate is what is devoid of thought, of the Notion, something in which justice and injustice disappear in abstraction; in tragedy, on the other hand, destiny moves within
a certain sphere of moral justice. We find this truth
expressed in the noblest form in the Tragedies of Sophocles. Fate and necessity are both referred to there. The
destiny of individuals is represented as something incomprehensible, but necessity is not a blind justice; on the
contrary, it is recognised as the true justice. And just
because of this these Tragedies are the immortal spiritual
productions of moral understanding and comprehension,
the eternal patterns or models of the moral Notion. Blind
destiny is something unsatisfying. In these Tragedies
justice is grasped by thought. The collision between
the two highest moral powers is set forth in a plastic
fashion in that supreme and absolute example of tragedy,
Antigone. In this case, family love, what is holy, what
belongs to the inner life and to inner feeling, and which
because of this is also called the law of the nether gods,
comes into collision with the law of the State. Creon is
not a tyrant, but really a moral power; Creon is not in
the wrong; he maintains that the law of the State, the
authority of government, is to be held in respect, and
that punishment follows the infraction of the law. Each
of these two sides realises only one of the moral powers,
and has only one of these as its content; this is the
element of one-sidedness here, and the meaning of eternal
justice is shown in this, that both end in injustice just
because they are one-sided, though at the same time
both obtain justice too. Both are recognised as having
a value of their own in the untroubled course of morality.

Here they both have their own validity, but a validity which is equalised. It is only the one-sidedness in their claims which justice comes forward to oppose.

We have another example of collision in the case of Œdipus, for instance. He has slain his father, is apparently guilty, but guilty because his moral power is one-sided; that is to say, he falls into the commission of his horrible deed unconsciously. He, however, is the man who has solved the riddle of the Sphinx; he is the man distinguished for knowledge, and so a kind of balance is introduced in the shape of a Nemesis. He, who is so gifted in knowledge, is in the power of what is unconscious, so that he falls into a guilt which is deep in proportion to the height on which he stood. Here, therefore, we have the opposition of the two powers, that of consciousness and unconsciousness.

To mention still another case of collision. Hippolytus becomes unfortunate because he pays honour to Diana only, and despises Love, which accordingly revenges itself on him. It is an absurdity to ascribe to Hippolytus another amour, as is done in the French version of the story by Racine, for in that case what he suffers is no punishment of Love with any pathos in it, but is merely a certain misfortune arising from the fact that he is enamoured of one maiden, and gives no heed to another woman; for though the latter is indeed his father's wife, still the moral hindrance implied in this is obscured by the love he has for Aricia. The real cause of his destruction is the injury he has done by his neglect of a universal Power as such; it is nothing moral, but is, on the contrary, something particular and accidental.

The conclusion of this Tragedy is reconciliation, rational necessity, the necessity which here begins to mediate itself; it is justice which is in this way satisfied with the maxim, "There is nothing which is not Zeus," that is, eternal justice. Here there is an active necessity, but it is one which is completely moral; the

misfortune endured is perfectly clear ; here there is
nothing blind and unconscious. To such clearness of
insight and of artistic presentation did Greece attain at
her highest stage of culture. Yet there remains here
something unsolved in that the higher element does not
appear as the infinitely spiritual power ; we still have
here an unsatisfied sorrow arising from the fact that an
individual perishes.

The higher form of reconciliation would be that the
attitude of one-sidedness should be done away with *in
the Subject,* that the subject should have the consciousness of his wrong-doing, and that he should in his own
heart put away his wrong-doing. To recognise this his
guilt, his one-sidedness, and to discard them, is not,
however, natural to this sphere of thought. This higher
point of view makes the outward punishment, namely,
natural death, superfluous. Beginnings, faint echoes of
this reconciliation, do undoubtedly make their appearance
here, but nevertheless this inward change or conversion
appears more as outward purification. A son of Minos
was slain in Athens, and its purification was thus
rendered necessary. This deed was declared to be
undone. It is Spirit which seeks to render what has
been done undone.

In the *Eumenides* Orestes is acquitted by the Areopagus; here we have, on the one hand, the greatest
possible crime against filial piety, while on the other we
see that he did justice to his father, for he was not only
head of the family, but also of the State. In one action
he both committed a crime and at the same time acted
in accordance with perfect and essential necessity.
Acquittal just means that something is made undone,
made as though it had not happened.

In the case of Œdipus Coloneus reconciliation is
hinted at, and more particularly the Christian idea of
reconciliation. He is taken into favour by the gods, the
gods call him to themselves. In the present day we

demand more, since with us the idea of reconciliation is of a higher kind, and because we are conscious that this conversion can occur in the inner life, whereby that which is done can be rendered undone.

The man who is "converted" gives up his one-sidedness; he has extirpated it himself in his will, which was the permanent seat of the deed, the place of its abode; that is, he destroys the act in its root. It is congenial to our way of feeling that tragedies should have conclusions which have in them the element of reconciliation.

(*b.*) *Worship as Service.*—If the real point accordingly is that subjectivity should consciously pronounce its identity with the divine which confronts it, then both parts must give up something of their determinateness. God comes down from his throne of the universe and delivers Himself up, and man must, in the act of receiving the gift, accomplish the negation of subjective self-consciousness—that is, he must acknowledge God or take the gift with an acknowledgment of the essentiality which is in it. The service of God is consequently a reciprocal giving and receiving. Each side gives up something of the particularity which separates it from the other.

1. The outward relation of the two sides to one another in its most extreme form is that God has in Himself a natural element, and exists independently relatively to self-consciousness in an immediate definite fashion; or, to put it otherwise, God has His existence in an external, natural manifestation. In this relation the service of God is on the one side an acknowledgment that natural things are an Essence in themselves. On the other side, the deity offers itself up, sacrifices itself in the power of Nature in which it appears, and allows itself to be taken possession of by self-consciousness.

If then the divine powers give themselves up as gifts of Nature and graciously offer themselves for use, the

service in which man comes to have a consciousness of
unity with his powers has the following signification :—

As for those fruits, those springs, which exist in
Nature, they allow themselves to be used and drawn
upon without hindrance, or to be laid hold of and used
as nourishment.   These gifts fall freely into the lap of
man ; man eats the gifts, drinks the wine, and gets from
them invigoration and stimulus, and this invigoration in
which they are an element, is their work, the effect they
produce.   In this relationship it is not a case of mere
reciprocal action, the melancholy, continuous, self-pro-
ducing uniformity of what is mechanical.   On the
contrary, these gifts are rendered honourable because
man eats them and drinks of them ; for to what higher
honour can natural things attain than to appear as the
inspiring force of spiritual action ?   Wine inspires, but it
is man who first exalts it to the rank of an inspiring
and power-giving agent.   So far the relationship of bare
need disappears.   In connection with the sense of need
man gives thanks to the gods for the receiving of the
gifts, and these needs presuppose a separation which it is
not in the power of man to do away with.   Need, strictly
so called, first makes its appearance owing to property
and the retention of something by one will, but man does
not stand in such a relation of need to the gifts of
Nature ; on the contrary, they have to thank him that
they come to be something, that anything is made of
them ; without him they would rot and dry up and pass
away in uselessness.

The sacrifice which is connected with the enjoyment
of these natural gifts has not here the sense of the
offering up of what is inward or of the concrete fulness
of Spirit ; on the contrary, it is just this very fulness
which is affirmed and enjoyed.   Sacrifice in this case
can only signify that acknowledgment of the universal
Power which expresses the theoretical giving up of a
part of what is to be enjoyed, *i.e.*, the acknowledgment

here is a useless and aimless kind of giving up, a
renunciation which is not practical and has not reference
to the self; as, for example, the pouring out of a bowl of
wine. The sacrifice is itself at the same time the enjoyment of the thing; the wine is drunk, the meat is eaten,
and it is the power of Nature itself whose individual
existence and external form are offered up and destroyed.
Eating means sacrifice, and sacrifice just means eating.

Thus this higher sense of sacrifice and the enjoyment
found in it attach themselves to all the actions of life;
every occupation, every enjoyment of daily life is a
sacrifice. Worship is not renunciation, not the offering
up of a possession, of something belonging to oneself, but
is rather idealised, theoretical and artistic enjoyment.
Freedom and spirituality are spread over the entire daily
and immediate life of man, and worship is in short a
continuous poetry of life.

The worship of these gods is accordingly not to be
called service in the proper sense of the word, as something having reference to a foreign independent will from
whose chance decision is to be obtained what is desired.
On the contrary, the act of adoration itself already
implies a previous granting of something, or, in other
words, it is itself enjoyment. It is, therefore, not a
question of calling a power back to oneself from its place
beyond what is here and now, nor of renouncing what,
on the subjective side of self-consciousness, constitutes
the separation, in order that man may be receptive of
the power. It is thus not a question of deprivation or
renunciation, or of the laying aside of something subjective belonging to the individual, nor does the idea of
anguish, of self-tormenting, of self-torture come in here.
The worship of Bacchus or of Ceres is the possession, the
enjoyment of bread and wine, the consumption of these,
and is therefore itself the immediate granting of these
things. The Muse to which Homer appeals is in the
same way his genius, and so on.

The universal powers, however, in this case certainly retire farther into the background again, so far as the individual is concerned. The spring allows itself to be drawn upon unhindered, and the sea allows itself to be freely frequented, but it also rises in storm; it and the stars are not only not serviceable to man, but inspire fear, and are a source of disaster. Nor is the Muse always gracious to the poet either; she goes away and serves him badly, though, properly speaking, the poet really appeals to her only when he is composing his poem, and the appeal to and praise of the Muse is itself Poetry. Even Athene—Spirit, God—is unfaithful to herself. The Tyrians bound their Hercules with chains, so that he should not desert their city, which represented his reality and actual real existence; and yet Tyre fell. But such estrangement on the part of men from their essentiality or embodiment of essential Being does not lead to absolute division, not to that inward laceration of heart which would compel men to draw down their deity, so to speak, by the force of spirit to themselves in worship, and with which the lapse into magic would be connected. The individual cannot go on living in endless opposition to these particular powers, because as particular ends they lose themselves in necessity, and are themselves surrendered in this necessity.

Service hence consists in the fact that the universal powers are given a place of honour on their own account and are duly acknowledged. Thought grasps the essential, substantial element of its concrete life, and hence is neither sunk in a state of torpor in the empirical details of life and dissipated amongst these, nor does it turn from these merely to the abstract One, to the infinite "Beyond." On the contrary, just because Spirit sets before itself the true element, the Idea of its manifold existence, it is, in the very act of acknowledging and doing reverence to this universal, in the state of enjoyment, and remains in the presence of its own nature.

This presence of Spirit in its essentialities is on the one hand its truly valuable, thinking, theoretic relationship, and on the other hand is that happiness, joyousness, and freedom which is securely conscious of itself in this state, and is here in presence of its self, or together with its own self.

2. Service as a certain relationship to the gods on their spiritual side does not mean either that man appropriates these powers for the first time, or that man for the first time becomes conscious of his identity with them. For this identity is already present, and man finds these powers already realised in his consciousness. The spiritual in a definite form, as right, morality, law, or in the form of universal essential beings, such as Love, Aphrodite, attains actual existence in individuals, moral individuals, who know and love. They are the will, the inclination, the passion of these individuals themselves, their own willing, active, life. Consequently what is left for worship to do is merely to acknowledge these powers, to revere them, and together with this, to raise the identity into the form of consciousness, and to make it into theoretic objectivity.

If we compare this objectivity with our idea, we at the same time lift the universal out of our immediate consciousness and think it. We can also go on to raise these universal powers into the sphere of the ideal and give them spiritual form. But when it comes to offering prayer or bringing sacrifices to such creations, we reach the point at which we abandon the material view referred to. We cannot go so far as to give those images, which yet are no mere fancies but real powers, individual separate independence and ascribe personality to them as over against ourselves. Our consciousness of infinite subjectivity as something universal absorbs those particular powers and reduces them to the level of beautiful pictures of fancy, whose substance and significance we are indeed able to appreciate, but which cannot be held by us to have true independence.

In Greek life, however, poetry, the thinking imagination, is itself the essential Service of God. Viewed from one side, these powers split up *ad infinitum*, and, although they constitute an exclusive circle, just because they are particular powers they themselves come almost to have the infinitude of the qualities belonging to them when they are thought of as actually existing. What a number of particular relations are comprised in Pallas, for instance! Viewed from the other side, again, we see that it is the human, sensuous-spiritual form in which the ideal is to be represented, and as a consequence of all this, this representation is inexhaustible, and must ever continue to go on and renew itself, for the religious sense is itself this continuous transition from empirical existence to the ideal. There is here no fixed, spiritually definite doctrinal system, no doctrine; we have not truth as such in the form of thought; on the contrary, we see the divine in this immanent connection with reality, and hence always raising itself up anew and producing itself in and out of this reality. If this active production is brought to perfection by art, imagination has reached its ultimate fixed form, so that the ideal is set up, and then we find that there is a close connection between this and the decay of religious life.

So long, however, as the productive force which characterises this standpoint is fresh and active, the highest form of the assimilation of the divine consists in this, that the subject makes the god present through himself, and makes the god manifest in his own self. Because in this connection the recognised subjectivity of the god at the same time remains on one side as a " Beyond," this representation of the divine is at the same time the acknowledgment and the adoration of his own substantial essentiality. Thus accordingly the divine is revered and acknowledged when it is represented in festivals, games, plays, songs—in art, in short. For any one is honoured in so far as a lofty idea is formed of him, and in so far

too as this idea is made visible through action and is
allowed to appear outwardly in his conduct.

Now since the nation in the productions of art, in the
honour paid in songs and festivals, allows the idea of the
divine to appear in itself, it has its worship in itself,
i.e., it directly shows what is really *its own* excellence; it
shows the best it has, that which it has been capable of
making itself. Men adorn themselves; pageantry, dress,
adornment, dance, song, battle—all are connected with
the desire to show honour to the gods. Man shows his
spiritual and bodily ability and skill, his riches; he
exhibits himself in all the glory of God, and thus enjoys
the manifestation of God in the individual himself. This
characterises festivals even yet. This general description
may suffice to show that man allows the idea of the
gods to appear to him through himself, and that he represents himself in the most splendid possible way, and thus
shows his reverential recognition of the gods. High
honour was ascribed to the victors in battle; they were
the most honoured of the nation; on festive occasions
they sat beside the Archons, and it even happened that
in their lifetime they were revered as gods, inasmuch as
they had given outward manifestation to the divine in
themselves through the skill which they had shown. In
this way individuals make the divine manifest in themselves. In practice individuals honour the gods, are moral
—that which is the will of the gods is what is moral—
and thus they bring the divine into the sphere of actual
reality. The people of Athens, for example, who held
a procession at the festival of Pallas, represented the
presence of Athene, the spirit of the people, and this
people is the living spirit which represents and exhibits
in itself all the skill of Athene and all that is done
by her.

3. But man may be ever so certain of his immediate
identity with the essential powers, and may thoroughly
appropriate divinity to himself and rejoice in its presence

in him, and in the presence of himself in it; he may
continue to absorb those natural gods, and represent the
moral gods in morality and in the life of the State, or
he may in practice live a godly life and bring into view
the outward embodiment and manifestation of divinity in
festivals in his own subjectivity; still there yet remains
for consciousness a " Beyond," that is to say, the entire
particular element in action and in the circumstances
and relations of the individual, and the connection of
these relations with God.   Our belief that Providence in
its action reaches even to the individual, finds its confirmation in the fact that God has become man, and
this in the actual and temporal mode within which
consequently all particular individuality is comprehended,
for it is owing to this that subjectivity has received
the absolute moral justification by which it is subjectivity of the infinite self-consciousness.   In the beautiful form given to the gods, in the images, stories, and
local representations connected with them, the element
of infinite individuality, of particularity in its most
extreme form, is doubtless directly contained and expressed, still it is a particularity which in one aspect of
it is one of the chief defects charged against the mythology of Homer and Hesiod, while in another aspect these
stories belong so specially to the gods represented that
they have no reference to other gods or to men, just as
amongst men each individual has his own particular
experiences, doings, circumstances, and history, which
belong wholly and entirely to his particular life.   The
moment of subjectivity does not appear as infinite subjectivity, it is not Spirit as such which is contemplated
in the objective forms given to the divine; and wisdom
is what must constitute the fundamental characteristic of
the divine.   This, as working in accordance with ends,
must be comprised within one infinite wisdom, within
one subjectivity.   The truth that human things are
ruled over by the gods is thus no doubt involved in that

religion, but in an indeterminate, general sense, for it is just the gods who are the ruling powers in all that concerns man. The gods too are certainly just, but justice, so far as it is one Power, is a titanic power and pertains to the ancient gods. The beautiful gods have a valid existence of their own in their particular forms and come to be in collision, and these collisions are only settled by equal honour being given to all—a method, however, which certainly gives no immanent settlement.

From gods such as these, in whom the absolute return into self has not made its appearance, the individual could not look for absolute wisdom and ordered design in connection with what happened to him in life. Man, however, still feels the need of having above his particular acts and particular lot, an objective determining principle. He does not possess this in the thought of divine wisdom and Providence so as to be able to trust it in general, and for the rest to depend upon his own formal knowledge and will, and to await the absolute and entire consummation of these, or else to seek some compensation for the loss and failure of his particular interests and ends, or for his misfortune, in an eternal end.

When the particular interests of man, his happiness or misery, are concerned, we find that this outward element in what happens still depends on whether a man does this or that, goes to this or that other place. This is *his* act, his decision, which he, however, in turn knows to be contingent. As regards the circumstances which I actually know, I can doubtless decide one way or other. But besides these thus known to me, others may exist through which the realisation of my end is completely defeated. In connection with these actions I am thus in the world of contingency. Within this sphere knowledge is accordingly contingent; it has no relation to what is ethical, and truly substantial, to the duties to country, the State, and so on; man cannot, however, get to know this contingent element. The decision conse-

quently cannot so far have anything fixed about it, nor
be in any way grounded in the nature of things, but in
deciding I know at the same time that I am dependent
on what is other than myself, on what is unknown.
Now, since neither in the divine nor in the individual
is the moment of infinite subjectivity present, it does not
fall to the individual to take the final decision of himself,
to perform of himself the final act of will, for instance,
to give battle to-day, to marry, to travel; for the man is
conscious that objectivity does not reside in this willing
of his, and that it is formal merely. To satisfy the longing for this completion and to add on this objectivity, a
direction from without is required coming from one higher
than the individual, that is, the direction of an external,
decisive, and definite sign. It is the inner free will
which, that it may not be mere free will, makes itself
objective, *i.e.*, makes itself inalienably into what is other
than itself and accepts the external free will as higher
than itself. It is, speaking generally, some power of
Nature, a natural phenomenon, which now decides. The
man, amazed at what he sees, finds in such a natural
phenomenon something relative to himself, because he
does not yet see in it any objective essential significance,
or, to put it otherwise, he does not see in Nature an
inherently perfect system of laws. The formal rational
element, the feeling and the belief in the identity of the
inward and outward, lies at the basis of his conception,
but the inward element of Nature, or the universal to
which it stands related, is not the connection of its laws;
on the contrary, it is a human end, a human interest.

When, accordingly, any one wills anything, he demands,
in order actually to take his resolution, an external objective confirmation or assurance; he asks that he should
know his resolution to be one which is a unity of the
subjective and objective, one which is assured and rati-
fied. And here this ratification is the unexpected, something which happens suddenly, a materially significant,

unconnected change in things, a flash in a clear sky, a
bird rising up in a wide uniform horizon, and which
breaks in upon the indeterminateness of the inner irre-
solution. This is an appeal to what is inward, an appeal
to act suddenly, and to come to a determination within
the mind in a chance way without a knowledge of the
connection and grounds, for this is just the point at which
the grounds or reasons stop short, or at which they are
in fact absent.

The outward phenomenon which is nearest at hand
for the accomplishment of the end in view, namely, the
finding out of what is to determine action, is a sound, a
noise, a voice, ὄμφη, whence Delphi has got the name
ὄμφαλος, a supposition which is certainly more correct
than that which would find in it the other meaning of the
word, namely, the navel of the earth. In Dodona there
were three kinds of sounds—the sound produced by the
movement of the leaves in the sacred oak, the murmuring
of a spring, and the sound coming from a brazen vessel
struck by rods of brass moved by the wind. At Delos
the laurel rustled ; at Delphi the wind which blew on
the brazen tripod was the principal element. It was not
till later on that the Pythia had to be stupefied by vapours,
when in her raving she emitted words without any connection, and which had first to be explained by the priest.
It was the priest, too, who interpreted dreams. In the
cave of Trophonius the inquirer saw visions, and these
were interpreted to him. In Achaia, as Pausanias relates,
there was a statue of Mars, and the question was spoken
into its ear, after which the questioner went away from
the market with his fingers in his ears. The first word
heard by him after his ears were opened was the answer,
which was then connected with the question by interpretation. To the same class of signs belong also the
questioning of the entrails of sacrificial animals, the
signification of the flight of birds, and several other such
purely external rites. Animals were slaughtered in sacri-

fice till auspicious tokens were got. In the case of the oracles, two things went to constitute the verdict—the outward word and the explanation. With regard to the former, the mind took up a receptive attitude, but with regard to the latter, its attitude, as being the interpreter, was an active one, for the outward element in itself was supposed to be indeterminate. (Αἰ τῶν δαιμόνων φωναὶ ἄναρθροὶ εἰσιν.) But even as representing the concrete expression of the decision of the god, the oracles have a double meaning. Man acts in accordance with them while taking the words in *one* of their aspects. The other meaning, however, appears in opposition to the first, and so man comes into collision with the oracle. The oracles just mean that man shows himself to be ignorant, and shows that the god has knowledge; as ignorant, man accepts the utterance of the god who has knowledge. He consequently does not represent the knowledge of something revealed, but the absence of the knowledge of this. He does not act with knowledge in accordance with the revelation of the god, which, as being general, has no inherent determinate meaning, and thus, where there is a possibility of two meanings, it must be ambiguous. The oracle says, "Depart, and the enemy will be conquered." Here both enemies are "the enemy." The revelation of the divine is general, and must be general; man interprets it as one who is ignorant, he acts in accordance with it. The action is his own, and thus he knows himself to be responsible. The flight of birds, the rustling of oaks, are general signs. To the definite question, the god, as representing the divine in general, gives a general answer, for it is only what is general, and not the individual as such, that is included in the end aimed at by the gods. The general is, however, indeterminate, ambiguous, capable of a double meaning, for it comprises both sides.

(*c.*) What came first in worship was religious sentiment; then, secondly, we had worship as service, the concrete relationship, where, however, negativity as such has not yet appeared. The third form of the service of God is the divine service of reconciliation. The gods must be realised in the soul, in the subject, which is hypothetically estranged, *i.e.*, negatively determined relatively to the divine, and in opposition to it. The agreement cannot take place in the immediate way characteristic of the foregoing form ; on the contrary, it demands a mediation-in which that must be sacrificed which was formerly held to be fixed and independent. This negative element, which must be yielded up in order that the estrangement and alienation of the two sides may be removed, is of a twofold kind. In the first place, the soul, in its character as the natural or untutored soul, is negative relatively to Spirit; the second negative element is accordingly the positive-negative element, so to speak, that is, any misfortune whatever, and more definitely, in the third place, a moral misfortune or crime, the extreme alienation of the subjective self-consciousness relatively to the divine.

1. The soul in its natural state is not as it should be ; it ought to be free Spirit, but the soul is Spirit only through the abrogation of the natural will, of the desires. This abrogation, this subjection of itself to what is moral, and the habituation to this so that the moral or spiritual becomes the second nature of the individual, is, above all, the work of education and culture. The thought of this reconstruction of man's nature must accordingly come into consciousness at this standpoint, because it is the standpoint of self-conscious freedom, and come into it in such a way as to show that this change or conversion is recognised as requisite. If this training and conversion are represented as essential moments, and as essentially living, we get the idea of a road which the soul has to traverse, and as a consequence we get the idea of some outward arrangement in which it is supplied with the pictorial representation of this road. But if the course followed by this conversion, this self-negation and dying

to self, is to be set forth for perception or pictorial contemplation as absolute and essential, it must be beheld in
the divine objects themselves. The ·need for this has,
as a matter of fact, been obviated by means of a process
which, in the pictorial representation of the world of the
gods, has been carried out in the following way.

It is a fact intimately connected with the adoration of
the many divinities,—which, however, just because they
are many are limited divine beings,—that there is also a
transition to the universality of the divine power. The
limited character of the gods itself leads directly to the
idea of a transcendence, a rising above them, and to
the attempt to unite them in one concrete picture, and
not merely in abstract necessity, for the latter is not
anything objective. As yet this transcendence cannot
here be the absolute inherently concrete subjectivity as
Spirit, but neither can it be the return to the pictorial
representation or perception of the power of the One and
to the negative service of the Lord. On the contrary,
the One which is the object for self-consciousness at this
standpoint is a unity which is in a concrete fashion
all-embracing; it is universal Nature as a whole, or,
a totality of gods, the content of the sensuous-spiritual
world united in a material fashion. Inasmuch as self-
consciousness cannot advance to infinite subjectivity,
which as Spirit would be inherently concrete, the perception or picturing of substantial unity is something
already present so far as this stage is concerned and
preserved from the older religions. For the older original religions are the definite nature-religions, in which
this Spinozism, namely, the immediate unity of the
spiritual and the natural, constitutes the foundation.
But further, the older form of religion, however much it
may be locally defined and limited in its outward representation and in the mode in which it is conceived of,
is, before it reaches its developed form, still inherently
indefinite and general. Each local god in its deter-

mination of locality has at the same time the significance
of universality, and since this is firmly clung to as
against the splitting up and particularisation into characters and individualities developed in the Religion of
Beauty, it is in what is rude and primitive, in what is
unbeautiful and uncultured, that the service of a deeper,
inner universal, maintains itself, a universal which is at
the same time not abstract thought, but which, on the contrary, retains in itself that external and contingent form.

This older religion may, on account of its simplicity
and substantial intensity, be called deeper, purer, stronger,
more substantial, and its meaning may be termed a truer
one, but its meaning is essentially enveloped in a kind of
haze, and is not developed into thought, that is, is not
developed into that clearness which marks the particular
gods in whom the day of Spirit has dawned, and which
have in consequence attained to character and spiritual
form.   The service of this deeper and universal element
involves, however, in it, the opposition of this deeper and
universal element itself to the particular, limited, and
revealed powers.   It is, regarded from one side, a return
from these to what is deeper, more inward, and so far
higher, the bringing back of the many scattered gods
into the unity of Nature, but it also involves the antithesis which is expressed by saying that this deeper
element is as opposed to clear self-consciousness, to the
serenity of day and rationality, something dull and torpid,
unconscious, crude, and .barbarous.   The perception, or
pictorial contemplation, in this kind of worship, is accordingly in one aspect the perception of the universal life of
Nature and of natural force, a return to inward substantiality; but in another aspect it is equally the perception of
the process, of the transition from savagery to a state of
law, from barbarousness to morality, from mental torpor
to the clear growing certainty of self-consciousness, from
the Titanic to the Spiritual.   It is consequently not a
god in his finished form who is beheld here, no abstract

doctrine is propounded ; on the contrary, the content of
perception is the conflict of what is original and primitive,
which is brought forth from its undeveloped state into
clearness, into form, into the daylight of consciousness.
This idea is already present in many exoteric and pictorial forms in mythology.   The war of the gods and
the conquests of the Titans is just this divine issuing
forth of the spiritual from the overcoming of the rude
powers of Nature.

It is here accordingly that the action of the subjective
side and its movement receive their deeper determination.   Worship cannot here be merely serene enjoyment,
the enjoyment of present immediate unity with the
particular powers ; for since the divine passes out of its
particularity over to universality, and since self-consciousness is reversed or inverted within itself, opposition is
consequently present, and the union starts from a separation greater than that presupposed by outward worship.
Worship here is rather the movement of an inward impression made on the soul, an introduction to and initia-
tion into an essentiality which is for it foreign and
abstract, an entrance into disclosures which its ordinary
life and the worship grounded on that do not contain.
Just because the soul enters into this sphere the demand
is made that it should give up its natural Being and
essence.   This worship is thus at the same time the purification of the soul, a path to this purification, and a
gradual progress towards it, the admission into the high
mystical Essence, and the attainment of a contemplation
in pictorial form of its secrets, which, however, have for
the initiated ceased to be secrets, and can only still
remain such in the sense that the pictures thus contemplated, and this content, are not introduced into the
sphere of ordinary existence and consciousness, that is,
into the sphere of ordinary action and reflection.   All
Athenian citizens were initiated into the Eleusinian
mysteries.   A secret is thus essentially something known,

only not by all. Here, however, there is something
known by all, which is merely treated as secret, *i.e.*,
secret only to this extent, that it is not made the talk of
everyday life, just as we see in the case of Jews, who do
not name the name Jehovah, or, to take an opposite case,
just as in daily life there are things known to all but of
which no one speaks. But these pictures of the divine
were not mystical in the sense in which the public
doctrines of Christendom have been called mysteries.
For in the case of the latter the mystical element is the
inward and speculative element. What had been seen by
the initiated had to remain secret, mainly because the Greeks
would not have been able to speak of it otherwise than in
myths, that is to say, not without altering what was old.

But even in this worship, although it starts from a
definite opposition, joyousness or serenity still continues
to constitute the basis. The path of purification is tra-
versed indeed, but that does not represent the infinite
pain and doubt in which the abstract self-consciousness
isolates itself from itself in its abstract knowledge, and
because of this moves and pulsates merely within itself
when in this empty abstract form, is merely a kind of
inward trembling, and in this abstract certainty of itself
cannot absolutely reach fixed truth and objectivity, nor
come to have the feeling of these. On the contrary, it
is always on the basis of that unity that this traversing
of the path exists and has value as the actually completed purification of the soul, as absolution, and having
this original unconscious basis remains rather an external
process of the soul, since the latter does not go down into
the innermost depths of negativity as is the case where
subjectivity is completely developed and attains to infinitude. If terrors, frightful images, forms inspiring dread,
and such like, are already employed here, and if, on the
other hand, and in contrast to this dark side, bright and
brilliant representations, significant pictures full of splendour are made use of to produce a deeper effect on the

mind, the initiated is purified in the very process of passing through the experience of seeing these pictorial forms and having these emotions.

These mystical perceptions or pictorial forms accordingly correspond to those pictorial forms of the divine life, the process of which is set forth in tragedy and comedy. The fear, the sympathy, the grief represented in tragedy, all those conditions in which self-consciousness is carried away, and in which it shares, are just what forms that process of purification which accomplishes all that should be accomplished. In the same way the pictorial representations of comedy, and the giving up by Spirit of its dignity, of its value, of its opinion of itself, and even of its fundamental powers, this entire surrender of all that belongs to self, is just this worship in which the spirit, through this surrender of all that is finite, enjoys and retains the indestructible certainty of itself.

In public worship even the main interest is not so much the paying of honour to the gods as the enjoyment of the divine. Since, however, in this worship of mysteries, the soul is on its own account elevated into an end and is regarded in this condition of contrast as abstract, independent, and, as it were, sundered from the divine, the idea of the immortality of the soul necessarily makes its appearance here. The completed purification raises it above the temporal, fleeting, present existence, and inasmuch as it is made permanently free, the idea of the passing over of the individual as one dead on his natural side, into an eternal life, is closely associated with this form of worship. The individual is made a citizen of the essential, ideal kingdom of the under world, in which temporal reality is reduced to the condition of a phantom world.

Since then the mysteries represent the return of the Greek spirit to its first beginnings, the form of what constitutes these is essentially symbolical, i.e., the signification is something other than the outward representation. The Greek gods themselves are not symbolical; they are what they represent, just as the conception of a work of art means the giving expression to what is meant, and does not mean that what is inward is something different from what is outwardly seen. Even if the beginnings of the Greek god are to be traced back to some such ancient symbolic representation, still what this is actually made into has become the work of art which perfectly expresses what it is intended to be. Many have sought, and especially Creuzer, to investigate the historical origin of the Greek gods, and the signification which lies at the basis of their character. But if the god is a subject for art, that alone is a good work of art which exhibits him as what he actually is. In the religions of nature this is a mystery, something inward, a symbol, because the outward form does not actually reveal the meaning which lies in this mystery, the idea rather being that it is merely *intended* to reveal it. Osiris is a symbol of the sun, and similarly Hercules and his twelve labours have reference to the months; thus he is a god of the calendar, and no longer the modern Greek god. In the mysteries, the content, the manifestation, is essentially symbolical. The principal symbols had reference to Ceres, Demeter, Bacchus, and the secrets connected with these. As Ceres, who seeks her daughter, is in the language of prose the seed that must die in order to retain its true essence and to bring it into life, so, too, the seed and the germination of the seed are in turn something symbolical; for, as in the Christian religion, they have the higher signification of resurrection, or they can be taken as meaning that the same holds good of Spirit, whose true essence or potential nature can bear blossoms only through the annulling of the natural will. Thus the meaning changes about; at one time this content signifies an idea, some process, and then again the idea, the signification, may itself be the symbol for something else. Osiris is the Nile which is dried up by Typhon, the

fire-world, and is again brought into existence; but he is
also a symbol of the sun, a universal life-giving power
of Nature. Osiris finally is also a spiritual figure, and
in this case the Nile and the sun are in turn symbols of
the spiritual. Such symbols are naturally mysterious.
The inward element is not clear as yet; it exists first as
meaning, signification, which has not yet attained to true
outward representation. The outward form does not perfectly express the content, so that the latter remains in
a partially expressed shape at the basis of the whole
without coming forth into existence. Hence it came
about that the mysteries could not give to the self-consciousness of the Greeks true reconciliation. Socrates
was declared by the oracle to be the wisest of the Greeks,
and to him is to be traced the real revolution which
took place in the Greek self-consciousness. This pivot,
so to speak, of self-consciousness was not, however, himself initiated into the mysteries; they stand far below
what he brought into the consciousness of the thinking
world. All this has to do with the first form of reconciliation.

2. The other negative element is misfortune in general,
sickness, dearth, or any other mishaps. This negative
element is explained by the prophets, and brought into
connection with some guilty act or transgression. A
negative of this kind first appears in the physical world
in the shape, for example, of an unfavourable wind. The
physical condition is then explained as having a spiritual
connection, and as involving in itself the ill-will and
wrath of the gods—that ill-will and wrath which are
brought upon men by some crime and by some offence
against the divine. Or it may be that lightning, thunder,
an earthquake, the appearance of snakes, and such-like
are interpreted to mean something negative which essentially attaches to a spiritual and moral Power. In this
case the injury has to be done away with through sacrifice,
and in such a way that he who has shown himself arro-

gant by committing the crime, imposes a forfeiture on himself, for arrogance is an injury done to a spiritual higher Power, to which accordingly humility has to sacrifice something in order to propitiate it and restore the equilibrium. In the case of the Greeks this idea seems rather to belong to primitive times. When the Greeks wished to depart from Aulis, and unfavourable winds held them back, Calchas interpreted the storm to be the wrath of Poseidon, who demands the daughter of Agamemnon as a sacrifice. Agamemnon is ready to give her up to the god. Diana saves the girl. In the *Œdipus Tyrannus* of Sophocles a certain disease is sent by means of which the deed of the parricide is disclosed. In later times such ideas no longer make their appearance. During the pestilence in the Peloponnesian war we hear nothing of the worship of the gods; no sacrifice was made during this war; we meet only with predictions of its conclusion. The appeal to the oracle implies that such a sacrifice has become antiquated. That is to say, if counsel is asked of the oracle, the result is viewed as determined by the god himself. Thus the result came to be regarded as something which has to happen, as a matter of necessity, a matter of fixed destiny, in connection with which no reconciliation could have a place, which could not be averted and could not be remedied.

3. The final form of reconciliation implies that the negative is really a crime, and is so regarded and declared to be such; not a crime which is only perceived to be such by the help of the explanation given through some misfortune. An individual, a state, a people commits a crime; from the human point of view the punishment is the propitiation for the crime either in the form of punishment or in the cruder form of revenge. The free spirit has the self-consciousness of its majesty, whereby it has to make what has happened as if·it had not happened, and to do this within itself. An outward act of pardon is something different, but that what has hap-

pened can within the mind itself come to be what has
not happened, is something which belongs to the higher
privilege of free self-consciousness, where evil is not merely
act, but is something fixed and settled, and has its seat
in the heart, in the guilty soul. The free soul can purify
itself from this evil. Faint resemblances of this inward
conversion do occur, but the general character of reconciliation here is rather outward purification. With the
Greeks this too is something belonging to ancient times.
A couple of instances of this are well known in connection with the history of Athens. A son of Minos was
slain in Athens, and on account of this deed a purification
was undertaken. Æschylus relates that the Areopagus
acquitted Orestes; the rock of Athena stood him in good
stead. The reconciliation here is regarded as something
outward, not as inward confession. The idea expressed
in *Œdipus at Colonos* savours of Christian thought; in
it this old Œdipus, who slew his father and married his
mother, and who was banished along with his sons, is
raised to a place of honour among the gods; the gods
call him to themselves. Other sacrifices belong still
more to the outward mode of reconciliation. This is the
case with the sacrifices to the dead, which are intended
to propitiate the Manes. Achilles, for example, slew a
number of Trojans on the grave of Patroclus, his intention being to restore the uniformity of destiny on both
sides.

III.

THE RELIGION OF UTILITY OR OF THE UNDERSTANDING.

A.

THE GENERAL CONCEPTION OF THIS STAGE.

In the Religion of Beauty empty necessity was the
ruling principle, and in the Religion of Sublimity unity
in. the form of abstract subjectivity. In the latter reli-

gion we find, besides unity, the infinitely limited real
end, and in the former again, besides necessity, we have
moral substantiality, the Right, the present and real in
empirical self-consciousness. In the bosom of necessity
repose the many particular powers and partake of its
essentiality. Represented as individuals, they are spiritual
concrete subjects, and each represents a particular national
spirit. They are living spirits, as, for instance, Athene
is for Athens, Bacchus for Thebes, and they are also
family gods, though they are at the same time transfer-
able, because they are in their nature universal powers.
Consequently the objects also with which such gods take
to do are particular towns, states, and, speaking generally,
a mass of particular ends.

Thus this particularity when brought under a " One "
or Unity represents determinateness in its more definite
form. The next demand of thought is for the union of
that universality and of this particularity of these ends,
in such wise that abstract necessity has its emptiness
filled within itself with the particularity, with the end.

In the Religion of Sublimity, the end, when it took
on a realised form, was an isolated end shutting off one
particular family from others. A higher stage is accordingly reached when this end is widened so as to correspond to the compass of the Power, and when at the
same time this Power itself is further developed. The
particularity which is developed in detail as a divine
aristocracy, and together with this the real national spirit
in its various forms, which as an end comes to form part
of the essential character of the Divine and is preserved
within it, must get a place also within the unity. This
cannot, however, be the truly spiritual unity such as we
have in the Religion of Sublimity. The characteristics
of the earlier stages are rather merely put back into a
relative totality in which, it is true, both the religions
which preceded lose their one-sidedness, but in which at
the same time each of the two principles is also perverted

into its opposite. The Religion of Beauty loses the concrete individuality of its gods, as well as their independent moral content or character. The gods are degraded to the rank of means. The Religion of Sublimity again loses its tendency to occupy itself with the One, the eternal, the supernatural. Their union, however, is a step in advance in this, that the single end and the particular ends are broadened out so as to form a universal end. This end has to be realised, and God is the Power which is to realise it.

Action in accordance with an end is a peculiarity not only of Spirit but of life in general. It is the action of the Idea, for it is an act of production which is no longer a passing over into something other or different, whether it is now characterised as other, or, as in the case of necessity, as potentially the same, though in its outward form, and as existing for others, it is an " other." In the end, any content, as being what is primary, is independent of the form which the transition takes, and of the alteration which takes place, so that it maintains itself within it. The impulse of this flower-like nature, which may take on an external form under the influence of the most manifold conditions, shows itself in the production only of its own development, and only in the simple form of the transition from subjectivity into objectivity. The form which reveals itself in the result is that which was formed before or pre-formed in the germ.

Action in accordance with an end is closely allied to the form of spiritual manifestation which we last considered ; but spiritual manifestation in that form is, to begin with, only the superficial mode in which anything having a definite nature and any spiritual determinateness appears, apart from the existence of this determinateness as such under the form or mode of the end or Idea. The abstract characterisation and the basis of the religion which went before were expressed by the idea of necessity, and outside of it was the fulness of Nature, spiritual and physical, which accordingly is broken up so as to have definite quality and to exist in definite time; while the unity is in its own nature devoid of content, roots itself within itself, and receives that serenity or joyousness which at once raises it above its determinateness and renders it indifferent towards it, only from the spiritual form and from ideality. Necessity is freedom potentially only, is not yet wisdom, and is devoid of an end. In it we find freedom only in so far as we yield up the content of freedom. Anything that is necessary, doubtless, represents something having a content, some occurrence or other, condition and consequence, &c.; but its content as such is something contingent. It may take this particular form, or it may take some other form; or, to put it otherwise, necessity is just a formal mode of existence, and its content consists merely in the fact that it *is*, but suggests nothing of *what* it is. It consists only in holding fast to this abstract form of existence.

Necessity, however, buries itself in the Notion. The Notion, or freedom, is the truth of necessity. To grasp anything in thought means that we conceive of it as a moment of a connected whole, which in its character as a connected whole has the element of difference in it, and has thus a definite and substantial nature. The connection between things which is expressed by cause and effect is itself as yet a connection of necessity, *i.e.*, it is as yet formal. What is wanting in it is that a content be posited as determined for itself, *traversant ce changement de cause en effect sans change,* a content which passes through the change of cause and effect without alteration. In this case, in fact, the external relation and reality as embodied in different forms are degraded to the condition of means. In order to the carrying out of an end it is necessary to have means, *i.e.*, something external with the power of producing effects, the essential mark of which consists in its being subordinate to the movement of the end, which preserves itself in its movement, and does away with its transitional character. In cause and effect we have potentially the same content, but it appears in the form of actual independent things which mutually affect each other. The end, however, is this content which is posited as identity with itself in contrast to the apparent difference between reality and the form in which reality appears. Accordingly, in the case of action carried out in accordance with an end, nothing can come out of it which was not already there.

So far as the end is concerned, it is just in this that the difference between the end and the reality is found. The end maintains itself, mediates itself only with itself, coincides only with itself, brings about the unity of itself in the form of the unity of what is subjective with reality; but it does this through means. It is the power which is above reality, the power which has at the same time a primary content determined in and for itself, and this content is what is first and continues to be what is last. The end is thus the necessity which has taken into itself the external, particular content, and holds it fast as against reality, which has a negative character and is degraded to a means.

This unity of the content which ever dominates reality, freeing itself from its power, and maintaining itself in opposition to it, is accordingly present in life. The content, however, is not free in its own nature, free for itself in the element of Thought; it has not been given a higher form in the mode of its identity, it is not spiritual. The same unity exists in the spiritually formed ideal; but inasmuch as it is represented as being present in a free form and as beauty, it belongs to a higher stage than what has life. The quality of this unity is, so far, to be regarded as an end, and what it produces is action in accordance with an end. Its qualities, however, are not represented under the mode of the end—*e.g.*, Apollo and Pallas do not set it before them as an end to produce and extend science and poetry; Ceres and the mystic Bacchus do not make the production and the teaching of

laws an end. They take under their protection what constitutes the laws, it is their special care; but here the
separation between end and reality does not exist. These
beings which have divine nature are those very powers
and activities themselves; the Muse is herself the com-
position of poetry; Athene herself is Athenian life—the
happiness and well-being of the city is not her end;
but, on the contrary, these powers rule in as immanent a
way in the reality with which they are connected as the
laws act within the planets.

And further, as the gods in the stage of thought represented by beauty are in no sense means, they are just as
little mutually opposed as independent; rather, they themselves disappear in necessity. If they do at a time act
on their own account, they soon submit again and allow
themselves to be put in their right place. While, accordingly, in necessity one determination depends on
another, and the determinate character passes away, the
end is posited as identity with difference and reality in
it, the unity which is determined in and for itself, and
which maintains itself in its determinate character as
against the determinate character of something else.

The Notion, accordingly, in so far as it is posited as
free in its own nature, or for self, is at first confronted
by reality, and this is characterised in reference to it as
negative. In the absolute Notion, the pure Idea, this
reality, this hostile element, melts away into unity, and
gets to be on a friendly footing with the Notion itself;
it throws off its peculiar individual character, and is itself
freed from the position of being merely a means. It is
this which is the true conformity to an end in which is
posited the unity of the Notion, of God, of the Divine
Subject or person, with that in which the Notion realises
itself, namely, objectivity and realisation, and it is the
very nature of God Himself which realises itself in objectivity, and is thus identical with itself viewed under
the aspect of reality.

At first, however, the end itself is as yet immediate, formal; its first determination consists in this that what is thus determined in itself should, in reference to reality, be for itself, should exist independently, and realise itself in it as something offering resistance to it. It is thus at first a finite end, and the relation between things expressed by it is a relation of the understanding, and the religion which is founded on such a basis is a religion of the understanding.

In the religion of the One we have already had an end somewhat of this sort, and something which had a close resemblance to this religion of the understanding. The religion of the One is also a religion of the understanding in so far as this One maintains itself as end as against reality of every kind, and the Jewish religion is on this account the religion of the understanding in its most rigid and lifeless form. This end consisting, as it does, in the glorification of the name of God, is formal, it has no absolutely definite character, but is only abstract manifestation. The people of God, it is true, represent a more definite end as an individual people; but this is a kind of end which it is wholly impossible to form a conception of, and is an end only in the sense in which the servant is an end for his Lord. It does not represent the nature of God Himself; it is not His end; it is not divine determinateness.

When we say that God is the Power which works in accordance with ends, and in accordance with the ends of wisdom, we are speaking in a sense different from that which at first attaches to this characterisation as applied to the stage of the development of the Notion at which we have arrived. What we mean is that those ends are undoubtedly also limited, finite ends, but that they are essentially ends of wisdom in general, and ends of one wisdom, *i.e.*, ends of the Good in and for itself, ends which have reference to one supreme final end. These ends are consequently subordinate simply to one end, or aim. The limited ends and the wisdom in them are of a subordinate character.

Here, however, the limitation of the ends is the fundamental characteristic, and this has no higher one above it.

Religion of this sort is consequently in no sense a religion of unity, but rather of multiplicity; it is neither one Power nor one wisdom, one Idea, which constitutes the fundamental determination of the divine nature.

Thus the ends which constitute the content of those forms of existence are definite ends, and these ends are not to be sought for in Nature; but, on the contrary, we find that amongst the many forms of existence, and of the relations between things, those that have reference to man are undoubtedly the really essential ones. What is human is inherently possessed of thought, and man, in pursuing his end, however unimportant it may be in itself, as, for instance, in seeking nourishment, &c., has the right of using up natural things and animal life without further ado and to whatever extent he may choose. Just for this very reason the ends are not to be sought for as if they existed objectively in the gods and in and for themselves. On the contrary, this religion, in so far as it is a definite religion, owes its origin to human ends, to human need or fortunate events and circumstances.

In the religion which went before this one, it was necessity which was the universal, and which floated above the particular.

This cannot be the case at the present stage; for in necessity finite ends disappear as in a higher form, while here, on the contrary, they represent what gives definite character to things and persists. At this stage the universal represents rather the consent to or agreement with particular ends, and, in fact, consent in general; for here the universal must remain undefined, because the ends remain individual ends, and their universality is only of the abstract sort, and is thus Happiness.

This happiness, however, is not to be distinguished

from necessity as belonging to the class of contingent things, for in that case it would be the necessity itself, in which those very finite ends are merely contingent; nor is it foreordination in general, and the directing of finite things in accordance with an end; but, rather, it is happiness with a definite content, with certain definite elements.

But a definite content, again, does not mean any kind of random content in general. On the contrary, although it is finite and actually present, it must be universal in its nature, and its existence must be justified on higher grounds—justified in and for itself. And this end accordingly is the State.

The State, however, as representing this end is, to begin with, only the abstract State—the union of men held together by some bond, but in such a way that this union is not yet in itself in the form of a rational organisation, and it does not yet take this form because God is not yet a rational organisation in Himself. Such conformity to an end as there is, is external; if it were conceived of as existing inwardly, it would represent the peculiar nature of God. Just because God is not yet this concrete Idea, because He does not yet represent in Himself the true fulness of Himself reached through Himself, this end, namely, the State, is not yet a rational totality in itself, and does not therefore deserve the name State, but is merely a kind of dominion or sovereignty, the union of individuals, of peoples, held together by some bond under one Power. Since, too, we have here the distinction between end and realisation, this end exists at first only in a subjective form, and not as end which has been carried out, and the realisation of it is represented by the acquiring of sovereignty, the realisation of an end which is of an *à priori* character, which, in the first instance, lays hold of the peoples and carries itself out.

As this quality of external utility or action in accordance with an end is different from the moral substan-

tiality of Greek life, and from the identity of the divine
Powers and their external existence, so, too, this sovereignty, this universal monarchy, this end is to be distinguished from that of the Mohammedan religion. In this
latter, sovereignty over the world is also the end sought
after; but what is to exercise sovereignty is the One of
Thought, the One of the Israelitish religion. Or when,
as in the Christian religion, it is said that God wills that
all men should come to a consciousness of the truth, the
nature of the end is spiritual. Each individual is thought
of as a thinking being, as spiritual, free, and actually present in the end, it possesses in him a central point, it is
not any kind of external end, and the subject embraces
within himself the entire extent of the end. Here, on
the contrary, it is still empirical, a sovereignty of the
world which embraces it in an external way. The end
which exists in this sovereignty is one which lies outside
of the individual, and the more it is realised the more
external does it become, so that the individual is brought
into subjection simply to this end, and serves it.

The union of universal power and universal individuality is, to begin with, implicitly contained here, but
it is, so to speak, only a crude union, devoid of Spirit.
The power is not wisdom, its reality is not a divine end
in and for itself. It is not the One who derives his
fulness from himself; this fulness is not conceived of
as existing in the realm of thought; the power is worldly
power, worldliness merely as sovereignty, and power in
this aspect is virtually irrational. In presence of the
power all that is particular accordingly crumbles away,
because it is not taken up into it in a rational way,
and it takes on the form of self-seeking on the part of
the individual, of satisfaction in an ungodly way in particular interests. The sovereignty is outside of reason,
and stands coldly, selfishly, on the one side, just as the
individual does on the other.

This is the general conception of this religion. The

demand for what is highest is implicitly stated in it, namely, the union of what has pure Being in itself and of particular ends; but the union here is of the ungodly, undivine, crude sort just described.

B.

THIS RELIGION AS IT APPEARS OUTWARDLY IN HISTORY IS REPRESENTED BY THE ROMAN RELIGION.

It is customary to take in a superficial way the Roman religion along with the Greek religion; but the spirit of the one is essentially different from that of the other. Even if they possess certain outward forms in common, still these occupy quite a different place in the religion we are dealing with; and the religions as a whole, and the religious sentiment connected with them, are essentially different, as is indeed already evident from an external, superficial, and empirical examination of them.

It is allowed in a general way that the State, the constitution of a State, the political destiny of any people, depends on its religion, that this is the basis, the substance of its actual spiritual life and the foundation of what we call its politics. The Greek and Roman spirit, culture, and character are, however, wholly and essentially different, and this fact must of itself bring us to the difference in the religions which form the substance of these.

The divine Beings belonging to this circle of thought are practical and not theoretical gods; prosaic, not poetical; although, as we shall presently see, this stage is the richest of all in the constantly new discovery and production of gods.

1. So far as regards abstract religious sentiment and spiritual tendencies, the earnestness of the Romans is what first calls for remark. Where one end exists, and that an essentially solid one which has to be realised, the understanding referred to comes into play, and along with

it the earnestness which clings firmly to this end, in opposition to a great deal else which is present in feeling or in external circumstances.

In the religion which comes before this one, the religion of abstract necessity and of particular individual beings who are beautiful and divine, it is freedom which constitutes the fundamental character of the gods and which gives to them their joyousness and bliss. They are not exclusively attached to any single form of existence, but are essential powers, and represent at the same time the irony which governs all that they seek to do; what is particular and empirical has no importance for them.

The joyousness of the Greek religion, which is the fundamental trait of the sentiment pervading it, is based on the circumstance that although an end certainly exists and is regarded with reverence, as holy, still there is present at the same time this freedom from the end, and it is directly based on the fact that the Greek gods are many in number. Each Greek god has more or less substantial attributes, moral substantiality; but just because there are many particular attributes, consciousness or Spirit is something above and beyond this manifold element, and exists outside of its particular forms. It abandons what is characterised as substantial and which can also be considered as end, and is itself the irony referred to.

The ideal beauty of these gods, and their universal character itself, is something higher than their particular character; thus Mars can find pleasure in peace as well as in war. They are gods of fancy existing for the moment, without consistency, now appearing on their own account, independently, and now returning again to Olympus.

Where, on the contrary, one principle, one supreme principle and one higher end exist, there can be no room for this joyousness or serenity.

Further, the Greek god is a concrete individuality, and each of these many particular individuals has itself again many different characteristics within it; there is here a rich individuality which must necessarily possess and give evidence of the existence in it of the element of contradiction, just because the two opposite elements in it have not yet been absolutely reconciled.

Since the gods have in themselves this wealth of external characteristics, we have a certain element of indifference existing in reference to those particular qualities, and they can be made sport of and be treated with levity. It is with this side of their nature that the element of contingency which we observed attached to them in the stories of the gods, is connected.

Dionysius of Halicarnassus, in drawing a comparison between the Greek and the Roman religion, extols the religious institutions of Rome, and points out the great superiority of the old Roman religion to the Greek. It has temples, altars, divine worship, sacrifice, solemn religious gatherings, festivals, symbols, &c., in common with the Greek religion; but the myths with their blasphemous features, the mutilations, the imprisonments, the wars, the squabbles, &c., of the gods, are excluded from it. These, however, belong to the gods in their joyous aspect, they lay themselves open to this, they are made sport of in comedy, and yet in all this they have a safe and undisturbed existence. When the element of seriousness comes in, then the outward form taken by gods, their actions and the events in their life, must appear in a way which is in conformity with a fixed principle. In free individuality, on the other hand, there are no such fixed ends, no such one-sided moral characterisations of the understanding. The gods, it is true, contain within them the moral element; but at the same time, since they have a particular definitely marked existence, they are possessed of a rich individuality, and are concrete. In this rich individuality the element of earnestness is not at all a necessary characteristic; on the contrary, it is free in all its separate manifestations, it

can roam about in a light-hearted way through everything, and it remains what it is. The stories which
appear to be unworthy of gods have reference to the
general aspects of the nature of things, the creation of the
world, &c. ; they have their origin in old traditions, in
abstract views regarding the processes of the elements.
The universal element in these views is obscured, but it
is hinted at; and in this external way of regarding things,
and in this want of order amongst things, a glimpse is
first got of the universal nature of the intelligence which
shows itself in them. In a religion, on the other hand,
in which a definite end is present, all reference to theoretical points of view from which intelligence may be
regarded disappears. No theories, and in fact nothing
universal, are to be found in the Religion of Utility. The
deity has here a definite character or content, namely, the
sovereignty of the world. The universality here is empirical, not moral or spiritual, but is rather a real, actual
universality.

The Roman god representing this sovereignty is to be
looked for in *Fortuna publica*, the necessity which for
others is a cold unsympathetic necessity ; the particular
necessity which contains the end concerned with Rome
itself is *Roma*, sovereignty, a holy and divine Being, and
this sovereign *Roma* in the form of a god who exercises
sovereignty is Jupiter Capitolinus, a particular Jupiter—
for there are many Jupiters, three hundred Joves in fact.

This Jupiter Capitolinus is not Zeus, who is the
father of gods and men; but rather, he simply stands for
the idea of sovereignty, and has his end in the world,
and it is for the Roman people that he carries out this
end. The Roman people is the *universal* family, while
in the Religion of Beauty the divine end was represented
by *many* families, and in the religion of the One, on the
other hand, by *one* family only.

2. This god is not the truly spiritual One, and just
because of this the Particular lies outside of this unity

of sovereignty. The Power is merely abstract, merely Power, and is not a rational organisation, a totality in itself, and just because of this the Particular appears as something which lies *outside* of the One, outside of the sovereign power.

This particular element appears partly, too, in the form taken by the Greek gods, or else we find that later on it was put side by side with them by the Romans themselves. Thus the Greeks, too, find their gods in Persia, Syria, and Babylonia, though, at the same time, this represents something different from the peculiar way in which they regarded their gods, and from the definite character of these gods, and it is only a superficial universality.

Looked at in a general way, the particular Roman deities, or at least many of them, are the same as the Greek. But still they have not the beautiful free individuality of the Greek gods; they seem to be grey, so to speak. We do not know where they come from, or else we know that they have been introduced in connection with some definite occasions. And besides, we must distinguish the real Roman gods from those Greek gods which the later poets such as Virgil and Horace have introduced into their artificial poetry in the form of lifeless imitations.

We do not find in them that consciousness, that humanity which is the substantial element in men as in the gods, and in the gods as in men. They appear like machines with nothing spiritual in them, and show themselves to be gods of the understanding which have no connection with a free beautiful spirit, with a free beautiful fancy. So, too, in those modern botches done by the French, they have the appearance of wooden figures or machines. It is, in fact, for this reason that the forms in which the Romans represent their gods have appealed more strongly to the moderns than those of the Greek gods, because the former have more the appearance of empty gods of the understanding which have no longer any connection with the free and living play of fancy.

Besides those particular gods which the Romans have in common with the Greeks, there are many gods and ways of worshipping God which are peculiar to the Romans. Sovereignty is the end sought after by the citizen; but the aims of the individual are not yet exhausted by this—he has also his own particular ends. The particular ends lie outside of this abstract end.

The particular ends, however, become perfectly prosaic particular ends, and it is the common particularity of man regarded in the manifold aspects of his necessities, or of his connection with Nature, which comes to the front here. God is not that concrete individuality above referred to. Jupiter is simply sovereignty; while the particular individual gods are dead, lifeless, without mind or spirit, or, what is more, they are got at second-hand.

Particularity thus bereft of universality, and existing on its own account, is something quite common; it is the prosaic particularity of man, but it is an end for man, and he uses this or that other thing to accomplish his end. Anything, however, which is an end for man is in this region of thought a characteristic of the Divine.

The end aimed at by man and the divine end are one, but it is an end which lies outside of the Idea; thus human ends rank as divine ends, and consequently as divine powers, and so we get these many particular and supremely prosaic deities.

We thus see on one side this universal Power which is sovereignty; in it the individuals are sacrificed and have no standing as individuals. Regarding the matter from the other side, we see that the definite element, just because that unity, God, is something abstract, lies outside of this unity, and thus it is what is human that is essentially the end; it is the human element which gives fulness to God by creating a content for Him.

In the Religion of Beauty, which represents the stage

preceding the present one, free, universal, and moral powers constitute the object of adoration. Although they are limited, still they have an objective, independently existing content, and in the very act of contemplating them the ends of individuality melt away, and the individual is raised above his needs and necessities. They are free, and the individual attains to freedom in them ; just because of this he glories in his identity with them, he enjoys their favour and is worthy of it, for he has no interests opposed to theirs, and in his needs and necessities, and in general in his particular existence, he is not an end to himself. Whether he will succeed in carrying out particular ends or not is a question he refers to the oracles only, or else he surrenders them to necessity. The individual ends here have, to begin with, a negative signification only, and are not something having a complete and independent existence.

In this religion of happiness, however, it is the *self-seeking* of the worshippers which is reflected in their practical gods in the shape of power, and which seeks in them and from them the satisfaction of its subjective interests. Self-seeking has in it a feeling of dependence, and just because it is purely *finite*, this feeling is peculiar to it. The Oriental who lives in light; the Hindu who sinks his self-consciousness in Brahma ; the Greek who yields up his particular ends in the presence of necessity, and beholds in the particular powers his own powers, powers which are friendly towards him, which inspire and animate him, and are in unity with him—lives in his religion without the feeling of dependence. Far from being dependent, he is free—free before his God. It is only in Him that he possesses his freedom, and he is dependent only outside of his religion, for in it he has thrown away his dependence. Self-seeking again, need, necessity, subjective happiness, the pleasure-seeking life, which wills *itself*, keeps to itself, feels itself oppressed, starts from the feeling that its interests are dependent on the deity. The Power which is above these interests has a positive signification, and has itself an interest for the subject, since it is to carry out its ends. So far it simply signifies that it is a means for the realisation of its ends. This is the sneaking hypocritical element in such humility ; for its own ends are and must be the content, the end of this Power. This kind of consciousness accordingly has no theoretical position in religion, *i.e.*, it does not consist in a free contemplation of objectivity, in an honouring of these powers, but only in practical selfishness, in a demand for the satisfaction of the individual interests of this life. It is the understanding which in this religion holds fast by its finite ends, by something which has been posited in a one-sided way by itself, and which is interesting only for it, and it neither sinks such abstractions and individual details in necessity nor resolves them in reason. Thus particular ends, needs, powers, appear also as gods. The content of these gods is practical utility ; they serve the common good or profit.

Thus (3) *the transition is made to gods who are wholly single or particular.*

The family gods belong to this or that particular citizen. The Lares, on the other hand, are connected with natural morality and piety, with the moral unity of the family. There are other gods, again, whose content or character has reference to utility pure and simple of a still more special kind.

Since human life and action of this kind appear also in a form from which the negative element of evil at all events is absent, the satisfaction of those needs which belong to life takes the shape of a simple, peaceful, primitive, natural state. The time of Saturn, the state of innocence, is the picture which floats before the mind of the Roman, and the satisfaction of the needs proper to such a condition of things is represented by a crowd of gods.

Thus the Romans had many festivals and a crowd
of gods, which were connected with the fruitfulness of
the earth as well as with the skill of men, who appropriate for their own use the operations of Nature.
Thus we find a Jupiter Pistor ; the art of baking ranks
as something divine, and the power connected with the
art as something having substantial existence. Fornax,
the oven in which the corn is dried, is a goddess by herself ; Vesta is the fire used for baking bread ; for in her
character as Ἑστία a higher meaning is attached to the
name, and one which has reference to family piety. The
Romans had their pig, sheep, and bullock festivals ; in the
rites connected with the worship of Pales they sought to
propitiate the goddess who caused the hay to thrive for
the cattle, and to whose protection the herds committed
their flocks in order to assure them against any kind of
injury. In the same way they had deities for the arts
which were connected with the State, *e.g.*, *Juno Moneta*,
since coins play an essential part in the regulated life
of a community.

When, however, such finite ends as the circumstances
and various interests of the State and prosperity in what
belongs to the physical necessities, the progress, and
material wellbeing of man, are regarded as the highest of
all ends ; and when the main concern is for the prosperity
and existence of an immediate reality, which as being
such can, in virtue of what constitutes it, be merely a
contingent reality ; it follows that by way of contrast to
what conduces to utility and prosperity, we have what
conduces to injury and failure. So far as regards finite
ends and circumstances man is dependent ; what he has,
or enjoys, or possesses, is something having a positive
existence, and when he is conscious of some opposing
limit or defect, and that what he has is in the power of
another, and when further he finds this negated or denied
to him, he has a feeling of dependence, and the legitimate development of this feeling leads him to revere the

power of what is injurious and evil, to pray to the devil
in fact. We do not at this stage get to the abstraction
called the devil, abstract evil and wickedness in an absolutely definite form, because here the characteristics are
finite, present realities with a limited content. It is
only some *special* form of damage or defect which is here
an object of fear and is revered. The concrete, which is
finite, is a state, a form of reality which passes away, a
kind and mode of Being which can be conceived of by
reflection as an external universal, such as peace (*Pax*),
tranquillity (*Tranquillitas*), the goddess *Vacuna* already
are, and which received a fixed form from the unimagi-
native Romans. Such powers, which are partly allegori-
cal and partly prosaic, are however chiefly and essentially
of the kind whose fundamental character is represented
by the ideas of defect and injury. Thus the Romans
dedicated altars to the plague, to fever (*Febris*), to care
(*Angerona*), and they revered hunger (*Fames*), and the
blight (*Robigo*) which attacked the grain. In the joyous
religion of art, this side of religion which consists of fear
of what brings misfortune, is put into the background ;
the infernal powers, which might be regarded as hostile
and powers to be dreaded, are represented by the Eumenides who are well disposed towards men.

It is difficult for us to understand how powers of that
kind should be honoured as divine. When we have
reached such ideas it is no longer possible to ascribe any
definite character to what is Divine, and they can become
objective only where the feeling of dependence and fear
exists. This state of things represents the total absence
of the Idea in any form, that decay of all truth which
can happen only in such circumstances. Such a phenomenon can be explained only by the fact that Spirit is
wholly shut up within the finite and the immediately
useful, as is evident when we consider how amongst
Romans arts and crafts connected with the most immediate needs and their satisfaction, are gods. Spirit has

forgotten everything inward and universal connected with thought, it has reached an utterly prosaic state, and what it aims at, what it seeks to raise itself to is nothing higher than what is supplied by the wholly formal understanding which puts together into one picture the circumstances, the character and mode of immediate Being, and knows no other mode of substantiality.

When power was thought of as existing in this prosaic condition, and when for the Romans the power which had to do with such finite ends and with immediate, real, and external circumstances, represented the welfare of the Roman Empire, it was no great step to go further and worship as God the actual present Power connected with such ends, the individual present form of such welfare, the Emperor in fact, who had this welfare in his hands. The Emperor, this monstrous individual, was the Power which presided over the life and happiness of individuals, of cities and of states, a power above law. He was a more wide reaching power than *Robigo ;* famine, and all kinds of distress of a public character were in his hands ; and more than that, rank, birth, wealth, nobility, all these were of his making. He was the supreme authority even above formal law and justice, upon the development of which the Roman spirit had expended so much energy.

All the special deities, however, are, on the other hand, again brought into subjection to the universal, real Power ; they fall into the background before the universal purely essential power of sovereignty, the greatness of the Empire, which spreads itself over the whole known civilised world. In this universality the destiny of the divine particularisation consists in the necessity there is that the particular divine powers should be disposed of and pass away in this abstract universality, just as the individual and divine national spirit of the various peoples is suppressed by being brought under the one sovereign authority. This comes out also in several practical or empirical features of the Roman spirit, and in Cicero we find this kind of cold reflection on the gods. Here reflection is the subjective power above the gods. Cicero institutes a comparison between their genealogies, their destinies, their actions; he enumerates many Vulcans, Apollos, Jupiters, and places them together in order to compare them. This is the kind of reflection which institutes comparisons, and in this way gives the hitherto fixed form belonging to the gods a dubious and vacillating character. The information which he gives in the treatise *De Natura Deorum* is in other respects of the highest importance, *e.g.*, in reference to the origin of myths; and yet at the same time the gods are in this way degraded by reflection, definite representation of them is no longer possible, and the foundation is laid for unbelief and mistrust.

If we regard the matter from the other side however, we find that it was a universal religious necessity and along with it the stifling power of the Roman fate, which collected the individual gods into a unity. Rome is a Pantheon in which the gods stand side by side, and here they mutually extinguish each other and are made subject to the one Jupiter Capitolinus.

The Romans conquer Magna Græcia, Egypt, &c., they plunder the temples, and then we see whole shiploads of gods hurried off to Rome. Rome thus becomes a collection of all religions, of the Greek, Persian, Egyptian, Christian, and Mithra forms of worship. This kind of tolerance exists in Rome; all religions there meet together and are mixed up. The Romans lay hold of all religions, and the general result is a state of confusion in which all kinds of worship are jumbled up, and the outward form which belongs to art is lost.

C. The character of the worship connected with this religion and its characterisation are involved in the foregoing description. God is served for the sake of an end and this end is a human one. The content does not start so to speak from God, it is not the content of what really is His nature, but on the contrary it starts from man, from something which is a human end.

For this reason the outward form taken by these gods can scarcely be considered as distinct from the worship paid to them; for this distinction together with free worship presupposes a truth which has a realised existence, a truth in and for self, something which is universal, objective, and truly divine, and which by means of its content rises above particular subjective necessities and exists on its own account, and thus worship is the process in which the individual gets for himself the enjoyment of his identity with what is universal and in which he commemorates this identity. Here, however, the interest originates in the subject or individual; his needs, and the fact that the satisfaction of these depends on another, produce piety, and worship is thus the positing of a Power which will relieve him and which exists because of his needs. These gods have thus essentially a subjective root and origin, and they have, as it were, an existence only in the worship paid to them; they possess substantiality in the festivals though scarcely in the conceptions formed of them. The truth, rather, is that the effort to overcome the need by the help of the power of the gods, and to get from them the satisfaction of the want and the hope of being able to do this, are merely the second part of worship, and the side which is otherwise objective comes to be included within the worship itself.

It is thus a religion of dependence and of the feeling of dependence. The dominant element in such a feeling of dependence is the absence of freedom. Man knows that he is free; but that in which he is in possession of himself is an end which remains outside of the individual, and this is still more the case with those particular ends, and it is just in reference to these that the feeling of dependence finds a place.

Here we have what is essentially superstition, because we are concerned with limited finite ends and objects, and those are treated as absolute which, so far as their content is concerned, are limited. Superstition, put generally, consists in giving to finitude, externality, common immediate reality as such, the value of power and substantiality. It originates in the sense of oppression felt by the spirit, in the feeling of dependence it has in connection with its ends.

Thus the Romans were always conscious of a thrill of fear in presence of anything unknown, anything which had no well-defined nature or consciousness. Everywhere they saw something full of mystery and experienced a vague kind of horror, which led them to feign the existence of something irrational which was reverenced as a kind of higher being. The Greeks on the contrary made everything clear, and constructed a beautiful and brilliant set of myths, which covered all the relations of life and Nature.

Cicero extols the Romans as being the most pious of nations, since in all departments of life they think on the gods, do everything under the sanction of religion, and thank the gods for everything. This is as a matter of fact actually the case. This abstract inwardness, this universality of the end, which is the fate in which the particular separate individual and the morality and humanity of the individual are suppressed, and in which they cannot be present in a concrete form and cannot develop—this universality, this inwardness is the basis of the Roman religion, and consequently since everything is related to this inwardness, religion is in everything. Thus Cicero, in complete accordance with the Roman spirit, derives religion from *religare*, for religion in all its relations has as a matter of fact become to the Roman something which binds and sways.

But this inwardness, this higher thing, this universal, is at the same time only form: the subject or content, the end, in fact, of this power is the human end and is suggested by men. The Romans revere the gods because they make use of them and when they make use of them, especially in the crisis of war.

The introduction of new gods takes place in times of difficulty and anxiety or because of vows. It is distress or trouble which in general constitutes with them the universal theogony. Connected with this also is the fact that the oracle, the Sibylline books are regarded as something divine, by means of which the people get to know what they should do or what ought to happen if they are to be benefited. Arrangements of this sort are in the hands of the State or the magistrate.

This religion is not at all a political religion in the sense in which all the religions already treated of are, in the sense that the nation has in religion the supreme consciousness of its life as a State and of its morality, and is indebted to the gods for the general arrangements connected with the State, such as agriculture, property, and marriage. In the Roman religion, on the contrary, reverence for and gratitude to the gods are closely connected, partly with definite individual cases, *e.g.*, deliverance from danger, and partly with public authority of all kinds and with state transactions, in a prosaic way, and religious feeling is in general mixed up in a finite way with finite ends and with the deliberations and resolutions connected with these.

Thus speaking generally the character of empirical particularity is impressed on necessity; it is divine, and from a religious feeling which is identical with superstition there springs up a collection of oracles, auspices, Sibylline Books, which on the one hand minister to the end aimed at by the State and on the other to particular interests. The individual on the one hand disappears in a universal element, in sovereignty, *Fortuna publica*, and on the other human ends are regarded as having value in themselves, and the human subject or individual has an independent,

substantial, and valid standing. It is within these
extremes and within the contradiction involved in them
that Roman life moves restlessly about.

Roman virtue, *virtus*, consists of that kind of cold
patriotism according to which the individual gives himself wholly up to advance anything that is a matter of
state or of sovereignty. The Romans too gave a visible
representation of this disappearance of the individual
in the universal, of this negativity, and it constitutes
an essential feature of their religious games.

In a religion which has no doctrine it is by means
specially of the representations given in festivals and
dramas that the truth concerning the god is brought before the eyes of men. In such a religion dramas have for
this reason a wholly different importance from what they
have with us. In ancient times their essential object is
to bring before the imagination the process of the substantial powers, the divine life in its movement and
action. The adoration of the images of the gods, and the
worship paid to them are connected with this divine life
in its state of repose or Being, and the movement of the
divine life is contained in the narratives connected with
the gods, in the myth, though it is thought of as existing
only for the inner subjective mental representation of the
truth. And just as the idea formed of the god in his
state of repose comes to find expression in some work of
art, in the manner characteristic of immediate imaginative perception, so, too, the idea formed of divine action
comes to be represented externally in the drama. Such
a way of representing the god was not indigenous to the
Romans; it was not something which sprang up on Roman
soil and Roman ground; and thus in adopting what was
for them originally foreign, they turned it into something
empty, ghastly, horrible—as we can see in the case of
Seneca—without making the moral divine Idea of it
their own. So, too, it was really only the later Greek
comedy which they took to do with, and they gave repre-

sentations merely of vicious scenes, and of private affairs springing out of the relations between fathers, sons, harlots, and slaves.

Amongst a people thus absorbed in the pursuit of finite ends, it was impossible that any lofty perception of moral and divine action, any theoretical or intellectual conception of those substantial powers could exist; and actions which might be theoretically interesting to them as spectators, although they had no reference to their practical interests, could have for them only an external crude reality, or, if they were to move them, a hideous reality.

In Greek drama it was what was spoken that was the main thing; the persons who acted retained a calm plastic attitude, and there was none of that mimic art, strictly so called, in which the face comes into play, but rather it was the spiritual element in the conceptions dramatised which produced the effect desired. Amongst the Romans, on the contrary, pantomime was the main thing—a form of giving expression to thoughts, which is not equal in value to the expression which can be clothed in speech.

The plays which ranked highest consisted, in fact, of nothing but the slaughter of animals and men, of the shedding of blood in streams, of life and death combats. They represent, as it were, the highest point to which imaginative conceptions could be brought amongst the Romans. There is in them no moral interest, no tragic collision in which misfortune or some ethical element constitutes the essential part. The spectators, who sought merely for entertainment, did not demand a representation of a *spiritual* history, but of one which was real and actual—a history, in fact, which represents the supreme change in what is finite, namely, barren, natural death— a history which is devoid of any substantial element, and is the quintessence of all that belongs to external life. These plays attained amongst the Romans such enormous proportions that hundreds of men, from four to five hundred lions, tigers, elephants, crocodiles were butchered by men who had to fight with them, and who in turn butchered each other. It is, above all, the history of cold, unspiritual death which is here brought before men's eyes—a death willed in an irrational, arbitrary way, and which serves to feast the eyes of others. It is necessity, which is purely arbitrary, murder without any substantial element or content, and which has only itself for content. It is this and this way of representing destiny which occupy the supreme place, the cold fact of dying, not a natural death, but a death brought about by an exercise of empty arbitrary will. It is not produced by some external necessity arising out of certain circumstances ; it is not a consequence of the violation of some moral principle. Dying was thus the only virtue which the noble Roman could practise, and he shared this virtue with slaves and with criminals who were condemned to death.

What is here pictured to the mind is that cold kind of murder which serves merely to feast the eyes upon, the nothingness of human individuality, and the worthlessness of the individual who has no moral life in himself. It is a picture of hollow, empty destiny, which in its relation to men is something contingent, a blind arbitrariness.

Contrasted with this extreme of empty destiny in which the individual disappears, a destiny which finally found a personal representation in the power of the Emperor, a power which is arbitrary and takes its own way, unhindered by moral considerations, we have the other extreme, the assertion of the worth of the pure particularity or separate life of subjectivity.

The power has, that is to say, at the same time an end also, but this power viewed in one aspect is blind; Spirit is not yet reconciled to itself, brought into harmony with itself in it, and both accordingly continue to occupy a one-sided position in reference to each other. This power is an end, and this end, the human, finite end, is the sovereignty of the world, and the realisation of this end is the sovereignty of men, of the Romans.

This universal end, taken in its real meaning, has its basis, its seat in self-consciousness, and this means that the independence of self-consciousness is posited, since the end is included within self-consciousness. On the one side we have a certain indifference in reference to concrete life, and on the other we have this reserve, this inwardness, which is an inwardness both of the divine nature and of the individual, though so far as the individual is concerned, it is a wholly abstract inwardness.

This explains what is a fundamental feature of Roman thought, namely, that the abstract person, the individual abstractly considered, is held to be of so much account. The abstract person is the individual regarded legally ; and accordingly, the development of law, of the essential characteristics of property, is an important feature of the Roman way of regarding things. This law, or right, is limited to juridical law, to the law or rights of property.

There are higher laws or rights ; the human conscience has its law or right, and this is as much a right as any other ; but the law of morality, the law of ethics is something far higher. Here, however, this right no longer possesses its concrete and proper meaning, the truth rather being that abstract right, the right of the person, expresses merely what is contained in the definition of property. It is certainly personality, but it is abstract personality only, subjectivity in the sense just explained, which is given this lofty place.

These are the fundamental features of this Religion of Utility or Conformity to an End. There are contained in it moments, the union of which constitutes the essential character of the next and last stage of religion. The moments which are isolated in the religion of outward utility, but which are related to each other, and consequently are in a condition of contradiction, are, though present here in an unspiritual form, the moments out of which, when united according to their true nature, arises the essential characteristic of the Religion of Spirit.

The Roman world forms the supremely important point of transition to the Christian religion, the indispensable middle term. It is that side of the Idea represented by reality, and, together with this, its potentially determinate character, which are developed at this stage of the religious spirit. At first we saw this reality held firm in immediate unity with the universal. Now, by giving itself a definite character, it has come out of the universal and detached itself from it, and has thus come to be completely realised externality, concrete individuality, and has consequently reached, in this its alienation carried to the furthest point, totality in itself. What now remains to be done, and what is necessary is, that this particularity or individuality, this determinate determinateness should be taken back again into the universal, so that it may reach its true determination, strip off the externality from itself, and consequently that the Idea as such may get its complete determination in itself.

The religion of external conformity to end or utility, viewed according to its inner signification, constitutes the closing stage of the finite religions. What is implied in finite reality is just that the notion of God should be or exist, that it should be posited, *i.e.*, that this notion or conception should be the truth for self-consciousness, and accordingly should be realised in self-consciousness, in its subjective aspect.

It is the notion or conception as thus posited which must develop itself on its own account until it reaches totality, for only then is it capable of being taken up into universality. It was this advance of determinateness to the stage of totality accordingly which took place in the Roman world, for here the determinateness is something concrete and finite, it is particularity, something which is inherently manifold, external, an actual condition, a kingdom, present objectivity, not beautiful objectivity, and consequently not complete or perfect subjectivity. It is through the end, the determinate determinateness, that the determinateness first returns into itself and is found in subjectivity.   At first, however, it is finite determinateness, and owing to the subjective return into itself, it is finitude without any measure or standard, the false infinite-finitude.

This measureless finite has two sides or aspects which we must get to understand and have a firm grasp of, its potentiality and its empirical manifestation.

If we consider perfect determinateness in its potential form, we see that it is the absolute form of the Notion, the Notion, namely, in its determinateness, when it has come back into itself.   The Notion is to begin with only the universal and abstract, the Notion in its potential form and as not yet posited.   It is the true universal when, by means of particularity, it unites itself with itself, *i.e.*, when by means of the mediation of particularity, of determinateness, by the act of going out of itself, and by the doing away with and absorption of this particularity, it returns to itself.   This negation of the negation is the absolute form, the truly infinite subjectivity, the reality in its infinitude.

In the Religion of Utility it is just this infinite form which self-consciousness has come to represent to itself. This absolute form is in a special sense the characterisation of self-consciousness, the characterisation of Spirit. This is what constitutes the infinite importance of and necessity for the Roman religion.

This infinite subjectivity, which is infinite form, is the grand moment which has been gained for Power; it is what was wanting in the idea of God as Power, in the God of substantiality.   It is true that in Power we had subjectivity, but Power has only single ends, or several

single ends, and its end is not yet infinite. It is only
infinite subjectivity which has an infinite end, *i.e.*, it is
itself the end, and it is only inwardness, this subjectivity
as such, which is its end. This characterisation of Spirit
was accordingly gained for thought in the Roman world.

This absolute form, however, is here still empirical, and
appears as a particular immediate person, and thus what
is highest when conceived of in a finite way, is what is
worst. The deeper the nature of Spirit and genius, the
more monstrous are their errors. When superficiality
errs, its error is correspondingly superficial and weak, and
it is only what possesses depth in itself that can become
the most evil and the worst. Thus it is this infinite
reflection and infinite form which, since it is devoid of
content and without substantiality, is the measureless and
unlimited finitude, the limitedness which is itself absolute
in its finitude. It is what appears in another shape in
the system of the Sophists as reality, for to them man
was the measure of all things, man, that is, regarded
according to his immediate acts of volition and immediate
feeling, from the point of view of his ends and interests.
In the Roman world we see that this thinking by man on
himself gets an important place, and is elevated to the
condition of the Being and consciousness of the world.
The act by which thought shuts itself up within finitude
and particularity means, to begin with, the total disappearance of all beautiful, moral life, the falling away from
true life into the infinitude of the desires, into momentary
enjoyment and pleasure, and this stage in the entire
shape in which it appears, constitutes a human animal-
kingdom, from which everything of a higher nature,
everything substantial has been removed. Such a state
of lapse into purely finite forms of existence, ends, and
interests, can certainly be maintained only by the inherently measureless authority and despotism of a single
individual whose means for maintaining this authority is
the cold unspiritual death of individuals, for only by this

means can negation be brought to bear on them, and only thus can they be kept in a condition of fear. The despot is one, a real present God, the singleness or individuality of will in the form of power exercising authority over all the other infinitely many single individualities.

The Emperor represents the Divinity, the divine essence, the Inner and Universal as it appears, and is revealed, and is actually present in the form of the singleness or particularity of the individual. This individual is the characterisation of Power advanced to the state of particularity, the descent of the Idea into the present, but it is a descent which means the loss on the part of the Idea of its inherent universality, of truth, of Being in-and-for self, and consequently of its divine nature. The universal has taken flight, and the Infinite is impressed in such a way on the finite that the finite is the subject of the proposition; this as something which has a fixed, permanent character, and is not negative, is placed within the Infinite.

This completion of finitude is thus pre-eminently the absolute misery and the absolute sorrow of Spirit, it is the opposition of Spirit to Spirit in its most complete form, and this state of opposition is not reduced to a state of reconciliation, this contradiction remains unsolved. But Spirit is what thinks, and so if it has lost itself in this reflection into itself as externality, in its character as thought it at the same time returns into itself through the loss of itself; it is reflected into itself, and in its depth as infinite form, as subjectivity,—but as subjectivity which thinks, and not as immediate subjectivity,— it has placed itself at the highest point which can be reached. In this abstract form it appears as philosophy, or speaking generally as the sorrow of virtue, as a longing and seeking for help.

The resolution and reconciliation of the opposing elements is what is everywhere demanded. This reconciliation becomes possible only when the external finitude, which has been set free, is taken up into the infinite universality of Thought, and is in this way purified from its immediacy, and raised to the condition of what has substantial validity. So, too, this infinite universality of thought which has no external existence or value of its own must in turn receive a present reality, and self-consciousness must at the same time come to be a consciousness of the reality of universality, so that it may see the Divine to be something with an actual definite existence, something belonging to the world and present in the world, and know that God and the world are reconciled.

We have seen how Olympus, that heaven of the gods, that region within which are found the fairest divine forms that were ever created by fancy, represented at the same time a free moral life, a free, though as yet a limited, national spirit. Greek life was split up into many small states, into those stars which themselves are only limited centres of light. In order that the free condition of Spirit may be reached, this state of limitation must be done away with, and the fate which floats in the distance above the world of the gods and above the national life must make its true authority felt in them in such a way that the national spirit of these free peoples is destroyed. The free spirit must get to know itself as free spirit in the entirety of its nature, free spirit in-and-for self. Its value no longer consists in its being simply the free spirit of the Greeks, of the citizens of this or the other state, but rather man must be known to be free as man, and God is thus the God of all men, the all-embracing, universal Spirit. This fate, accordingly, which exercises a kind of corrective discipline on the particular forms in which freedom shows itself and crushes the limited national spirit of the various peoples—so that the nations apostatise from their gods, and get to be conscious of their weakness and powerlessness, since their political life is destroyed by the one universal

Power—was the Roman world and its religion. In this religion of utility or conformity to end, the end was none other than the Roman State, which thus represents abstract Power exercising its authority over the national spirit of the various peoples. The gods of all nations are collected together in the Roman Pantheon, and mutually destroy each other, owing to their being thus united. The Roman spirit as representing this fate, destroyed the happiness and joyousness of the beautiful life and consciousness of the religions which went before, and crushed down all the various forms in which this consciousness showed itself into a condition of unity and uniformity. It was this abstract Power which produced the tremendous misery and the universal sorrow which existed in the Roman world, a sorrow which was to be the birth-throe of the religion of truth. The distinction between free men and slaves disappears in the presence of the all-embracing power of the Emperor; everything permanent, whether existing in an inward or in an outward form, is destroyed, and we are in the presence of the death of finitude, since the *Fortuna* of the one Empire itself succumbs too.

The true taking up of finitude into the Universal, and the perception of this unity, could not have their development within those religions, and could not originate in the Roman and Greek world.

The penitence of the world, the discarding of finitude, and the despair of finding satisfaction in what was temporal and finite which gained the upper hand in the spirit of the world, all served to prepare the soil for the true, spiritual religion, a preparation which had to be completed on the part of man, in order that "the time might be fulfilled." Granting that the principle of Thought was already developed, still the Universal was not yet an object for consciousness in all its purity, as is evident from the fact that even in philosophical speculation, Thought was united with ordinary externality, as, for

instance, when the Stoics made the world originate in
fire. The truth is that the reconciliation could appear
only amongst a people who possessed the purely abstract
idea of the One for itself, and had completely cast away
finitude in order to be able to conceive of it again in a
purified form. The Oriental principle of pure abstraction had to unite with the finitude and particularity of
the West. It was the Jewish nation which preserved
the idea of God as representing the ancient sorrow of the
world. For here we have the religion of abstract sorrow,
of the one Lord, and because of this the reality of life
appears relatively to this abstraction and in this abstraction, as the infinite wilfulness of self-consciousness, and is
at the same time bound up with the abstraction. The
old curse is removed and becomes the source of salvation,
and this just because finitude has on its part raised
itself to the condition of something positive, has become
infinite finitude, and has gained for itself a valid
existence.

PART III

THE ABSOLUTE RELIGION

PART III

THE ABSOLUTE RELIGION

WE have now reached the realised notion or conception of religion, the perfect religion, in which it is the notion itself that is its own object. We defined religion as being in the stricter sense the self-consciousness of God. Self-consciousness in its character as consciousness has an object, and it is conscious of itself in this object; this object is also consciousness, but it is consciousness as object, and is consequently finite consciousness, a consciousness which is distinct from God, from the Absolute. The element of determinateness is present in this form of consciousness, and consequently finitude is present in it; God is self-consciousness, He knows Himself in a consciousness which is distinct from Him, which is potentially the consciousness of God, but is also this actually, since it knows its identity with God, an identity which is, however, mediated by the negation of finitude. It is this notion or conception which constitutes the content of religion. We define God when we say, that He distinguishes Himself from Himself, and is an object for Himself, but that in this distinction He is purely identical with Himself, is in fact Spirit. This notion or conception is now realised, consciousness knows this content and knows that it is itself absolutely interwoven with this content; in the Notion which is the process of God, it is itself a moment. Finite consciousness knows God only to the extent to which God knows Himself in it; thus God is Spirit, the Spirit of His Church in fact, *i.e.*, of those who worship Him. This is the perfect religion, the Notion become objective to itself. Here it is revealed what God is; He is no longer a Being above and beyond this world, an Unknown, for He has told men what He is, and this not merely in an outward way in history, but in consciousness. We have here, accordingly, the religion of the manifestation of God, since God knows Himself in the finite spirit. This simply means that God is revealed. Here this is the essential circumstance. What the transition was we discovered when we saw how this knowledge of God as free Spirit was, so far as its substance is concerned, still tinged with finitude and immediacy; this finitude had further to be discarded by the labour of Spirit; it is nothingness, and we saw how this nothingness was revealed to consciousness. The misery, the sorrow of the world, was the condition, the preparation on the subjective side for the consciousness of free Spirit, as the absolutely free and consequently infinite Spirit.

We shall confine ourselves, to begin with (A), to the general aspects of this sphere of thought.

The Absolute Religion is—1. *The Revealed Religion.* Religion is something revealed, it is manifested, only when the notion or conception of religion itself exists for itself; or, to put it differently, religion or the notion of religion has become objective to itself, not in the form of limited finite objectivity, but rather in such a way that it is objective to itself in accordance with its notion.

This can be expressed in a more definite way by saying that religion, according to its general conception or notion, is the consciousness of the absolute Essence. It is the nature, however, of consciousness to distinguish, and thus we have two things, consciousness and absolute Essence. These two at first are in a state of mutual exclusion, standing in a finite relation to each other. We have the empirical consciousness, and the Essence taken in the sense of something different.

They stand in a finite relation to each other, and so far they are themselves both finite, and thus consciousness knows the absolute Essence only as something finite, not as something true. God is Himself consciousness, He distinguishes Himself from Himself within Himself, and as consciousness He gives Himself as object for what we call the side of consciousness.

Here we have always two elements in consciousness, which are related to each other in a finite and external fashion. When, however, as is the case at this stage, religion comes to have a true comprehension of itself, then it is seen that the content and the object of religion are made up of this very Whole, of the consciousness which brings itself into relation with its Essence, the knowledge of itself as the Essence and of the Essence as itself, *i.e.*, Spirit thus becomes the object in religion. We thus have two things, consciousness and the object; in the religion, however, the fulness of which is the fulness of its own nature, in the revealed religion, the religion which comprehends itself, it is religion, the content itself which is the object, and this object, namely, the Essence which knows itself, is Spirit. Here first is Spirit as such the object, the content of religion, and Spirit is only for Spirit. Since it is content and object, as Spirit it is what knows itself, what distinguishes itself from itself, and itself supplies the other side of subjective consciousness, that which appears as finite. It is the religion which derives its fulness from itself, which is complete in itself. This is the abstract characterisation of the Idea in this form, or, to put it otherwise, religion is, as a matter of fact, Idea. For Idea in the philosophical sense of the term is the Notion which has itself for object, *i.e.*, it is the Notion which has definite existence, reality, objectivity, and which is no longer anything inner or subjective, but gives itself an objective form. Its objectivity, however, is at the same time its return into itself, or, in so far as we describe the Notion as End, it is the realised, developed End, which is consequently objective.

Religion has just that which it itself is, the conscious-

ness of the Essence, for its object; it gets an objective
form in it, it actually *is*, just as, to begin with, it existed
as Notion and only as the Notion, or just as at first it
was *our* Notion.   The absolute religion is the *revealed*
religion, the religion which has itself for its content, its
fulness.

It is the Christian religion which is the perfect religion,
the religion which represents the Being of Spirit in a
realised form, or for itself, the religion in which religion
has itself become objective in relation to itself.   In it the
universal Spirit and the particular spirit, the infinite
Spirit and the finite spirit, are inseparably connected; it
is their absolute identity which constitutes this religion
and is its substance or content.   The universal Power is
the substance which, since it is potentially quite as much
subject as substance, now posits this potential being which
belongs to it, and in consequence distinguishes itself from
itself, communicates itself to knowledge, to the finite
spirit; but in so doing, just because it is a moment in its
own development, it remains with itself, and in the act of
dividing itself up returns undivided to itself.

The object of theology as generally understood is to
get to know God as the merely objective God, who is
absolutely separated from the subjective consciousness,
and is thus an outward object, just as the sun, the sky,
&c., are objects of consciousness, and here the object is
permanently characterised as an Other, as something
external.   In contrast to this the Notion of the absolute
religion can be so presented as to suggest that what we
have got to do with is not anything of this external sort,
but religion itself, *i.e.*, the unity of this idea which we
call God with the conscious subject.

We may regard this as representing also the standpoint of the present day, inasmuch as people are now
concerned with religion, religiousness, and piety, and
thus do not occupy themselves with the object in
religion.   Men have various religions, and the main

thing is for them to be pious. We cannot know God
as object, or get a real knowledge of Him, and the main
thing, what we are really concerned about, is merely the
subjective manner of knowing Him and our subjective
religious condition. We may recognise this standpoint
as described in what has just been said. It is the
standpoint of the age, but at the same time it represents a most important advance by which an infinite moment has had its due value recognised, for it
involves a recognition of the consciousness of the subject
as constituting an absolute moment. The same content
is seen to exist in both sides, and it is this potential or
true Being of the two sides which is religion. The great
advance which marks our time consists in the recognition of subjectivity as an absolute moment, and this is
therefore essentially determination or characterisation.
The whole question, however, turns on how subjectivity
is determined or characterised.

On this important advance we have to make the
following remarks. When religion is determined from
the point of view of consciousness, it is so constituted
that the content passes beyond consciousness, and in
appearance at least remains something strange or foreign
to consciousness. It does not matter what content religion has, this content, regarded solely from the standpoint of consciousness, is something which exists above
and outside of consciousness, and even if we add to it
the peculiar determination of Revelation, it is nevertheless for us something given and outward. The result of
such a conception of religion is that the Divine content
is regarded as something given independent of us, as
something which cannot be known but is to be received
and kept in a merely passive way in faith, and on the
other hand it lands us in the subjectivity of the feeling
which is the end and the result of the worship of God.
The standpoint of consciousness is therefore not the sole
and only standpoint. The devout man sinks himself in

his object, together with his heart, his devotion, and his will, and when he has attained to this height of devoutness he has got rid of the sense of separation which marks the standpoint of consciousness. It is possible also from the standpoint of consciousness to reach this subjectivity, this feeling that the object is not foreign to consciousness, this absorption of the spirit in those depths which do not represent something distant, but rather absolute nearness and presence.

This doing away with the separation can, however, in turn be conceived of as something foreign to consciousness, as the grace of God, which man has to acquiesce in as something foreign to his own nature, and his relation to which is of a passive sort. It is against this separation that the formula is directed which says that it is with religion as such we have got to do, *i.e.*, with the subjective consciousness which has in itself what God wills. It is in the subject accordingly that the inseparability of subjectivity and of the Other or objectivity exists; or, to put it otherwise, the subject as containing in itself the real relation is an essential element in the whole range of thought. Regarded from this standpoint, the subject is accordingly raised to the rank of an essential characteristic. It is in harmony with the freedom of Spirit that it should thus recover its freedom, that there should be no standpoint at. which it is not in company with itself. That it is religion which is objective to itself is a truth which is contained in the notion or conception of the absolute religion, but only in the conception. This conception or notion is one thing, and the consciousness of this notion is another.

Thus in the absolute religion as well the notion may potentially contain the truth referred to, but the consciousness of this is something different. This then is the phase of thought which has reached consciousness and come to the front in the formula which says that it is with religion we have to do. The Notion is itself still one-sided, is taken as merely implicit or potential; and so it appears in this one-sided shape where subjectivity itself is one-sided; it has the characteristic of one of two only, is only infinite form, pure self-consciousness, the pure knowledge of itself, it is potentially without content, because religion as such is conceived of only in its potential character, and is not the religion which is objective to itself, but is only religion in a shape which is not yet real, which has not yet made itself objective or given itself a content. What has no objectivity has no content.

It is one of the rights of truth that knowledge should have in religion the absolute content. Here, however, what we have is not the content in its true form, but only in a stunted form. Thus there must be a content. The content in the present case has, as we have seen, the character of something contingent, finite, empirical, and consequently we have a state of things similar to what existed in Roman times. The times of the Roman Emperors resembled ours in many points. The subject as it actually is, is conceived of as infinite; but as abstract, it changes into the direct opposite, and is merely finite and limited. Its freedom consequently is only of the sort which admits the existence of something beyond the present, an aspiration, a freedom which denies the existence of a distinction in consciousness, and consequently casts aside the essential moment of Spirit, and is thus unspiritual subjectivity, subjectivity without thought.

Religion is the knowledge which Spirit has of itself as Spirit; when it takes the form of pure knowledge it does not know itself as Spirit, and is consequently not substantial but subjective knowledge. The fact, however, that it is nothing more than this, and is therefore limited knowledge, is not apparent to subjectivity in its own form, *i.e.*, in the form or shape of knowledge, but rather it is its immediate potentiality which it finds, to begin with, in itself, and consequently in the knowledge of itself as being simply the infinite, the feeling of its finitude and consequently of its infinitude as well, as a kind of potential Being beyond and above it in contrast to its actual Being, or Being-for-self—the feeling, in short, of longing after something above and beyond it which is unexplained. The Absolute Religion, on the other hand, contains the characteristic, the note, of subjectivity or infinite form which is equivalent to substance. We may give the name of knowledge, of pure intelligence, to this subjectivity, this infinite form, this infinite elasticity of substance whereby it breaks itself up within itself, and makes itself an object for itself. Its content is therefore a content which is identical with itself, because it is the infinitely substantial subjectivity which makes itself both object and content. Then in this content itself the finite subject is further distinguished from the infinite object. God regarded as Spirit, when He remains above, when He is not present in His Church as a living Spirit, is Himself characterised in a merely one-sided way as object.

This is the Notion, it is the Notion of the Idea, of the absolute Idea, and the reality is now Spirit which exists for Spirit, which has made itself its object, and this religion is the revealed religion, the religion in which God reveals Himself. Revelation means this differentiation of the infinite form, the act of self-determination, the being for an Other, and this self-manifestation is of the very essence of Spirit. Spirit which is not revealed is not Spirit. We say that God has created the world, and we state this as a fact which has happened once and which will not happen again, and we thus ascribe to the event the character of something which may be or may not be. God, we say, might have revealed Himself or He might not. The character we ascribe to God's revelation of Himself is that of something arbitrary, accidental as it were, and not that of some-

thing belónging to the Notion of God. But God as
Spirit is essentially this very self-revelation; He does
not create the world once for all, but He is the eternal
Creator, this eternal self-revelation, this *actus*. This is
His Notion, His essential characteristic.

Religion, the revealed religion, Spirit as for Spirit, is
as such the Religion of Spirit. It is not something which
does not open itself out for an Other, which is an Other
merely momentarily. God posits or lays down the
Other, and takes it up again into His eternal movement.
Spirit just is what appears to itself or manifests itself;
this constitutes its act, or form of action, and its life;
this is its only act, and it is itself only its act. What
does God reveal, in fact, but just that He is this revelation of Himself? What He reveals is the infinite form.
Absolute subjectivity is determination, and this is the
positing or bringing into actual existence of distinctions
or difference. The positing of the content, what He
thus reveals, is that He is the one Power who can make
these distinctions in Himself. It is His Being to make
these distinctions eternally, to take them back and at
the same time to remain with Himself, not to go out of
Himself. What is revealed, is, that He is for an Other.
This is the essential character, the definition, of revelation.

2. This religion, which is manifest or revealed to
itself, is not only the revealed religion, but the religion
which is actually known as a religion which has been
revealed; and by this is understood, on the one hand,
that it has been revealed by God, that God has actually
communicated the knowledge of Himself to men; and, on
the other hand, that being a revealed religion, it is a
positive religion in the sense that it has come to men,
and has been given to them from the outside.

In view of this peculiarity which attaches to the idea
of what is positive, it becomes interesting to see what the
Positive is.

The absolute religion is undoubtedly a positive religion in the sense that everything which exists for consciousness is for it something objective. Everything must come to us in an outward way. What belongs to sense is thus something positive, and, to begin with, there is nothing so positive as what we have before us in immediate perception.

Everything spiritual, as a matter of fact, comes to us in this way also, as the spiritual in a finite form, the spiritual in the form of history, and the mode in which the spiritual is thus external and externalises itself is likewise positive.

A higher and purer form of the spiritual is found in what is moral, in the laws of freedom. This, however, is not in its real nature any such outward form of the spiritual as has just been referred to, it is not something external or accidental, but expresses the nature of pure Spirit itself. It too, however, comes to us in an outward way, at first in education, training, definite teaching; there its truth or validity is simply given to us, pointed out to us.

And so, too, laws, civil laws, the laws of the State, are something positive; they come to us, they exist for us, they have authority or validity, they *are*, not in the sense that we can leave them alone or pass by them, but as implying that in this external form of theirs they ought also to exist *for us* as something subjectively essential, subjectively binding.

When we get a grasp of the law that crime should be punished, when we recognise its validity and find it to be rational, it is not something essential for us in the sense that it has authority for us only *because* it is positive, because it is what it is; but it has authority for us inwardly as well, for our reason, as being something essential, because it is also inward and rational.

The fact of its being positive in no way deprives it of its character as something rational, as something which is our own. The laws of freedom, when they actually appear, have always a positive side, a side marked by reality, externality, and contingency. Laws must get a specific character, and into the specification, into the quality of the punishment, there already enters the element of externality, and still more into the quantity of the punishment.

In the case of punishment the positive element cannot at all be absent—it is absolutely necessary. This final determination or specification of the immediate is something positive which is in no sense rational. In the case of punishment, round numbers, for instance, decide the amount; you cannot find out by reason what is the absolutely just penalty. It is the irrational which is naturally positive. It must get a definite character, and it is characterised in a way which has nothing rational about it, or which contains nothing rational in it.

It is necessary to regard revealed religion in the following aspect also. Since in it there is present something historical, something which appears in an outward form, there is also present in it something positive, something contingent, which may take either one form or another. Thus it occurs in the case of religion as well, that owing to the externality, the appearance in an outward form which accompanies it, there is always something positive present.

But we must distinguish between the Positive as such, the abstract Positive, and the Positive in the form of and as the law of freedom. The law of freedom should not possess validity or authority because it is actually there, but rather because it is the essential characteristic of our rational nature itself. It is not, therefore, anything positive, not anything which simply has validity, if it is known to be a characteristic of this kind. Religion, too, appears in a positive form in all that constitutes its doctrines; but it is not meant to remain in this condition, or to be a matter of mere popular ideas or of pure memory.

The positive element connected with the verification

of religion consists in the idea that what is external should establish the truth of a religion, and should be regarded as the foundation of its truth. Here in this instance the verification takes the form of something positive as such. There are miracles and evidences which it is held prove the divinity of the person who reveals and prove that this person has communicated to men certain definite doctrines.

Miracles are changes connected with the world of sense, changes in the material world which are actually perceived, and this perception is itself connected with the senses because it has to do with changes in the world of sense. It has been already remarked in reference to this positive element of miracle, that it undoubtedly can produce a kind of verification for the man who is guided by his senses; but this is merely the beginning of verification, an unspiritual kind of verification by which what is spiritual cannot be verified.

The Spiritual, as such, cannot be directly verified or authenticated by what is unspiritual and connected with sense. The chief thing to be noticed in connection with this view of miracles is that in this way they are put on one side.

The understanding may attempt to explain miracles naturally, and may bring many plausible arguments against them—*i.e.*, it may confine its attention simply to the outward fact, to what has happened, and direct its criticism against this. The essential standpoint of reason in the matter of miracles is that the truth of the Spiritual cannot be attested in an outward way; for what is spiritual is higher than what is outward, its truth can be attested only by itself and in itself, and demonstrated only through itself and in itself. This is what has been called the witness of the Spirit.

This very truth has found expression in the history of religion. Moses performs miracles before Pharaoh, and the Egyptian sorcerers imitate them, and this very fact implies that no great value is to be put on them. The main thing, however, is that Christ Himself says, "Many will come who will do miracles in My name, but I know them not." Here He Himself rejects miracles as a true criterion of truth. This is the essential point of view in regard to this question, and we must hold fast to the principle that the verification of religion by means of miracles, as well as the attacking of miracles, belong to a sphere which has no interest for us. The Witness of the Spirit is the true witness.

This witness may take various forms; it may be indefinite, general, something which is, broadly speaking, in harmony with Spirit, and which awakens a deeper response within it. In history all that is noble, lofty, moral, and divine, appeals to us; our spirit bears witness to it. The witness may not be more than this general response, this assent of the inner life, this sympathy. But it may also be united to intellectual grasp, to thought; and this intellectual grasp, inasmuch as it has no element of sense in it, belongs directly to the sphere of thought. It appears in the form of reasons, distinctions, and such like; in the form of mental activity, exercised along with and according to the specific forms of thought, the categories. It may appear in a more matured form or in a less matured form. It may have the character of something which constitutes the necessary basis of a man's inner heart-life, of his spiritual life in general, the presupposition of general fundamental principles which have authoritative value for him and accompany him through life. These maxims don't require to be consciously followed; rather, they represent the mode and manner in which his character is formed, the universal element which has got a firm footing in his spirit, and which accordingly is something permanent within his mind and governs him.

Starting from a firm foundation or presupposition of this sort, he can begin to reason logically, to define or

arrange under categories. Here the stages of intellectual
advance and the methods of life are of very many kinds,
and the needs felt are very various. The highest need
of the human spirit, however, is thought—the witness
of the Spirit, which is not present only in the merely
responsive form of a kind of primary sympathy, nor in
that other form according to which such firm foundations
and fundamental principles do exist in the spirit, and
have reflective thought built upon them, firmly based
presuppositions from which conclusions can be drawn
and deductions made.

The witness of the Spirit in its highest form takes
the form of philosophy, according to which the Notion,
purely as such, and without the presence of any presupposition, develops the truth out of itself, and we recognise it as developing, and perceive the necessity of the
development in and through the development itself.

Belief has often been opposed to Thought in such a
way as to imply that we can have no true conviction
regarding God and the truths of religion by any other
method than that of Thought, and thus the proofs of the
existence of God have been pointed to as supplying the
only method by which we can know and be convinced
of the truth.

The witness of the Spirit may, however, be present in
manifold and various ways ; we have no right to demand
that the truth should in the case of all men be got at in
a philosophical way. The spiritual necessities of men
vary according to their culture and free development;
and so, too, the demand, the conviction that we should
believe on authority, varies according to the different
stages of development reached.

Even miracles have their place here, and it is interesting to observe that they have been reduced down to
this minimum. There is thus still something positive
present in this form of the witness of the Spirit as well.
Sympathy, which is immediate certainty, is itself some-

thing positive in virtue of its immediacy, and the process of inference which starts from something laid down or given has a similar basis. It is man only who has a religion, and religion has its seat and its soil in thought. Heart or feeling is not the heart or feeling of an animal, but the heart of *thinking* man, a thinking heart, or feeling; and what shows itself in the heart as the feeling for religion, exists in the thinking element of the heart, or feeling. In so far as we begin to draw conclusions, to draw inferences, to suggest reasons, to advance to thought - determinations or categories of thought, we do this always by the exercise of thought.

Inasmuch as the doctrines of the Christian religion are found in the Bible, they are given in a positive way; and if they become subjective, if the Spirit bears witness to their truth, this can happen only in a purely immediate way, by a man's inner nature, his spirit, his thought, his reason being impressed with their truth and assenting to it. Thus, for the Christian it is the Bible which is this basis, the fundamental basis, and which has upon him the effect referred to, which touches a chord in his heart, and gives firmness to his convictions.

We get a stage further, however, when it is seen that just because he is a thinking being he cannot rest in this state of immediate consent or witnessing to truth, but turns it over by thinking, meditating, and reflecting upon it. This accordingly leads to a further development in religion; and in its highest and most developed form it is theology, scientific religion; it is this content of religion known in a scientific way as the witness of Spirit.

But here a principle which is the opposite of this comes in, and which is expressed by saying that we should simply keep to the Bible. Looked at in one aspect, that is a perfectly correct principle. There are people who are very religious, who do nothing but read the Bible and repeat sayings out of it, and whose piety and religious feeling are of a lofty kind, but they are not

theologians; religion does not, so far, take with them a
scientific form, the form of theology. Götze, the
Lutheran zealot, had a celebrated collection of Bibles;
the devil, too, quotes the Bible, but that by no means
makes the theologian.

As soon, however, as this ceases to be simply the
reading and repetition of passages, as soon as what is
called explanation begins, as soon as an attempt is made
by reasoning and exegesis to find out the meaning of
what is in the Bible, then we pass into the region of
inference, reflection, and thought, and then the question
comes to be as to whether our thinking is correct or not,
and as to *how* we exercise this power of thought.

It is of no use to say that these particular thoughts
or these principles are based on the Bible. As soon as
they cease to be anything more than the mere words of
the Bible, a definite form is given to what constitutes
them, to their content; this content gets a logical form,
or, to put it otherwise, certain presuppositions are formed
in connection with this content, and we approach the
explanation of the passages with these presuppositions
which represent the permanent element so far as the
explanation is concerned. We bring with us certain
ideas which guide us in the explanation given. The
explanation of the Bible exhibits the substance or
content of the Bible in the form or style of thought belonging to each 'particular age. The explanation which
was first given was wholly different from that given now.

These presuppositions consist, for instance, of such an
idea as this, that man is naturally good, or that we
cannot know God. Consider how any one with such
preconceived ideas in his mind must distort the Bible.
Yet people bring such ideas to the interpretation of the
Bible, although the Christian religion just means that we
know God, and is just the religion in which God has
revealed Himself and has shown what He is.

Thus here again the positive element may enter in

in another form, and in this connection it is a matter of great importance to determine whether this content, these ideas and principles, are true or not.

It is no longer the Bible which we have here, but the words as these have been conceived of within the mind or spirit. If the spirit gives expression to them, then they have already a form got from the spirit, the form of thought. It is necessary to examine this form which is thus given to the content of these words. Here again the positive element comes in. In this connection it means, for instance, that the existence of the formal logic of syllogistic reasoning, of the relations of thought belonging to what is finite, has been presupposed.

According to the ordinary view of the nature of reasoning, it is only what is finite, only what may be grasped by the understanding, that can be conceived of and known. Reason, as ordinarily understood, is not adequate to deal with a divine element or content. Thus this content is rendered totally useless.

As soon as theology ceases to be a rehearsal of what is in the Bible, and goes beyond the words of the Bible, and concerns itself with the character of the feelings within the heart, it employs forms of thought and passes into thought. If, however, it uses these forms in a haphazard way so that it has presuppositions and preconceived ideas, then its use of them is of an accidental and arbitrary kind, and it is the examination of these forms of thought which alone makes philosophy.

When theology turns against philosophy, it is either not conscious that it uses such forms, that it thinks itself, and that its main concern is to advance in accordance with thought, or else its opposition is not seriously meant, but is simply deception; it wishes to reserve for itself the right to think as it chooses, to indulge in thinking which does not follow laws and which is here the positive element.

The recognition of the true nature of thought lessens

the value of this arbitrary kind of thought. This sort of thought, which is a matter of choice and does not follow strict laws, is the positive element which comes in here. It is only the Notion in its true nature, the Notion for itself, which truly frees itself absolutely from this positive element, for both in philosophy and religion freedom in its highest form is thought itself as such.

The doctrine or content also takes on the form of something positive ; it is something having a valid existence, and it passes as such in society. All law, all that is rational, and in general all that has true value or validity, takes the form of something which exists or is possessed of being, and as such it is for each one something essential, something having true value or validity. This, however, is merely the form in which what is positive appears ; the content or substance must be constituted by the true Spirit.

The Bible represents the Positive in this form ; but it is one of its own sayings, that the letter killeth, while the spirit giveth life ; and here the important point is the kind of spirit which is brought into connection with the letter, what kind of spirit gives life to the word. We must know that we bring with us a concrete spirit, a thinking, reflecting, or feeling spirit, and we must have a consciousness of the presence of this spirit which is active and forms a conception of the content before it.

This act of apprehending or forming a conception is not a passive reception of something into the mind, but, on the contrary, just because the spirit forms a conception, this conceiving of something is at the same time a manifestation of its activity. It is only in the mechanical sphere that one of the sides remains passive in connection with the process of reception. Thus Spirit plays a part here, and this spirit has its ideas and conceptions, it is a logical Essence, a form of thinking activity, and the spirit must know this activity. Thought in this form, however, can also pass into the various categories of finitude.

It is Spirit which after this fashion starts from what is positive but is essentially in it; it must be the true, right spirit, the Holy Spirit which apprehends and knows the Divine, and which apprehends and knows this content as divine. This is the witness of the Spirit, and it may have a more or less developed form.

The main thing, therefore, so far as the Positive is concerned, is that Spirit occupies a thinking relation to things, that it appears in an active form in the categories or specific forms of thought, that Spirit is active here and may take the shape of feeling, reasoning, &c. Some don't know this, and are not conscious when they have impressions that they are active in receiving them.

Many theologians, while treating their subject exegetically, and as they imagine taking up a purely receptive attitude to what is in the Bible, are not aware that they are at the same time thinking actively and reflecting. Since this kind of thinking is accidental, governed by no necessary laws, it yields itself up to the guidance of the categories of finitude, and is consequently incapable of grasping the divine element in the content; it is not the divine but the human spirit which is actively present in such categories.

It is owing to this finite way of conceiving of the Divine, of what has full and complete Being, what is in and for itself, and to this finite way of thinking of the absolute content, that the fundamental doctrines of Christianity have for the most part disappeared from Dogmatics. At the present time it is philosophy which is not only orthodox, but orthodox *par excellence;* and it is it which maintains and preserves the principles which have always held good, the fundamental truths of Christianity.

In treating of this religion we do not go to work historically after the fashion of that form of mental action which starts from what is outward, but, on the contrary, we start from the Notion. That form of activity which starts from what is outward takes the shape of something which apprehends or receives impressions only when we look at it in *one* of its two aspects, while looked at in the other it is activity.

Our attitude here is essentially an attitude of activity of this kind; we are, in fact, conscious that we are thinking on thought itself, on the course taken by the categories of thought, a kind of thinking which has tested itself and knows itself, which knows how it thinks, and knows which are the finite and which the true categories of thought. That, regarding the matter from the other point of view, we start from what is positive, is true in reference to education, and is even necessary; but here we must abandon this mode of procedure in so far as we employ the scientific method.

3. The absolute religion is thus the religion of Truth and Freedom. For truth means that the mind does not take up such an attitude to the objective as would imply that this is something foreign to it. Freedom brings out the real meaning of truth, and gives it a specific character by means of negation. Spirit is for Spirit; that expresses its nature, and it is thus its own presupposition. We start with Spirit as subject, it is identical with itself, it is the eternal perception of itself, and it is at the same time conceived of only as a result, as the end of a process. It is the presupposition of itself, and it is at the same time the result, and it exists only as the end of a process. This is truth, this condition of being adequate, of being object and subject. The fact that it is itself the object makes it the reality, the Notion, the Idea, and it is this which makes the Truth. So, too, it is the religion of freedom. Freedom considered abstractly means that the mind is related to something objective which is not regarded as foreign to its nature, its essential character is the same as that of truth, only that in the case of freedom the negation of the difference of Otherness has been done away with and absorbed in something higher, and thus it appears in the form of Reconciliation. Re-

conciliation starts from the fact that there are different forms of existence which stand to each other in a relation of opposition, namely, God, who has opposed to Him an estranged world, and a world which is estranged from its own essential Being. Reconciliation is the negation of this separation, of this division; it means that each recognises itself, finds itself and its essential nature, in the other. Reconciliation is thus freedom; but it is not something in a state of repose, something which simply is; on the contrary, it is activity. All that we mean by reconciliation, truth, freedom, represents a universal process, and cannot therefore be expressed in a single proposition without becoming one-sided. The main idea which in a popular form expresses the truth, is that of the unity of the divine and human natures; God has become Man. This unity is at first *potential* only, but being such it has to be eternally produced or brought into actual existence; and this act of production is the freeing process, the reconciliation which in fact is possible only by means of the potentiality. The Substance which is identical with itself is this unity, which as such is the basis, but which as subjectivity is what eternally produces itself.

The final result of the whole of philosophy is that this Idea only is the absolute truth. In its pure form it is the logical result, but it is likewise the result of a study of the concrete world. What constitutes the truth is that Nature, life, Spirit, are thoroughly organic, that each separate thing is merely the mirror of this Idea, in such a way that the Idea exhibits itself in it as in something isolated, as a process in it, and thus it manifests this unity in itself.

The Religion of Nature is the religion which occupies the standpoint of consciousness only. This standpoint is to be found in the Absolute Religion as well, but it exists within it only as a transitory moment. In the Religion of Nature God is represented as an "Other," as present in a natural shape; or, to put it otherwise, religion appears in the form merely of consciousness. The second form was that of the spiritual religion, of Spirit which does not get beyond finite characterisation. So far it is the religion of self-consciousness, that is, of absolute power, of necessity in the sense which we have given to these terms. The One, the Power, is something defective, because it is abstract Power only, and is not in virtue of its content absolute subjectivity, but is only abstract necessity, abstract, simple, undifferentiated Being.

The condition of abstraction in which the Power and the necessity are conceived of as still existing at this stage, constitutes their finitude, and it is the particular powers, namely, the gods who when characterised in accordance with their spiritual content first make totality, since they add a real content to that abstraction. Lastly, we have the third form of religion, the religion of freedom, of self-consciousness, which, however, is at the same time a consciousness of the all-embracing reality which constitutes the determinateness of the eternal Idea of God Himself, and a consciousness which does not go outside of itself, which remains beside itself in this objectivity. Freedom is the essential characteristic of self-consciousness.

B.

THE METAPHYSICAL NOTION OR CONCEPTION OF THE IDEA OF GOD.

The metaphysical notion of God here means that we have to speak only of the pure Notion which is real through its own self. And thus the determination or definition of God here is that He is the Absolute Idea, *i.e.*, that He is Spirit. Spirit, however, or the Absolute Idea, is what appears simply as the unity of the Notion and reality in such a way that the Notion in itself represents totality, while the reality does the same. This reality, however, is Revelation, actual manifestation, manifestation which is for self. Since manifestation, too, has in itself the moment of difference, it contains the note or characteristic of finite Spirit, of human nature, which being finite stands opposed to the Notion above mentioned. Since, however, we call the Absolute Notion the divine nature, the Idea of Spirit means the unity of divine and human nature. But the divine nature itself is merely something which is to be Absolute Spirit, and thus it is just the unity of divine and human nature which is itself the Absolute Spirit. The truth, however, cannot be expressed in a single proposition. The absolute Notion and the Idea as the absolute unity of their reality, are different the one from the other. Spirit is accordingly the living Process by which the implicit unity of the divine and human natures becomes actual and comes to have a definite existence.

Thus the abstract character or description of this Idea is the unity of the Notion with Reality. One of the Proofs of the Existence of God takes the form of a proof which represents this transition or mediation according to which the Being of God follows from the notion or conception of God. It is to be observed that in the case of the other proofs we started from finite Being as representing something immediate, and inferred from its existence the existence of the Infinite, or true Being, which appeared in the form of infinitude, necessity, absolute power which is at the same time wisdom and has ends within itself. Here, on the contrary, we start from the notion or conception, and go on to Being. Both methods are necessary, and it is necessary to point out the existence of this unity, since we may start from either side with equal propriety, for it is the identity of the two which is the truth. The Notion as well as Being, the world, the finite, are equally one-sided determinations, each of which changes round into the other, and appears at one time as a moment without independence, and at another as producing the other determination which it carries within itself. Their truth is to be found in the Idea only, *i.e.*, both are to be regarded as things posited, as dependent for their existence on something else. Neither of the two can be characterised simply as something which continues to begin or is permanently original, but must show itself in the character of something which passes over into the other, *i.e.*, it must show itself to be something posited. This transition has two opposite meanings, each is represented as a moment, *i.e.*, as something which passes over from immediacy to the Other, so that each is something posited. On the other hand, it has the signification also of something which produces the Other, inasmuch as it posits the Other, or brings it forward into actual existence. Thus one of these two elements represents movement; but so, too, does the other.

If, accordingly, the transition to Being is to be exhibited in the Notion, it is necessary to point out, to begin with, that the characterisation or determination we call Being is of an utterly poor kind. It is abstract equality with self, that last form of abstraction which is indeed affirmation, but affirmation in its most abstract form, purely indeterminate, characterless immediacy. If there were nothing more in the Notion it would be necessary to put into it at least this most extreme form of abstraction, namely, that the Notion *is*. Even when it is defined simply as infinitude, or with a more concrete meaning as the unity of the Universal and the Particular, as universality which particularises itself and thus returns into itself, this negation of the negative, this reference to self, is Being taken in a purely abstract sense. This identity with self, this characterisation just described, is directly contained in the Notion as an essential element.

Still it is necessary to state that the transition from the Notion to Being has a rich and varied character, and contains what most deeply concerns reason. The understanding of this relation between the Notion and Being is something, too, which very specially concerns our time. We must indicate more definitely the reason why this transition possesses such an interest for us. The appearance of this state of contrast or opposition is a sign that subjectivity has reached the furthest point of its Being for self or independent Being, and has arrived at the condition of Totality, in which it knows itself as infinite and absolute in itself. The essential characteristic of revealed religion appears in the form of something by means of which Substance is Spirit. Of the two opposite sides one is represented by the subject itself which is the realisation of the Idea taken in its concrete meaning. The reason why this opposition seems so hard to overcome and seems to be infinite is that this particular side or aspect of reality, the side of subjectivity, the finite spirit in itself, has reached the point at which it is able to comprehend its infinity. It is only when the subject is a totality, when it has attained to this inner freedom, that it is Being; but then it is also the case that Being in this form is indifferent relatively to this subject, the subject is for itself, and Being stands above it as an Other which is indifferent to it. It is this which more particularly constitutes the reason why the opposition can appear to be of an infinite kind, and it is because of this and as an immediate result of this that there exists in all that has life an impulse to reconcile the opposing elements. The demand that these opposing elements should be reconciled is directly involved in the totality which belongs to them ; but the abolition of the opposition has become infinitely difficult, because the opposition is of such an infinite kind, and because the Other is so entirely free, being something which exists in another sphere, in a sphere beyond.

Thus the grandeur of the standpoint of the modern world consists in this going down of the subject into itself whereby the finite knows itself to be the Infinite and is yet hampered with the antithesis or opposition which it is forced to solve. For the Infinite has an Infinite opposed to it, and thus the Infinite itself takes on the form of something finite, so that the subject, because of its infinitude, is driven to do away with this antithesis or opposition which is just what has so deepened it as to make it realise its infinitude.   The antithesis consists in this, that I am subject, free, a person existing for myself, and therefore I leave the Other free as something which is in another sphere and remains there. The ancients did not attain to a consciousness of this antithesis or division, which can be tolerated only by Spirit when it exists for itself.   Spirit, in fact, simply means that which comprehends itself in an infinite way in antithesis or opposition.   Our present standpoint implies that we have on the one side the notion of God, and on the other Being as opposed to the Notion. What accordingly is demanded is the reconciliation of the two in such a way that the Notion will force itself to take on the form of Being, or that the nature of Being will be deduced from the Notion and the Other, the antithesis or contrasted element will proceed out of the Notion.   It is necessary to explain briefly the mode and manner in which this takes place, as also the forms of the understanding which belong to it.

The form in which this mediation appears is that of the Ontological Proof of the existence of God, in which we start from the Notion.   What then is the notion of God ? It is the most real of all things, it is to be conceived of affirmatively only, it is determined in itself, its content has no limitation, it is all reality, and only as reality is it without limit, and consequently all that really remains outside of it is a dead abstraction, as has been already remarked.   The possibility of this Notion, i.e., its identity having in it no element of contradiction, is exhibited in the form proper to the Understanding.   The second point is involved in the statement, Being is a reality, Non-being is negation, defect, simply the opposite of Being.   The third point consists of the conclusion, Being is therefore reality, and this belongs to the notion or conception of God.

The objections brought by Kant against this mode of

reasoning amount to an annihilation of the Proof, and
their correctness has come to be taken for granted.
Kant tells us that the Being of God cannot be got out
of the notion or conception of God, for Being is something different from the Notion; we distinguish between
the two, they are mutually opposed, and thus the Notion
cannot contain Being, which is something outside of it
and beyond it. He says further, that Being is not in any
sense reality, it is to God that all reality is to be attributed, consequently Being is not contained in the notion
of God, and thus it does not stand for any specific content
or determination of content, but, on the contrary, is pure
Form. I may imagine I have a hundred thalers, or may
actually possess them, but in either case the thalers are
not altered, and consequently the content is always the
same whether I have them or not. Kant thus under-
stands by the content what constitutes the notion or
conception, although the meaning attached to the latter
is not what is usually implied in the Notion. We may
certainly put it so, if by the Notion we understand the
determination of the content, and make a distinction
between the content and the form which contains the
thought, and, on the other side, Being. In this way
all content is referred to the Notion, and all that is
left to the other side is simply the characteristic of
Being. Put shortly, it amounts to saying that the
Notion is not Being, but that the two are different. We
cannot understand anything about God, or get any knowledge of Him; we can, it is true, form notions or conceptions about Him, but this by no means implies that there
is anything actually corresponding to these notions.

As a matter of fact, we know that it is possible to
build castles in the air, which, all the same, don't exist.
Kant thus appeals to popular ideas so far, and in this
way he has, in the general judgment, annihilated the Ontological Proof, and has won great applause for himself.

Anselm of Canterbury, a thoroughly learned theologian.

presented the Proof in the following form. God is the
most perfect of all existences, the substance of all reality ;
but if God is simply an idea, a subjective idea, then He
is not the most perfect of beings, for we only regard as
perfect something which we do not merely picture to ourselves by an idea, but which has in addition Being. This
is perfectly correct, and it contains a presupposition
which everybody has in his mind, namely, that what is
merely represented in the form of a mental picture is
imperfect, and that that alone is perfect which has reality
as well, that that only is true which exists just as really
as it is thought of. God is thus the most perfect of
beings, and must therefore be as truly real and truly
exist as He is conception or notion. But it is further
implied in the idea, as thus understood, that the ordinary
idea and the notion are different, and consequently we
get the idea that what is merely pictured to the mind as
an idea is imperfect, while God, again, is the most perfect
of beings. Kant does not demonstrate the difference
between notion or conception and Being; it is understood in a popular sense, its truth is granted, but the
healthy human understanding forms pictorial ideas only
in connection with imperfect things.

Anselm's proof, as well as the form given to it in the
Ontological Proof, contains the thought that God is the
substance of all reality, and consequently contains Being
as well. This is perfectly correct. Being is such a poor
characteristic or quality that it directly attaches to the
Notion. The other point is that Being and Notion are
also different from each other. Being and Thought,
ideality and reality, are different from and opposed to
each other ; the true difference is opposition as well, and
this contrast is to be done away with, and the unity of
the two characteristics is to be exhibited in such a way
that it will be seen to be what results from the negation
of the contrast. Being is contained in the Notion. This
reality when it is unlimited gives us only empty words,

empty abstractions. Thus it has to be shown that the characteristic or quality of Being is affirmatively contained in the Notion, and so we get the unity of the Notion and Being.

They are, however, different, too, and thus their unity is the negative unity of both, and what we are concerned with is the abolition of the difference. The difference must be discussed, and the existence of the unity must be established and exhibited in accordance with this difference. It belongs to logic to exhibit the unity in this way—that the Notion is this movement according to which it characterises itself and takes on the form of Being, and that this dialectic, this movement in accordance with which the Notion gives itself the characteristics of Being, of its opposite, and which we may call the logical element, is a further development of thought which is accordingly not found in the Ontological Proof. It is this which constitutes the defect of the latter.

As regards the form of Anselm's thought, it has been remarked that it is implied in the content that the notion or conception of God presupposes reality, because God is the most perfect of beings. The real point is that the notion gives itself an objective form on its own account; but God is thus the most perfect of beings only in idea, or popular thought. It is when measured with the idea of the most perfect being that the bare conception of God appears defective. The conception of perfection is the standard, and thus it is seen that God as simply notion or thought does not come up to this standard.

Perfection is a merely indeterminate idea. What is really meant when anything is called perfect? The essential quality of the perfect may be directly seen in something which is the opposite of that to which it is here applied, that is to say, imperfection represents merely the thought of God, and thus perfection is the unity of thought or the Notion with reality, and this unity is therefore presupposed or pre-posited here. In

that God is posited as the Most Perfect. He has here
no further determination or characterisation, He is the
perfect one only, He exists only as such, and this represents His determinate character. It is clear from this
that the real point is only this unity of the Notion and
reality. This unity is the characteristic of perfection
and at the same time of the Godhead itself, and it is
in fact the characteristic of the Idea too. It certainly,
however, belongs still more to the determination of God.

The presupposition which really underlies the Notion,
as it was understood by Anselm, is that of the unity of
the Notion and reality, and thus we see why this proof
cannot satisfy reason, because it is just this very presupposition that is in question. The view according to
which the Notion determines itself in itself, gives itself an objective form or realises itself, is one which is
reached later, and proceeds from the nature of the Notion
itself, and cannot exist apart from this. This is the
view which raises the question as to how far the Notion
can itself do away with its one-sidedness.

If we compare this view with that which belongs to
our own day, and which in a very special sense originated with Kant, it may be put thus : Man thinks, perceives, wills, and his acts of will are connected with his
acts of thought, he both thinks and forms conceptions,
and is a being both with a concrete sense nature and a
rational nature. Then, further, the notion of God, the
Idea, the Infinite, the Unlimited, is, according to this
view, a notion merely which we construct; but we must
not forget that it is only a notion which exists in our
heads. Why is it said that it is *only* a notion ? The
notion is something imperfect since thought is only one
quality, one form of human activity amongst others, *i.e.*,
we measure the notion by the reality which we have
actually before us in concrete individuals. Man is certainly not merely a thinking being; he is a being with a
sense nature as well, and may have sense objects even

in his thought. This is, in fact, merely the subjective element in the notion. We find it to be imperfect on account of the standard applied to it, because this standard is the concrete man. It might be said that we declare the Notion to be nothing more than a notion, and what is perceived by the senses to be reality, and assert that reality means what we see, feel, or perceive in sensation. This might possibly be maintained, and there are many who do maintain this, and who recognise nothing as reality unless what is felt or tasted; only it is not conceivable that men should fall so low as to ascribe reality only to what is perceived by the senses, and not to what is spiritual. It is the concrete total subjectivity of man which is floating before the mind, and which is taken as the standard, measured by which the grasping of things in the Notion is nothing more than a forming of notions or conceptions.

If, accordingly, we compare the two views—that of Anselm, and that which belongs to the present time—we see that what they have in common is that both make presuppositions. Anselm presupposes indeterminate perfection, the modern view the concrete subjectivity of men in general. As compared with that perfection, and, on the other hand, as compared with that empirical and concrete subjectivity, the Notion appears to be something one-sided and unsatisfying. In Anselm's view, the characteristic of perfection really means, too, that it is the unity of the Notion and reality. With Descartes and Spinoza, too, God is the First, the absolute unity of thought and Being, *cogito, ergo sum*, the absolute Substance; and this is also the view of Leibnitz. What we thus have on one side is a presupposition, which is in reality something concrete, the unity of subject and object, and judged by this the Notion seems to be defective. According to the modern view, we must hold to the thought that the Notion is merely the Notion, and does not correspond to the concrete. Anselm, on the other hand, tells us that we must abandon the thought of regarding the subjective notion as something fixed and independent, and that, on the contrary, we must start from its one-sidedness. Both views have this in common, that they contain presuppositions, and what is distinctive in each is that the modern world makes the concrete the basis, while, according to Anselm's view—the metaphysical view—on the other hand, it is absolute thought, the absolute Idea which is the unity of the Notion and reality, that forms the basis. This old view is, so far, superior, inasmuch as it does not take the concrete in the sense of empirical men, empirical reality, but as thought; and it is superior to the other also, because it does not keep to the idea of something imperfect. In the modern view the contradiction between the concrete and what is only notion or conception is not solved; the subjective notion exists, it has a real value, it must be considered as subjective, it is what is real. Thus the older point of view is greatly to be preferred, because its keynote rests on the Idea. The modern view, again, has one characteristic of a broader kind, since it represents the concrete as the unity of the Notion and of reality ; while, in contrast to this, the older view does not get beyond an abstraction of perfection.

END OF VOL. II.